LANA
The Lady, The Legend, The Truth

LANA

The Lady, The Legend, The Truth

Lana Turner

NEW ENGLISH LIBRARY

First published in the United States of America by E. P. Dutton, Inc. in 1982

First published in Great Britain in 1983 by New English Library,
Mill Road, Dunton Green, Sevenoaks, Kent.
Editorial Office: 47 Bedford Square, London WC1B 3DP.

Typeset by Hewer Text Composition Services, Edinburgh
Printed by The Thetford Press Ltd., Thetford, Norfolk

ISBN: 0 450 06019 5

For my beloved mother.
You didn't live to read it, Mama,
but you lived every minute of it with me.

Grateful acknowledgment is made to Lou Valentino
for providing the photographs in this book
except for those individually credited and
the photo of Lana today.

Foreword

AT WHAT age does a lady become a legend? For me it was fifty-four. In 1975 John Springer, well-known publicist and film historian, was presenting a series at New York's Town Hall called *Legendary Ladies of the Screen*. Each show was a tribute to a lifetime career, and he'd already featured Bette Davis, Rosalind Russell, and Joan Crawford. Now he was inviting me. It meant a personal appearance.

'I'm a little on the young side to be a legend,' I protested.

'Nothing wrong with being a very live legend,' he countered. 'And Bette enjoyed it so much she's doing it in other cities, too.'

At the time I was preparing to do another play, *The Pleasure of His Company*, at the Arlington Park Theater in Illinois. Louis Jourdan was to be my costar, and John Bowab, who'd directed me in *Forty Carats*, was again directing. But there was a big difference between appearing on the stage in a role and turning up as myself, Lana Turner, to answer questions submitted by an audience.

'Look, John,' I said nervously, 'there are bound to be some pretty strong questions, and I make it a point not to answer those.'

Springer nodded; he knew the questions I meant. But he had planned to have the audience write them out in advance, and he would collect and screen them. My objections were evaporating fast, but my natural shyness—yes, I am shy—still rebelled against so public an exposure of myself. Doubts began to nibble away at me. Town Hall had about fifteen hundred seats; would enough people show up? If they came, would they like me? Or would there be some smart aleck who'd come to heckle and turn the audience against me? What questions would they ask? Could I answer them impromptu, just like that?

Yet I was flattered and I was thrilled—and I did agree to come to New York for an evening of re-creating Myth Turner as Miss Turner.

I went ahead and ordered a new evening dress and wig, although I wasn't happy with my appearance then. My weight was up to 115, hardly what anybody would call fat or even plump, but still 10 pounds more than I like. I'm only five-feet-three-and-a-half inches tall. Nothing this special had ever been offered to me, yet I had very mixed emotions. I was scared.

Finally the day arrived, and before I could think the whole thing through, there I was at the Plaza, trying to decide whether or not to wear a new wig. I was running so late that John Springer kept phoning the hotel every few minutes, in a sweat, and my secretary, Taylor Pero, kept telling him, 'We'll be there. Don't worry. We'll be there.'

I'd been ready for hours, but I couldn't finish dressing. Whenever I was nervous about anything, I ran late. Rudely late, although rudeness was far from my intention. These days, the new me can say, 'Look, girl, you've got to do it, so get going.' But in those days I'd do anything to put off the moment I dreaded. And here I was late for a program completely devoted to me.

Taylor came into my bedroom to say, 'You've done that ten times. Your eyes look beautiful, your lipstick is on straight, your makeup is perfect. Now do you want to wear the damn wig or not?'

And I yelled at him, 'You're making me nervous!' And I was dropping things, almost sick to my stomach with apprehension.

Then Springer phoned to say he couldn't stall the crowd any longer. The audience was restless. He would have to begin running the clips from my movies he had arranged to introduce the program.

It was too late to bother about the wig. I combed out my longish pageboy, gave it a final unhappy glance, and allowed Taylor to take me to Town Hall.

I was wearing diamond jewelry and a luscious floor-length white mink coat over slacks and a shirt. My shimmering white evening dress was safely tucked into Taylor's suit bag, so it wouldn't wrinkle in the limo. Everything was ready, but I was still terrified and shaking. On that short drive from the Plaza, every doubt I'd had about the evening's program rose up to torment me.

What was the mob outside Town Hall? There must have been thousands of people there, spilling off the sidewalks into the street. And there were lots of police. Some held back the crowd while others whisked me from the limo to the stage door. I couldn't believe it! A crowd that size had come to see me!

Inside there was standing room only, even in the balcony. Now I was in my dressing room, with Taylor zipping me up the back— that damn dress! It was the first and last time I ever wore it—as I sipped a vodka and tonic for courage. John Springer began knocking

8

at the door. 'It's time, Lana.' Did I want my purse? No! Yes! I had to hang on to *something*. We went down the stairs. Then into the wings to watch the end of the film clips, beginning with my famous walk down the street in *They Won't Forget*, through *Ziegfeld Girl*, the films with Clark Gable, *Johnny Eager* with Robert Taylor; and on to *Peyton Place*, *Imitation of Life*, and my hysterical scene in *The Bad and the Beautiful*. On the stage I could see a table with two microphones, an ashtray, water and glasses, and two chairs for John Springer and me. I couldn't see far enough around the black curtains to glimpse the full audience; I could see only the people down in front.

I kept thinking, 'I'll never get through this, I'll never get *through* this.' My entire body was trembling. Now I was taking deep breaths and praying, 'Please, God, don't let me trip. Don't let me fall on my face.'

Other actors have butterflies in their stomachs. I have eagles, with flapping wings and tearing claws. And the eagles were awake and angry.

Now it was my turn. I had to go out there and lay it on the line. I put my hand on the curtain to pull it back. The next day, a reviewer described it in rather picturesque terms: 'A thin, pale hand pushed aside the black curtain . . .'

Well, the minute the people saw the hand, the applause began. And then I moved my body, and Taylor grabbed the curtain so I wouldn't get caught, and I took two steps onto the stage, and there was this *roar*, and I froze. Froze dead on the spot, hearing only this *roar*. It was like the Atlantic Ocean—loud and powerful and swelling and overwhelming. The lights were on me, so I couldn't see much of the audience. All I could see was a blur of faces and waving arms.

John was beckoning to me—come, come on—and I looked from him to the audience, from the audience to him. I was *stuck* on this little square of stage, and I thought, 'My God, my shoes are nailed to the floor.' I had turned to stone—the cheers and the applause, the *intensity* of it, had taken me by surprise. I'd heard applause before, after the final curtain had come down on my plays, and after entertaining the troops in the Far East, but nothing to equal this! When I do a play, they applaud my role and the way I play it, but *this* applause was for *me*!

John Springer, laughing, came up to me with his hand stretched out and took my arm, leading me onto the stage. I couldn't have moved without him. And the whistles! And, 'We love you, Lana!' and '*I* love you, Lana!' It's a good thing I'm not the fainting type.

I stood in the middle of that stage and I placed my hand on my heart, then swung out my arm to include everybody there in the darkness, and I mouthed the words, 'My heart . . . to you!' That brought another roar. Then John guided me to my seat.

Never had I been so glad to sit down, because my legs were barely holding me up. I sat with a 'whew,' which brought laughter, lovely laughter, and more applause. I kept shaking my head, mouthing, 'I can't believe it.' John Springer was standing by my chair, clapping, and I gestured to him to get on with it.

Now, if I'd been on time, I'd have had some opportunity to read the question cards in advance, and try to come up with some answers. But I was late, so all the questions were surprises—some of them not so pleasant.

But they were with me all the way, that beautiful audience. I could feel the waves of love, nothing negative at all. Some of the questions stumped me—such as, Why did you marry so many times? 'How the hell,' I wondered, 'did *that* one slip through?' But I answered: 'Let me put it this way. With each marriage, I thought that that would be *it*. In my wildest dreams I never, never thought that I would have seven husbands. If you can believe it, I thought at the time that each marriage would last forever. You see, with one bitterly painful exception, when I fell in love, I married.'

And that last question: If your life was to be filmed, who would you pick to play you? I didn't think about it for even two seconds; I don't know where the answer came from. I just leaned forward with my arm on the table and told them, 'She hasn't been born yet.' Well, I'd never said that before in my life, but then nobody had ever asked me. But it was the truth, the *me* came out with that answer, and nobody was more surprised than I was. The audience shrieked with laughter.

And when it was over they came running, running down the aisles to the stage, grabbing at my hands to shake them. Once I nearly fell over the edge of the stage, and I was afraid my diamond rings would slip off and be lost. The people kept reaching for me, and I was touching their fingers. It seemed that it was never going to end, they just would not let me go. Finally, I couldn't take any more, I simply couldn't. I began to blow kisses and say good-bye.

'No, Lana! Stay, stay! Don't go, Lana!'

But it had been a long evening for them, too, an emotional one.

10

Backstage was bedlam. Springer was raving that he'd never seen a Town Hall audience like that one. Stage managers and other backstage people were crowding into the dressing room, congratulating me. The fans were trying to rush up the stairs, and the police were holding them back.

And me, still dazzled, still insecure. 'Did I do all right? Was it okay?'

Getting out of Town Hall was excruciating, I was shielded by policemen fore and aft, but somehow a woman slipped past the guards. As she reached me, her right hand grabbed one of my earrings—I was wearing long earrings, diamond baguettes, with pearls dangling from the ends. That hand yanked so hard at the earring it spun my head around. God, the pain! My ears are pierced, and I was terrified that the lobe would be ripped. She wouldn't let go, despite my screams, so I pounded on the back of the police officer in front of me.

'Make her let go!' I screamed. He could barely hear me because the fans were still yelling, 'Lana, we love you!' at top volume. But he felt my hands on his back, and he whirled around, sized up the situation, and hit her so hard that she had to let go. All I heard was a resounding crack.

What a madhouse. I was literally pushed through that crowd to the limousine while the fans thrust autograph books into my face. The police shoved me into the limo and I wound up sprawled on my side on the backseat. Then it was drive, drive, with fans chasing after me.

John Bowab gave a party for me, and when we arrived at his apartment the hallway was lined with people trying to get a look at me. Every room, even the kitchen, was packed like a sardine can.

What a night! Taylor and I didn't get back to the Plaza until four in the morning, still high and floating from the emotional charge of the evening, yet at the same time drained. I changed into a loose cuddly robe, and Taylor climbed into his pajamas and bathrobe in his room, then we met in the living room for a nightcap. Taylor flopped onto the couch and I fell into a big chair. I looked at Taylor and said in a marveling tone, 'Now what the hell was that all about?'

I couldn't get over it. Even the reviewers (all but one, Sally Quinn, I believe her name was) had been kind—more than kind. Some of them were downright embarrassing as they rehashed the evening.

11

I kept shaking my head. That audience had applauded a woman they had watched on the screen for decades. But they only knew the legend. They didn't know me. They had no idea that behind the façade was a scared, quaking child, a woman insecure and filled with doubts. I am not just a manufactured something, a 'star' from Hollywood's golden age. I am a real, live, breathing human being, with faults and good points like anybody else. Sure, I have made mistakes, plenty of them; some I have paid for dearly. But what I thought as I sipped my drink after that glorious evening was, 'Hmm, I wonder if the fans would applaud the *real* Lana if they knew her?'

1

One June evening in 1937 I sat in a Hollywood theater, waiting for a preview of *They Won't Forget*. I played a Southern schoolgirl, Mary Clay, who would be raped and murdered. An innocent teacher would be blamed and lynched before he came to trial. I hadn't really understood the significance of the script, but I remember what I wore—a close-fitting sweater with a patent-leather belt and a well-contoured skirt.

When the lights went down, I slumped in my seat and grabbed my mother's hand. The sound track's jazzy, earthy beat magnified the image on the screen. It was a young girl—was it me?—but, my God, the way she walked!

The audience began to stir as the camera angle shifted. That walk was more than teasing—it was seductive. Her breasts and backside were not that full, but when she walked, they bounced. From behind me came an audible growl, and a chorus of wolf whistles filled the hall.

'Who's the girl?' I heard someone ask, but I had tears in my eyes. I slipped down farther in my seat until I was resting on my spine. Only the brim of my new hat stopped me from sliding to the floor.

At the end of the reel, when the credits rolled up, my name was listed sixth. *Lana Turner*—the first time it had ever appeared on the screen. 'Let's get out of here,' I urged my mother, who seemed to be in a daze. A production assistant swept us out before the lights came on.

As we hurried to a waiting car, I clutched the young man's sleeve. 'Listen,' I said. 'Tell me. I don't really look like that . . .'

He cut me off with a slight smile. 'Fortunately,' he said, 'you do.'

When I learned more about filmmaking, I understood what director Mervyn LeRoy had done. He had emphasized my sexiness to fix me in the viewers' minds. He gave me what they call 'flesh impact,' to let a tight sweater imply what couldn't be said on the screen. But that walk down the street of a Southern town would completely change my life.

That image clung to me for the rest of my career. I was the sexual promise, the object of desire. And as I matured, my façade did too, to an image of coolness and glamour—the movie star in diamonds, swathed in white mink. There was another side to that picture—screaming sordid headlines, the seven marriages that failed. Those are the things people remember. But the rest—the inner agony, my suicide attempt; my desperate struggle to have children, the still-births, miscarriages, the two abortions I was forced to have; my disappointments in love, one after another—all these things I kept inside. Even my husbands seemed satisfied to possess the external me, the 'star.' Despite the reams of copy that have been written about me, even the supposedly private Lana, the press has never had any sense of who I am; they've even missed my humor, my love of gaiety and color. I am a romantic, and I was an optimist about my relationships with men. Even when times were tough, as they so often were, my friends knew that I could come up with a funny story, acting out all the parts, with voices for each of the players. Humor has been the balm of my life, but it's been reserved for those close to me, not part of the public Lana. In my public life I've had to be stoic. My inner self—my mind and heart, my thoughts, opinions, and beliefs—I have kept for myself alone.

For years publishers have begged me to tell my own story, but up to now, I've always turned them down. What I usually said was, 'I'm too damned busy living my life to write about it.'

But the truth is that, for all these years, I have had to live with headlines, and gossip columns, and intrusions into my personal life. I've despised those invasions of my secret, private self, and even more, the distortions and lies. I have had to turn my back on outrageous fabrications, some of them sadistically cruel. I simply took the punches without fighting back.

I have come a long way since 1937. I almost can't believe how far. I think it's because I've been so close to God these last two years. I wasn't born like this, the woman I am today. This new woman is no longer confused, she knows who she is. I've always told the truth, but never before have I dug down deep and told *all* the truth about myself. I refuse to leave this earth with that pile of movie-magazine trash, scandal and slander, as my epitaph. So now I'm ready to share what I've always kept private, to set the record straight. As you'll see, I'm willing to tell it all.

14

And I'll begin with my birth date, which was never printed accurately. I am one year younger than the records show. Now, if I were going to lie about my age, I might as well make it two, three, or five years. Why they always got it wrong by one year, I'll never understand. Anyway, there it is on my birth certificate: Julia Jean Turner, born in Wallace, Idaho, February 8, 1921.

My mother, a reticent lady, never told me much about how I came to be born there. Until recently I had supposed that she was a native of Wallace, too, But no, she was born Mildred Frances Cowan in Lamar, Arkansas, in 1904. My grandfather worked as a mining engineer, and later a ship's engineer. His wife had died in childbirth, probably because of a congenital Rh blood factor, which I have suffered with, too. My mother was raised by her great-aunt, her father's mother's sister.

Often she traveled with her father on mine-inspection tours. One of those stops was Picher, Oklahoma. In a roof-garden restaurant in Picher's rather plain downtown, a man asked her to dance. His name was John Virgil Turner.

Originally from Montgomery, Alabama, he had a Southern accent so thick he once entered an Amos 'n' Andy sound-alike contest—he didn't win. His ancestry was what my mother called Low Dutch, which I assumed meant his background was humble. Later I made a film in Holland, and I learned that the term referred to the lowlands of that country. My mother was a mixture of Scottish, Irish, and English—so I'm a proper American hybrid.

Anyway, my father was just out of the Army. He had served as an infantry platoon sergeant in World War I and had received several medals for valor. He was heading westward, working in the mines, and I guess that's how *he* got to Picher. After a night of dancing, he and my mother fell in love.

He was twenty-four, but she was only fifteen. When he began to court her, my grandfather put his foot down. So, what could they do? They eloped.

I arrived about a year later. My father, with a partner, had opened a dry-cleaning establishment in Wallace. When the business failed, it was back to the mines for my father. One of my earliest memories is of him arriving home grimy and weary. Though life wasn't easy for either my mother or my father, we still had good times. At night my father would turn on the record player and laugh and dance around the room with my mother and me. Many times right after dinner my father would scoop me off my chair and dance with me alone. I was thrilled. He taught me a few simple steps and was generous with compliments as I picked up a few. Maybe that's where my love of music and sense of rhythm got its start. Today I keep both my stereos tuned to one FM station that plays the kind of music I like, and every now and then a beat will catch my ear and I'll stand up and dance around all by myself.

My father was an excellent cardplayer, and his success at the occasional poker game may well have helped to support us. We must have been poor at times, for we lived near the railroad tracks. I have one strange memory from a time before I was three. My mother would carry me out to the yard to watch the trains go by. We would wave at the people we saw at the train windows. Once she was holding me in her arms while the train went by, and she said, 'Do you see that lady in the long white gloves? Wave to her.'

'Why?'

'Just wave to her. Now blow her a kiss.'

'Why?'

'Just do it.'

I did, and the lady waved back at me.

After the train passed, I asked, 'Why did I wave at that lady?'

'Because,' she said, 'that is your real mother.'

I burst into tears. 'No,' I sobbed, 'you're my real mother.'

'No,' she said again. 'I'm just taking care of you.'

I screamed and kicked and pushed her away until she dragged me into the house. There she rocked and petted me, and told me she'd only been teasing. But what fright and anguish that little episode caused me! I felt so lost, so insecure. Was she acting out some wayward fantasy of her own? Did she imagine herself as a lady in long white gloves, traveling to a far-off place?

Recently I learned that my mother remembered the incident, too, when my secretary, Lorry Sherwood, mentioned that my mother had told her. 'How could I have played such a trick on her?' she had asked Lorry. 'I have wondered and wondered about it, and to this day I regret it.'

Although for most of my life we were extremely close, there are secrets that my mother never revealed. Yet she was all the roots I had, and for years she was the only one in the world whom I could totally trust.

My mother was so much in awe of my father that she called him Mr. Turner. After they were married she called him Turner, instead of John or Virgil. Once I asked her why, and she answered quickly,

'Out of respect.' But I found him lots of fun, a delightful father. After sitting me on his lap he'd stand me on the floor and teach me how to tap-dance the way he did in the Elks Club shows in Wallace. He could sing well, too—he was alive with talent.

From the photos I can see that I look just like my father. I have his bright blue eyes and small nose, and I'm even built like him, with broad shoulders and slim hips. Both he and my mother were handsome, and they always dressed well, even when we had practically no money.

Once when the club had a fashion show, my mother modeled some furs. I was watching from backstage. I was so impressed with the way she looked that I put on a fur jacket and minced onstage, imitating her. I was four years old. They tell me I brought down the house.

It's funny what memories come back to you from your earliest childhood. For example, I can remember as clearly as if it was yesterday how proud I was, how elated, when I learned to tie my own shoes. I couldn't have been more than five years old. How I practiced tying them over and over until I could do it right every time, and so neatly! It was a challenge, and I conquered it! It gave me a real sense of accomplishment.

And once when my grandfather came to visit me, I asked him, 'How do you wipe your back?'

'What?' He looked at me, astonished and puzzled at the question.

'How do you wipe your back?' I repeated.

'Why do you want to know?'

'Because when mama bathes me, she always dries my back for me, and I want to learn how to do it for myself.'

Laughing, he took up a towel and held it by the corners behind him, showing me how to rub it back and forth, while I watched him solemnly and nodded. It seems to me I remember these things because they were little steps—well, not such little steps when you're less than six years old—on the road to independence. I wanted to learn to do things without help.

When I was six we piled possessions into a car and set out for San Francisco. Bored just sitting between my parents, I coaxed my father to put me on his lap. 'Oh, all right,' he said. But once I was there, I wanted to drive, too. So he placed both my hands on the steering wheel, saying, 'We'll both drive.' I thought it was great fun.

Suddenly my mother, who had been watching the scenery, glanced

17

our way and gave a yelp of alarm. My father's eyes were closed, and I was steering the car alone—doing quite well, I thought. My mother grabbed the wheel, my father came to, and that was the end of my first driving experience. Yet I treasure the memory, for I did not have my father around much longer.

Another memory—my father promised that when we got to San Francisco I would see the Golden Gate. What a vision my child's mind created! I imagined a radiant golden gate, shining, topped with pearls. As we drew near my father called out excitedly, 'There it is!' But all I saw was a large expanse of water.

I peered out, disbelieving. 'Where?' I asked accusingly. 'You said it would be a *golden gate*.' Crushed, I started to cry.

But there would be other disappointments, and graver ones than that. The trip had used up all our money, and work was hard to find. First we stayed in an auto court, then in some furnished rooms, and then in a small house in Stockton.

I suspected something was going on in the basement there in Stockton. I had heard strange discussions, and I made out the word *still*. I begged my father until he took me down to show me the contraption. It was a huge copper vat with rubber tubes. 'Now you must promise never to mention this,' he warned me. 'Never a word to anyone, understand?'

Of course I promised, thrilled to think that my father and I shared a secret. I didn't say a word to my mother about it. I had no idea what the still was for, and I'd never heard of Prohibition. I certainly didn't know it was illegal.

But one day I was sitting on the curb with a few of my playmates, and they started bragging about what their parents did. After a while I said, 'That's nothing. *My* father has a still.' I'd forgotten about my promise.

One of them must have gone home and repeated what I'd said. Some official-looking men came one day and took my father downtown. They chopped up the still and carted the pieces away. My father eventually got off with a reprimand and a fine.

When he came home he took me for a walk and asked me what had happened. I confessed that I hadn't meant to tell, but that I couldn't let those other kids think their fathers were better than mine. 'Oh, my God,' he said, shaking his head, and let the matter drop.

18

Soon afterward he went away. When I asked my mother where he'd gone, she said that he was traveling, selling insurance. Not long after that my parents split up. There was never a divorce. I know that my mother always loved him, and she never told me why they separated. She went to work in a beauty parlor in San Francisco and later found a better job in Sacramento.

After we moved there, I was sent to a Catholic school, even though I had not been baptized Catholic. One day I came home scratching my head furiously. I had a thick head of dark auburn hair in those days. Burrowing into it with her fingers, my mother found that I had lice! She doused my head with some nasty-smelling stuff called Black Mange Cure and wrapped my hair in a towel. I had to stay home from school for a week until my lousy head was sanitized. She wouldn't even let me go out and play.

Times were hard, and there were days when the money ran out. Once we lived on crackers and milk for half a week. Eventually we had to return to San Francisco, where my mother found an apartment to share with two young women. There wasn't much space. When their men friends came to visit, the women would bed me down on the floor of a large closet, to get me out of the way. My mother wasn't happy with that, and finally she found a home for me with a family in Stockton, the Hislops. I could share a room with the daughter, Beverly, who was close to my age, and I could play in the large backyard. She would come to visit every other week.

Most of the time Beverly and I were kept busy with household chores. One Saturday my hand got caught in the wringer of the washing machine, and my howls could be heard a block away. They had to dismantle the wringer to get me out. I can remember the pain to this day.

On Sundays I went to the Catholic church with the Hislops. The ritual thrilled me so that I wanted to convert, and my mother agreed. I had originally been christened Julia Jean, and now I needed some saints' names. I chose Frances—actually Mildred Frances—after my mother.

When my father heard about it he was furious. He came to see me every now and then. On one of his visits he took me back to San Francisco with him because I told him I needed shoes. In a store called The Emporium I saw just what I wanted—patent-leather pumps with little Cuban heels. 'Aren't they too snappy?' he asked me. I assured him that they weren't, and they fit best, so he bought them. When my mother saw them, she said that they were much too mature for me, blamed my father for his lack of taste, and insisted that he take them back and get me something more sensible. I cried, but it did no good; and the bawling out my mother gave my father made it all the worse.

When I became a film star, I developed the spendthrift habit of buying shoes in quantity—two, three, or four colours in the same style. At one time I had a special room, with shelves from floor to ceiling, filled with shoes. I had one of those library ladders so I could climb up to select a pair. Once I counted them all, and I discovered I owned 698 pairs of shoes. That jolted me! Since then I've tried to control the impulse.

On another visit I asked father to buy me a bicycle, and he promised that one day he would. A few days later Julia Hislop came into my room and said to me, 'Put on your nice dress. We're going to San Francisco.'

'Why?' I asked.

She looked at me strangely, but all she said was, 'Never mind.'

I knew the trip had to be important, and on the way I searched my mind for what it could mean. Finally it occurred to me to ask, 'Is my mother having a baby?' I've since wondered why I thought that. I suppose I had always wanted a brother or sister, or both. It was part of my secret wish that my parents would reunite.

Later that day we met my mother in a hotel. She seemed unusually quiet, even for her, and there was a drawn look around her mouth. As we ate in a Chinese restaurant, she didn't say a word and she ignored all my questions. In silence we went back to the hotel, where she and I shared a bed.

How long I had been asleep I don't know, but suddenly I was sitting up straight in the darkness. Before me was a vision so intense that it seemed to be alive. I saw a huge medallion of shining gold, and on it was embossed the face of God, a shimmering countenance, comforting, benign. A voice said, 'Your father is dead.' I was filled with awe, but also with a strange sense of peace as I closed my eyes and went back to sleep.

When I awoke in the morning, my mother and Julia Hislop were whispering in a corner. They didn't have to tell me why. I already knew that my father was dead. And when the feeling of peace wore off, the surprise at having *known* intensified my sense of loss and sorrow. Although I was only nine, I could imagine what death meant. I knew he was gone forever.

At the funeral home I saw him in the casket, his face waxen, his eyes closed, and I was terrified. I had never seen anyone dead. My mother asked, 'Do you want to kiss your father good-bye?' Gingerly I reached out and touched his hand. It was cold, so cold. It didn't feel real. Frightened, I pulled back and hid in my mother's skirts.

My father's burial in the Presidio followed, an oddly formal ceremony. Uniformed soldiers fired their rifles in a salute. My mother explained they did that because my father had been a hero in the war.

When I was older I read a news clip about my father's death. He sometimes played in a travelling crap game. On the night of December 14, 1930, the game was held in the basement of the *San Francisco Chronicle* building. He hit a winning streak, and he mentioned that he planned to buy his little girl a bicycle. Collecting most of the bets, he stuffed his winnings into his left sock. The next morning they found him slumped against a wall at Mariposa and Minnesota streets. He had been bashed in the head with a blackjack, and his left foot was bare. The murder was never solved.

With my father gone, I wanted more than ever to live with my mother, but I was stuck with the Hislops for almost a year. Then one day, Julia, who had her own problems, flew into a rage over some household chores that had gone undone. She blamed me, and grabbing a stick of kindling wood, beat me black and blue. I screamed until she came to her senses. When she realized what she had done, she threatened me with a worse beating if I told my mother.

That weekend my mother came to take me shopping. When she suggested new underthings, I backed away, saying I didn't need any. That made her suspicious, so she pulled up my dress and saw the bruises, as I sobbed out the story.

Back at the Hislops', I found a hiding place behind a large Philco radio cabinet while my mother had it out with Julia in the kitchen.

'Go pack your suitcase,' my mother ordered, and that day she took me back to San Francisco. She then found me a place to stay with an Italian family in Lodi, not far from Stockton. At first they seemed strange and rather scary; I'd never been with such a large family before. But they were warm and hospitable, and their doors were open to everyone in town. I had my first taste of wine

21

there—the children drank a little mixed with water at meals—and once again I attended a parochial school.

I longed to be with my mother, although I was happy enough, and before long she found a place for both of us. She had been working in a beauty parlor owned by a pleasant woman named Chila Meadows, who rented us a share of her Richmond district apartment. Her daughter Hazel and her son George accepted me as a kid sister. I couldn't have wished for more—I was living with my mother, and I'd gained a brother and sister, too. And soon I would enter Presidio Junior High School.

On Saturdays there were matinees at the local movie house. I'd save a nickel of my lunch money every day to raise the quarter to go. I loved the actresses and the beautiful clothes they wore, especially Kay Francis. I loved her because my mother looked exactly like her. She even wore her hair like Kay Francis. And Norma Shearer . . . so beautiful, so glamorous. That was real entertainment.

The Meadows family had a piano, and sometimes we'd gather around it and sing. Everyone claimed to like my voice, even though it was very small, and urged me to audition for the Major Bowes Amateur Hour, which was broadcast from San Francisco in those days. I guess I must have been around thirteen or fourteen. Egged on by peer pressure, I agreed, and the song I performed was 'The Basin Street Blues,' although only heaven knows why. I was too young to understand what the lyrics were all about, and of course I'd never been to New Orleans's Basin Street. Well, I was scared to death, and you know I didn't win. But on I went and off I went, with only the thinnest polite smattering of applause. I was mortified! What a waste of time. All the ambitious dreams my friends had for me turned into nothing but embarrassment, just a dumb plan for a tiny voice!

Oh, the kids were kind enough to say consoling, encouraging things like, 'What the heck do *they* know about talent?' and 'You're better and cuter than those others, Judy,' but none of those words could make the big ache in my tummy go away. But I did learn something from my humiliation—no more trying to be what I couldn't be. Namely a singer.

I decided just to float along, trying to do well in school. Or to do enough work to keep my grades up, if not the *A*'s, at least at the *B* and *B*+ level. Now and then a *C* would turn up or occasionally a dreadful *D*. And once, in mathematics, the fatal *F*, and you know that *F* didn't stand for *fun*. I'd plead with my friends to help me. I really needed help in math—those numbers might have been in Chinese for all I could make of them. But more than that I needed help in making my mother understand why, when my other subjects were passable, math wasn't. Of course, they were subjects I really enjoyed—history, geography, English, languages (even Latin—boy, was *that* ever a challenge). I especially enjoyed the Romance languages, French, Spanish, Italian.

Because my chum Aspasia was Greek, I even tried to learn the Greek alphabet and picked up a few phrases that were almost understandable. I remember going around muttering Greek to myself, 'Alpha, beta, gamma . . .' until there was my mother standing in front of me, demanding to know if I had a speech impediment.

'I was speaking Greek.'

'Whatever for?' But there was a twinkle in mother's eye.

I found myself wriggling in embarrassment. 'Well . . .' I told her finally, because I always told my mother the truth. 'It's so Aspasia and I can talk about . . . girls . . . and boys . . . and things, without anybody else knowing what we're saying.'

'Well, what about pig Latin? Wouldn't pig Latin be easier?'

'Aw, everybody at school knows pig Latin!'

My mother just smiled and wished me luck. She understood that teenagers often wish for a private language with their best friends, so they can keep their childish secrets.

If I had any real talent then, it was for designing clothes. I loved the costumes in the movies, and my first adolescent crush—if that's the word for it—was on my homeroom teacher, Miss Petch, because of the way she dressed. I still remember my favorite outfit—she wore a tailored gray flannel skirt, a blue and white blouse with a bow at the neck, and a grey cashmere sweater.

If I hadn't gone into the movies, I'd have become a dress designer; that's where I seemed to be heading. And I think I'd have been a damn fine one. My mother always dressed beautifully, whether she was well-off or poor. Somehow she got herself together. She always had style and class.

When we were living in Sacramento—I must have been about twelve years old—I got a long roll of paper from the butcher. It was white, shiny on one side, dull on the other. With a ruler and pencils and crayons, I planned to draw one or two store windows for my mother's birthday. But I kept on going and ended up doing more.

First I outlined the backgrounds and the mannequins in pencil, then I colored them in with the crayons. I drew every kind of outfit you could imagine, for all four seasons. The mannequins wore dresses, suits, coats, hats, gloves, purses, pumps or ankle-strap shoes—even pearls and furs. And I created the backgrounds to match the outfits—a snowscape for the ski suit, and so on.

And when I was finished, there were twelve store windows side by side, with no details left out. This, then, was to be my gift. I rolled it up and tied it in a red ribbon. I'd worked on it secretly after school until my mother came home from work. Now I stashed it under my bed, because I wanted it to be a surprise.

I can't explain the feeling I had when my mother took off the ribbon and began to unroll the paper, asking, 'What is it? What is it?' I was hugging myself with happiness, as excited as she was, maybe even more. As she unrolled it she looked at one picture, and then unrolled a little more and looked at the next, then looked at me, then back at the paper, with such wonderment in her eyes. When it was all unrolled, and she'd seen all twelve of the store windows, all she could say was 'Ohhhh, my!' and 'Ohhhh, Lord! Darling, that is so beautiful!' Then she grabbed me and hugged me.

When people came to visit, my mother would show off my present so proudly, and they were all amazed. And to everybody I would declare that someday, when I had money, my mother would have beautiful clothes like the ones I drew, and even more.

And, by golly, she did.

2

I' VE FINALLY learned the source of the legend that I was discovered at Schwab's. The Hollywood columnist Sidney Skolsky often ate lunch there. One day, as he sat at the fountain, a busty blonde came up and asked which stool was Lana Turner's. Skolsky simply picked one and pointed it out. Just like that, Schwab's became mecca to thousands of would-be movie stars, and Hollywood gained another persistent myth. I doubt that anyone was ever discovered there, but Schwab's should give me a percentage of their earnings.

But I *was* discovered sitting at a soda fountain. I was fifteen-going-on-sixteen at the time.

We had moved to Los Angeles in 1936, in the midst of the Great Depression. For me and my mother, the greatest change in our style of living had come when my father left, several years before the Crash. I was really too young to remember a time of national prosperity; even in the best of times my parents had never been comfortable. As I remember, my adolescent perceptions of the world around me focused on the spectacular events of the day—the bizarre claims of the evangelist Aimee Semple McPherson, whose strange disappearance had been the greatest scandal of the late 1920s; President Roosevelt's 1935 trip to California; the celebration of the first electric power from Boulder Dam, which would usher in a new era of progress.

Mostly I was aware of the economic woes of the country through adult conversations I overheard and from the worries my school-mates picked up from their parents—reports of the 400,000 people unemployed and homeless in Los Angeles alone; of the police stationed at the Nevada border to turn back thousands of impoverished immigrants from the Dust Bowl, desperate for a new start in California. Then there was the earthquake in 1933 that claimed 2,000 lives and devastated the meager hopes of countless others, already on the verge of despair. Later that year there were the terrible rains on New Year's Eve that submerged whole areas of southern California in mud, intensifying the sufferings of thousands.

My mother did her best to insulate me from the anxieties that must have tormented her in those lean times. And compared to millions of others we were lucky, for she managed to keep working fairly steadily. Looking back I can only marvel at the strength and determination that pulled her through the depression years—a woman alone, with a child to support. And she was in poor health, too, always prone to respiratory ailments. Finally she suffered a severe bout of the San Joaquin Valley fever, which left her with a racking cough. The doctor had advised her to seek a drier climate. So she called a friend, Gladys Taylor, who lived in Los Angeles. Without a moment's hesitation Gladys had replied, 'Come on down. I have room.'

We had packed our few possessions into a borrowed car. Our two suitcases we tied on top with rope, and my mother and I squeezed into the backseat with our boxes of books and linens. Throughout the trip the woman at the wheel kept up a constant stream of chatter, spasmodically hitting the brakes whenever another car approached. As we neared the town of Paso Robles it began to drizzle. Our driver hit the brakes one time too many, and we skidded off the slick road into a ditch. As if in slow motion the car flipped over on its side.

I remember hearing someone scream, and then we were all shaking and crying. We managed to wriggle out of the car into the mud. As we sat by the roadside in the rain, a truck-driver came to our aid and called a garage to tow the car to Paso Robles. My head ached from a nasty bump, and I was covered with scrapes and bruises. My mother had cracked a few ribs. After they bandaged her up in the emergency room, we found an auto court where we bedded down for the night.

By the next morning the car was upright again, but it was caked with mud and wobbled and clanked. Thank God it still ran! We rattled our way into Los Angeles—the biggest city I'd ever seen, its wide streets lined with ornate stone buildings, with bright, imposing signs. The women dropped us off at the corner of Sunset Boulevard and Highland Avenue, where we untied our muddy suitcases and unloaded our dented boxes and crumpled bags. Amid this scanty luggage, we sat on the curb until Gladys picked us up.

That was my introduction to Hollywood, movie capital of the world! But it hardly struck me then. All I noticed were those glorious art deco buildings on Sunset and Wilshire boulevards,.with

26

their gleaming fluted stone and chrome—so modern, so sophisticated. And I was really impressed with the new building there on the corner where we waited, with a façade as broad and white as a movie screen. It was Hollywood High, my new school.

I had been going there less than a month when I decided to cut typing class and run across Highland for a soda. Not a strawberry soda or a chocolate malted, the way the story goes. It was only a Coke, because Coke cost a nickel, and that was all the money I had. The place was the Top Hat Café. I think it's a gas station now.

As I sipped the Coke, a man at the fountain kept staring at me. He was well dressed and in his mid-forties, with sharp features, a mustache, and dark hair. I heard him talking to the counterman, who leaned over toward me and said, 'There's a gentleman who wants to meet you. He's all right. He works down the street and eats here all the time. Do you mind if he speaks to you?'

I said okay, and the counterman introduced him as Mr. Wilkerson. In turn I gave him my nickname, Judy Turner. He didn't seem to want to pick me up, because he didn't make idle chatter. He came straight to the point: 'Would you like to be in the movies?'

Completely shocked, all I could do was answer him truthfully. 'I don't know. I'd have to ask my mother.'

'Yes,' Mr Wilkerson said, as he gave me his business card. 'Ask your mother about it, and have her call me.'

It was nearly time for my next class, so I shoved the card into a notebook, gathered up my things, and ran back to Hollywood High.

We were living with Gladys Taylor then in her small, Spanish-style house on Glencoe Way. It had two bedrooms and a utility room, where Gladys did her ironing. That was where I slept, on a cot. My mother worked in a beauty parlor far away, so she left early in the morning and came home late. She was tired when I showed her Wilkerson's card, and so she shrugged it off. But Gladys took it more seriously.

'He publishes the *Hollywood Reporter*,' she said. 'It's a respectable paper, and he seems legitimate. Mildred, you should find out what he wants.'

'I've got to get up early,' my mother said. 'I don't know what we should do. If you think it's the right thing, Gladys, would you please give him a call?'

27

So Gladys phoned and made an appointment for the next day, at Mr. Wilkerson's office on Sunset Boulevard.

When W. R. Wilkerson gave me his card, he had been publishing the *Reporter* for six years. He had come to Hollywood in the 1920s with nightclub and restaurant interests. For a while he owned part of the Trocadero, popular with movie folks, and he often played poker on Wednesday nights with Louis B. Mayer and Nicholas Schenck. Despite Wilkerson's connections, the *Reporter* was banned from some studios. It criticized their practices—it told the truth.

It was housed in an old, elegant barbershop and haberdashery, one of Wilkerson's failed businesses. When Gladys brought me for my appointment—my mother had to work—I couldn't help staring at the decor. The offices had strange, ornate furnishings and glamorous rococo details. Mr. Wilkerson explained that, while he couldn't get me a job, he thought I had an excellent chance. He told me I was a very pretty girl.

I'd never thought of myself that way, although I had learned I was cute from flirting with boys, so I blushed and giggled. And though I liked the movies—still because of the clothes—I didn't read screen magazines. In no sense at all was I starstruck.

I would need an agent, Mr. Wilkerson was explaining, and he could recommend a good one. He told me to call Zeppo Marx, who had left the Marx Brothers' act to open a talent agency. Then he wrote Zeppo Marx a letter, put it in an envelope, and sealed it, saying, 'This will get you into Zeppo's office.'

What was in that letter, I'll never know. But a few days later Gladys and I presented it to Zeppo Marx himself. When he finished reading, he looked up and said, 'Tell me, Judy, how old are you?'

'Fifteen, Mr. Marx,' I said.

He slapped his hand down sharply on the desk, and he barked, 'Oh no, you're not.'

'Yes, I really am. Honest.'

'Don't ever say that again. As far as this industry goes, you're eighteen.'

We didn't know then why my age was so important, but later on I found out. Meanwhile Zeppo Marx agreed to represent me and assigned me to his agent Henry Willson. Henry took me around to meet the casting directors, but nobody offered me a job—not even as an extra. So he turned me over to another young man named Solly Biano.

By now it was almost Christmas, and I was working after school wrapping presents in a ladies' wear shop. One day Solly met me at work and told me to come with him. 'We'll go over to Warner's and see what's happening.'

He drove me to a studio in Burbank. When the casting director called me in, all he said was, 'Lift your skirt, walk, and turn around.'

Furious, embarrassed, and trying not to cry, I kept my eyes on the floor. No one had ever asked me to do that before. When I was just about to protest, he suddenly dismissed us. Then Solly got another idea.

'Mervyn LeRoy is looking for a girl,' he said. 'A sixteen-year-old. Let's go over to his bungalow.'

In the waiting room at the bungalow, Mervyn LeRoy's good-looking young assistant, Barron Polan, gave me an apple. I ate it while Solly went inside. Then he beckoned me in, and I met a short man in his middle thirties who paced the floor restlessly, chewing on a very large cigar.

He regarded me quizzically, and then he said, 'Well, you're very pretty. Tell me what you've done.'

I gave Solly a blank look. He only shrugged, and I answered, 'Nothing.'

'What about at school?'

I had been a cheerleader and I had played on the girls' softball team in San Francisco. I had good grades in English, Latin, and Spanish. But when it came to school plays or pageants or recitations, there was nothing I could say. So I smiled.

'No elocution class, no acting lessons?'

'No, sir.'

'She really *is* new,' he said, turning to Solly. Then he asked me to wait outside. As I sat there I fumed about the Warner's casting director who'd made me show him my thighs. My face burned with shame and disgust—and fear at what LeRoy might ask. But Barron Polan smiled at me from time to time. He must have known that my fate was being determined.

Out in the sun-blanched studio street, Solly told me, 'You're in the picture. It's a small part, but a good one, and we're getting you fifty a week.'

29

Fifty a week! That really impressed me, even more than getting the part. It was more than twice what my mother made. I could hardly wait to tell her.

And the day I received my first check, I met my mother coming home from work. I told her to sit down and close her eyes. Then I place the $50 in her hands. 'Now,' I said, 'you'll never have to work again.'

As things turned out, it was true.

Mervyn LeRoy once described our first meeting: 'She was so nervous her hands were shaking. She wasn't wearing any makeup, and she was so shy she could hardly look me in the face. Yet there was something so endearing about her that I knew she was the right girl. She had tremendous appeal, which I knew the audience would feel.'

Eventually I learned a bit about his personal history. He was the nephew of a famous industry figure, Jesse Lasky, who refused to give him a job. So he changed his last name, Levy, to LeRoy and looked for work as an actor. After a few bit parts, he began to write gags for Colleen Moore films, then graduated to directing. *Little Caesar*, starring Edward G. Robinson, was his first big film. It is now a screen classic.

By the time I met him he'd already become one of the most respected directors at Warner's, with *Public Enemy* and *I Am a Fugitive* among his credits. He hired me for a social melodrama about prejudice and political corruption, based on Ward Greene's *Death in the Deep South*, titled *They Won't Forget*. I signed the contract February 12, 1937, four days after I turned sixteen. He put me on a personal contract, not on the studio roster, and I couldn't know then how much that decision would alter my career.

The cameras would roll on March 6, but before we started shooting, Mervyn called a meeting with Solly, Barron, and me. 'We've decided you need a new name,' he told me. 'Judy Turner doesn't sound right. It's too ordinary, nothing really special.'

'Julia Jean?' I suggested.

'Nope. That's almost as bad. Turner sounds nice and American. But we need a new first name.'

Since it was just for the movie, I didn't have any objections. Mervyn brought out a dictionary of names, which we skimmed up to the *Ls*. 'Leonore?' Mervyn said. 'Lurlene?' I didn't like either one.

Then, out of nowhere, a name came into my head—as clearly as though God had decided to speak to me. I said to Mervyn (whom I still called Mr. LeRoy), 'What about—Lana?'

I'd heard it in my head as 'Lah-nah,' and I don't like hearing it pronounced any other way.

'Spell it,' Mervyn said.

I spelled it out, and he repeated it several times. 'Lana Turner. Lana Turner.' Then he gave a decisive nod. 'It sounds right. That's it. You're Lana Turner.'

It wasn't until some years later that I changed my name legally from Julia Jean Mildred Frances to Lana Turner. Sometimes the name *Lana* strikes me as having an almost magical significance. Although I had studied Spanish, I didn't know then that *lana* means 'wool'—the warm and comforting material of that fateful tight sweater—or that in Mexico it's a slang term for money, which eventually came in quantity.

Now that I had a name, I was slated for wardrobe tests. Besides the skirt and sweater, I wore high-heeled pumps and a perky tam. Everything came from wardrobe, even my brassiere. Yes, I did wear a bra, and no, it wasn't padded. A few more myths shot to hell. It was a blue silk bra to match the blue sweater.

During shooting I was rather uneasy—partly because the girl I played was going to be killed—but I did as I was told. My lines seemed natural and easy. After all, I was a schoolgirl just like Mary Clay. One scene took place at a soda fountain, where I asked the soda jerk for a malted—'and drop an egg in it as fresh as you.' That line may explain the chocolate malted I was allegedly sipping at Schwab's.

Mervyn spent most of the time watching the way I moved. 'Just walk,' he would tell me. 'Walk from here to there.' And Arthur Edeson, the cameraman, would follow me around, filming the way I walked. Of course it wasn't until the screening that I understood why or heard the sound track that would heighten the effect.

The first review I saw of *They Won't Forget* appeared in the *Hollywood Reporter*, under Billy Wilkerson's byline. 'Short on playing time,' it read, 'is the role of the murdered schoolgirl. But as played by Lana Turner it is worthy of more than passing note. This young lady has vivid beauty, personality, and charm.'

Once I recovered from my initial surprise at being in a movie, I

31

just assumed that this was how things happened. My mother was as much of an innocent as I was. Gladys was more sophisticated, but neither she nor my mother urged me to think of movies as a career. Whatever the reviews said, I didn't see myself as an actress. The movie was a one-shot job.

But that one review snowballed into an avalanche of publicity that the three of us could never have expected. During the filming, I had posed for lots of photos that were being distributed far and wide. Once, for instance, I was dressed in a riding costume and sent out to the studio ranch, to take some shots with a nice young man named Ronald Reagan. Because I was a featured player, my name and face appeared in ads, posters, and trailers. The publicists planted 'items' about me in newspapers and magazines. The more often I appeared in print, the better the studio liked me—which is not to say I approved of their campaign. The publicity shots all seemed to highlight my bosom. I was tagged 'the sweater girl' to hype the movie. It took me years of hard work to overcome that 'sweater girl' label.

Still, it shocked me when, instead of saying good-bye, Mervyn LeRoy cast me in his next film, *The Great Garrick*, a romantic comedy. I played a member of the Comédie Française masquerading as a country chambermaid. All I did was squeal, giggle, and curtsy through several scenes.

Since I traveled to the studio every day, my mother bought me my first car, which was hardly glamorous or speedy. It was a little Willys Knight that cost $50 third- or fourth-hand. It shimmied all the way out to the Warner studio in Burbank on tires not much wider than a bicycle's.

I'd thought of *The Great Garrick* mainly as one more job, but when I finished it, Mervyn loaned me to Samuel Goldwyn. Another picture! *The Adventures of Marco Polo*, a big, glittering production. Impressed though I was by the glamor and scope of the film, I hated my costumes and my makeup. I was a Eurasian handmaiden who had caught the eye of a warrior chief, played by Alan Hale. I wore a fancy, black Oriental wig, which had to be glued around my face with spirit gum. I didn't mind the wig so much—it was actually quite beautiful—but the costumes made me feel too undressed. And, worse yet, they shaved off my eyebrows, at the insistence of Goldwyn himself, and replaced them with false, slanting black ones. After three weeks of regular shaving, my eyebrows never grew back. I've had to draw or paste them on to this day.

32

The film's major star was Gary Cooper, but I never once saw him during the shooting. Ironically, when the film was released years later, I was billed as his costar, although most of my scenes had been cut. Why Goldwyn had asked for me, I can't even guess—hardly a glimpse of me remained.

Meanwhile letters from fans were beginning to arrive at Warner's—just a trickle at first, but before long, a tide. What a thrill! I had never gotten letters from strangers before, so I tried to answer them all. My mother and I spent whole evenings figuring out what to say. I liked responding, but the day soon came when I could no longer handle the volume myself.

Now almost seventeen, I had just started to date—sometimes Wayne Morris from the studio, or Bud Westmore, then a young makeup trainee, who became a good friend. The escort my mother especially liked was Don Barry, an actor in Westerns, who had red hair and somewhat resembled my father. With Don I attended the premiere of *The Life of Emile Zola* at that magical pagoda, Grauman's Chinese Theater.

A Hollywood premiere was a gala event in those days. Movies opened to a select audience resplendent in tuxedos and stunning evening gowns. A long red carpet was rolled out to the curb for the film's stars and studio personalities, who swept up in sleek limousines. The press turned out in force, and cheering crowds of fans greeted the arrival of each celebrity. Don and I wore evening dress, as part of the studio entourage, and I borrowed a fur coat from wardrobe. As we entered the theater George Jessel, master of ceremonies for a radio broadcast from the lobby, introduced me as a 'rising young star.' What a shock! All I could do was mumble something into the microphone about my eagerness to see this wonderful new picture.

Around this time Mervyn LeRoy told me that he was leaving Warner's for MGM, and that he would take me with him. My new salary would be $100 a week. Imagine—$100 a week! The raise meant that my mother and I could rent a house of our own.

We found one on Kirkwood Drive, high up in Laurel Canyon. We had to climb seventeen steps to get to the front door. The house had three bedrooms and a marble fireplace, and it was partially furnished—all in white. My room had a huge four-poster bed. On the living room floor lay a white bear rug, with a large grinning mouth filled with teeth. Sometimes my robe would catch on the teeth, as though the bear were snapping at me.

Compared to our cramped apartments, the house seemed vast and glamorous. But now I think of it with sadness—my mother's father stayed there with us when he was ill, and it was there that he died.

I officially signed on at MGM twelve days after I turned seventeen, on February 20, 1938. I was immediately cast in *Love Finds Andy Hardy*, with Mickey Rooney and Judy Garland. I played a new girl in the neighborhood, who was a precocious vamp and liked to kiss boys. From the start I told Carey Wilson, the producer, that I didn't like the 'sweater girl' label. His answer was to put me into a bathing suit. All the same, I realized that I had come to MGM under very special auspices. Word had gotten around that I was Mervyn LeRoy's protégé. Nobody ever made a pass at me. I was not just a six-month-option girl to be passed around the executive offices.

Often in those early years at MGM I'd see a young actress with more experience than I had, and I'd think, 'Oh boy, there's competition for me.' Six months later she would have fallen by the wayside. When I asked, people would say, 'You're so dumb!' It had to be spelled out for me that those six-month-option girls would never go on to a movie career—they were there for the benefit of management. That was what Zeppo Marx had meant when he told me to say I was eighteen. If I got one of those six-month-option deals, I'd better lie about my age—for *their* protection.

For those of us who were underage, the state required the studios to provide educational facilities. No more Hollywood High for me. Not that I missed it—I hadn't been there long, and I hadn't really made any friends. Both Alexis Smith and Nanette Fabray claim to have seen me there and thought that I would wind up in movies. But I never knew either of them until later, and I doubt that anyone really noticed me, except for the boy or two who made a fresh remark.

There had been a school at Warner's taught by Miss Carol Horn. But the Andy Hardy movie had a low budget and such a tight schedule that we did a lot of our schoolwork right on the set, supervised by an educational social worker. Sometimes we'd study for only fifteen minutes, with the assistants watching the clock, then go right back to the camera. Somehow I managed to earn my high school diploma that way.

34

My typical day began at six in the morning, in time for makeup and hairdressing at seven. The day's scene rehearsals were at nine. We'd read through once, then break, then hold a final rehearsal with actual props. Of course our hair would wilt and our makeup would smudge, so we'd have constant rounds of touch-ups before we ever got into costume. If we were lucky we'd be able to squeeze in a few shots before lunch. Only then, when the camera was rolling, would it be time to *act*. Sometimes the shooting continued until two or three in the morning. I could have slept in my dressing room, as Judy Garland and Mickey Rooney sometimes did—but I always insisted on driving home.

Part of that first year I attended MGM's 'little red schoolhouse.' I felt ridiculous there because most of the students, among them Mickey and Judy and Freddie Bartholomew, were a few years younger that I was. I rebelled against the childish restrictions— after all, I was seventeen. So one day I took the teacher, Miss Macdonald, aside and told her that I smoked.

'Not in the classroom,' she said firmly.

'That's not what I mean. I'll raise my hand to go to the bathroom, and have a cigarette there. Then I'll come right back. Would that be all right?'

She agreed. To the other students I must have seemed to be some kind of Peck's bad girl—and I suppose in fact I wasn't exactly an angel. I was going out a lot, mostly in groups, and staying out later than I should have. To appear older I'd sometimes ask for a drink, but after one sip I'd leave it sitting on the table. My mother was strict about drinking, and I didn't intend to defy her.

Although I still wasn't starstruck, I was amazed at the famous faces I saw in the Metro commissary. Once I spotted Greta Garbo walking on a studio street. Later I actually met her at a friend's house over tea. She spoke very little, but I was thrilled whenever her gaze or her smile fell on me.

Mervyn LeRoy's first picture for MGM was *Dramatic School*, which he produced but didn't direct. I played one of the student actresses, along with Paulette Goddard, Ann Rutherford, and Virginia Grey. Virginia and I became lifetime friends. It was hard to make friends on the set. We had to concentrate so hard when we worked, and we'd move on to the next film in a month, so there was very little time for camaraderie.

Dramatic School was set in Paris, probably because of Luise

Rainer's accent. She was the star. And during the shooting I witnessed some star temperament in action.

Winner of two Academy Awards, Luise Rainer was notorious for her difficult behavior. She hadn't wanted to do the picture from the outset; it turned out to be her last one for MGM. She and the director, Robert Sinclair, squabbled continually, and he took it out on us. One day Luise simply wouldn't or couldn't play a scene the way he wanted. She pleaded a headache and nausea, so we had to stop shooting.

The next day Sinclair's brooding grew ominous when Luise arrived late. Rehearsals began, and just when Luise seemed to have the right mood, he ordered a take. They corrected the lighting; everything was set. But when the camera started rolling, she suddenly went rigid and toppled straight to the floor.

'Cut! Kill the lights!' Sinclair was livid as he bent over Luise. But instead of checking her pulse, he exploded, 'You goddamned bitch! Get up of the floor! I'm sick of your tricks!'

She didn't move. She lay there like a corpse. We were herded out of the way, but we watched at a distance as studio assistants tried to lift her. Finally a kind of stretcher was constructed out of planks so the crew could carry her, still totally rigid, off the set. Although the word around the studio was that she was ill, I knew in my heart that what she had done was deliberate.

Paulette Goddard didn't produce that kind of tension, but it was clear that she was also a star. Besides her strong part, she had a bigger dressing room than the rest of us, and her costumes were *made* for her, while ours came out of wardrobe. The jewelry she wore was real—and her own. I'd never seen anyone quite so beautiful and elegant, except at a distance. Although she had a delicious sense of humor, she still occupied a pedestal, and I was quite in awe of her. Someday, I told myself, I would be like her.

Around this time I was invited to a party at Ann and Jack Warner's house in Beverly Hills. A Warner party, and I was just starting out at MGM! I remember that Ann Warner had just had her dressing room done over, and that I was amazed at such opulence. I began to feel that, by working hard, I'd be able to have not only security but luxuries. And by getting those I would be proving something about myself—that I was worth something. Possessions in Hollywood became very important, a way of entering those golden gates I'd imagined in my childhood. Deep down, I had a curious feeling that in some previous incarnation I'd known wealth. 'Lana,' a wise friend once told me, 'you're a very old soul.' And I do believe he was right—that I've been here before, that this isn't my first time around.

While I was still in my first year at MGM, I tested for the role of Scarlett O'Hara in *Gone with the Wind*. I had read the book and knew perfectly well that I could never play the role. That George Cukor himself was doing the test made it all the more embarrassing, for I knew his importance as a director. I felt completely out of my league. I prayed for the test to be finished, just so I could get out of there. Years later, much to my horror, many of the tests for the role were shown on TV, mine included! Needless to say, I wasn't the slightest competition for the lady who eventually got it.

The letters still poured in, and though the sacks of mail no longer came to me, I continued to keep up with some of the early fans. To each I sent a little note and a new photograph. Lana Turner fan clubs were springing up in different parts of the country. Later on, when I traveled, I met the presidents of some of them, and over the years we corresponded faithfully.

The studio continued to keep me busy. In *Calling Dr. Kildare*, I had the opportunity to work with Lionel Barrymore. An incredible man! How I admired and feared him. But at the same time I couldn't help liking him. Everyone on the set paid him deference, and he would shrug it off as though he were just a fellow actor. He would be wheeled onto the set because of his bad knee, and he would pretend to be crotchety and cantankerous, but in playing a scene with me he'd look up from under his brows with an adorable twinkle in his eyes. He enjoyed teasing me because I blushed easily. But he kept me on my toes, and I loved doing scenes with him.

Laraine Day was billed above me in that picture, and perhaps because my role was flashier, I felt some chilly vibrations from her direction. I responded in kind. Years later we did another film together, *Keep Your Powder Dry*, after our careers had advanced at different rates. Now I was the star. I tried to tease her out of her iciness, and now and then I succeeded—but not too often. Many people found her a strange cold fish of a woman.

All these early pictures—except for Goldwyn's, of course—I played with my own auburn hair. Usually I was described as a redhead. But then I got the chance to appear with the King himself, Clark Gable, in *Idiot's Delight*. In one dance number Gable performed with a straw hat and a cane, surrounded by four blondes. I hated the thought of bleaching my hair, but when the studio commanded, you obeyed. From that day on I was a golden blonde.

But despite the dye job, I didn't do the picture. Instead I went into the hospital for an operation. I'd had my appendix removed back in San Francisco, after an acute attack when I was fourteen. An incompetent surgeon had cut me open from just below the navel to near the pubic hairline, and later inserted tubes when peritonitis developed. Because of that botched operation, I had so much scar tissue that my ovaries and my colon were both affected. I suffered terribly during menstruation. My Los Angeles doctor finally had to operate to clean it up.

While I was in the hospital, I got a bonus check from the studio and the news that stacks of fan letters had accumulated in the hospital's mailroom. The press release reported that I had appendicitis. How amazing and touching that all those fans took the trouble to find out where I was.

By now Los Angeles was starting to shed the cocoon of the depression. Even young Englishmen traveled in small groups to Hollywood by way of Canada for flight training in the cloudless skies of south California. I heard many stories about those romantic young men, many of whom returned home in time to fight the Battle of Britain. Unfortunately I never got to know any of these heroic flyers who were adopted by Ronald Colman and other members of Hollywood's English colony. The war in Europe was allowing FDR to revitalize the economy. Although the United States wasn't involved yet, Roosevelt had ordered ten thousand airplanes from the city's manufacturers. There were jobs again, there was money again, the city was booming. Construction began on the new Union Station and the new Spanish-style post office, the largest mail-handling center in the West. The city swelled with hope and pride—once again, California was the shining land of opportunity.

The new prosperity brought celebrations, festivals, parades—the reawakening of a festive spirit. Glittering restaurants and nightclubs sprang up to serve a clientele starving for entertainment. That was a golden era for me, too, when I was seventeen, and not serious about anybody. How I loved to go out! I ran with a crowd that included Linda Darnell, Bonita Granville, Ann Rutherford (who was especially sharp and funny), Jackie Cooper, and Mickey Rooney. I never dated Mickey, that adorable nut. He had unmistakable talent, and he knew he was a star.

We had youth, we had beauty, we had money, we had doors open to us. Four, or six, or eight of us—Betty Grable, Mary Carlisle, and the others—would meet for lunch at, say, Romanoff's, just to watch the people, gossip, and giggle. We had our own booth, and everyone in the restaurant stared at us.

And after lunch we'd go shopping, even if it meant only window shopping. And we dressed to the nines, in hats, gloves, alligator purses with matching shoes, and sometimes fur pieces. No blue jeans for us in those days. We were glamorous and we looked it. And Beverly Hills, though really a small town then, seemed to be elegance itself.

We were so alive and so caught up in business. What are you working on? What's coming up next? Do you like the story? No, I hate it, but I have to do it. Industry talk made us feel so grown-up.

We'd play tennis, or go roller skating. You'd get a party of twenty or thirty of us down at the big roller rink on Sunset Boulevard. We'd always go in groups, big groups. Young people didn't pair off then as they do today.

And we jitterbugged and danced the Big Apple. I loved to dance and was good at it. Or sometimes we'd go to a matinee when we weren't working. But, believe it or not, we never did anything naughty. The worst thing we did was go 'cruising.' That word has a different meaning now, a sexual connotation. But then cruising simply meant that a few girls would pile into somebody's convertible and ride with the top down to the drive-in. It would be eight or nine in the evening, ten at the latest. And when we'd see a car full of boys, we'd flirt. That was cruising. If, God forbid, somebody asked me, 'Say, aren't you that Lana Whatshername,' I'd say, 'Oh, no, no. I've been told I look like her.' Then we'd step on the gas pedal and get the hell out of there.

There used to be an amusement pier on the Santa Monica beach. Sometimes we'd drive down there and go on the rides. We'd enjoy it until we were recognized, and then we'd have to run from the autograph seekers.

But it was all innocent fun, nothing harmful and nothing serious.

Even so, my nights on the town were getting more press than

39

MGM's publicity people were churning out. Though I'd been shy as a young girl, once I came out of my shell I wanted to live it up. But now every time I dated someone, it made headlines as a 'hot new romance.'

Eventually Louis B. Mayer himself took notice. He summoned me to his office, along with my mother. In an emotional, disappointed tone he told me that keeping late hours and making the papers were risking my wonderful future. He actually had tears in his eyes at one point, so I started crying too. Then he jumped up and shouted. 'The only thing you're interested in is . . .' and he pointed to his crotch.

Outraged, my mother rose from her seat. 'How dare you. Mr. Mayer! In front of my daughter!'

Then, grabbing me by the arm, she marched me out of his office. After that I did try to slow down for a while.

My heady first year at MGM was drawing to a close. On Mervyn LeRoy's advice, I got a new agent to renegotiate my contract. By then I had established enough of a reputation to get Johnny Hyde, a vice-president at the William Morris Agency. Through his efforts, my salary was raised to $250 a week, with escalations every year. That was a huge sum in those days. I could buy the clothes I'd always dreamed of wearing. I could afford a maid. And no more Willys Knights for me—I owned a new fire-engine-red Chrysler coupe.

But by the end of 1938 I didn't care about money or movies or fame. I had found something more important. In a crazy, dizzy, girlish way I had fallen in love.

3

H IS NAME was **Greg Bautzer**. He was about thirty, tall and husky, with soulful dark eyes, a tanned complexion, and a flashing smile that showed a lot of white teeth. He was so smooth, so self-assured, that all the other boys I knew seemed like children. Greg was a lawyer who had already won a reputation for brilliance. His partner, Bently Ryan, handled the court work. Greg's talents lay in the business end of the practice and in his ability to trade on his social connections. He was a man who could get things done, sweep aside obstacles with effortless confidence. I wasn't surprised at all when I recently read that he is now the power behind the throne at MGM.

He seemed enchanted by my vivaciousness and lack of worldly wisdom. He loved to take me out and show me off. We went dancing at the most glamorous places, like Ciro's or the Trocadero. I'd always wanted to be older and know what life was all about. And Greg was so gentle, so considerate, how could I help falling in love?

I was seventeen, romantic, and a virgin. My only experience up to now had been necking, with very little petting. I'd always fought off my eager young dates when they wanted to touch my breasts. But Greg was far too sophisticated to wrestle in the front seat of a car or to steal a kiss at the front door.

When we went dancing, he would rub his body up against mine. It would thrill me, make me shiver, those first flushes and tinglings, and the wondering, when, oh, when would it happen? But I was scared at the same time. And Greg never rushed me, never tried to hustle me into bed, for which I thanked him then and thank him now. Yet it was inevitable, and we both knew it.

Finally one night we did make love. Greg didn't take me to a hotel but to his own home. His mother lived with him, but he thought she was out for the evening. Actually, she wasn't, but we didn't find out until much later, when we heard her moving around in her bedroom. By that time, it was too late.

Greg was loving and patient with me, even though I was awkward. I had no idea how to move or what to do. The act itself hurt like

41

hell, and I must confess that I didn't enjoy it at all. I didn't even know what an orgasm was. But I loved being close to Greg and holding him, and the feeling that now, at last, I was giving myself to him. I was giving him all of me. Now he would know how much I loved and adored and worshipped him. Now I was truly his.

To tell the truth, I wasn't looking forward to the next time. I did feel passion for him and eventually I did achieve orgasm, but what I really wanted was to have Greg hold me, keep me safe in his arms. And I didn't sleep with Greg very often. I was busier than ever at Metro with larger parts, which required more time for wardrobe details, makeup, and hairdressing. My billing went up a notch after *Calling Dr. Kildare*, so for my next picture, *These Glamour Girls*, I had more publicity chores. If I wasn't working at night, I often had early calls. That meant I'd have to be home by midnight.

Greg accepted my time limitations. He'd drop me off, say good night, and kiss me good-bye. What I was too young and inexperienced to realize was that Greg was getting his action on the side.

He'd always enjoyed a reputation as a playboy; he was so attractive and desirable that a lot of women threw themselves at him. But at first that didn't bother me. I was the one he was usually seen with, the woman who so proudly wore his little 'engagement' ring. Later I understood that to Greg the little diamond meant something more like friendship than devoted love and marriage. As a matter of fact, he remained a bachelor for years, always with some beautiful woman, usually a star, as his lover. No one could catch the elusive Greg Bautzer until Dana Wynter came along and married him. How she did it, none of us can figure out to this day. After all, he not only had the milk free, as the saying goes, but the cream and the cow as well.

One day I got a phone call from Joan Crawford. Greg had taken me to several parties at her house, but I didn't know her well. Those parties were all the same. After dinner the guests would be herded into a projection room to watch movies. Joan knitted constantly. During the film, you could always hear her needles clicking away.

I was surprised and intrigued by her call, but even more by her request. 'Lana, dear,' she cooed, 'I wonder if you'd drive out to my home. I'd like to talk to you about something very important.'

When I arrived she greeted me cordially and fussed over making me comfortable. 'Now, darling,' she began, 'you know I'm a bit

42

older than you, and so I may know some things you haven't learned yet . . .'

'Like what?' I asked, thinking that she was *quite* a bit older.

'Well, dear, when you're young you see things a certain way, but that's not always how they are. As you get older you realize that life can be very complex . . .' She continued rambling, as I grew more and more fidgety.

Finally I interrupted. 'Joan, what are you trying to tell me?'

Looking back, I sometimes marvel at the acting performance Joan delivered there in her living room. Sincerity overcame her. Her hand went to her forehead, then to her heart. Agitatedly, she reached for a cigarette, then fumbled with the matches. Finally she got it lit and drew in deeply, gearing herself for the thrust.

What a thrust! 'Well, darling, I feel it's only right to tell you that Greg doesn't love you anymore . . . that he hasn't for a long time.'

I could only stare at her, too stunned to speak.

'I couldn't let you go on, hoping, believing . . . Because, you see, Greg wouldn't tell you. Darling, you've simply got to know that what Greg and I have is real, and it's been going on for a long time. It's me he truly loves . . .' She gave me a direct look, and her eyes hardened. 'But he hasn't figured out how to get rid of you.'

By then I was outraged. 'Get rid of me! Trash is something you get rid of. Or disease, you get rid of. I'm not something you get rid of—'

'Dear, I know how you feel . . .'

'Don't you dare say that to me! You are lying about Greg. I know it isn't true—'

'But why should I lie to you, darling? He loves me, only me.'

My head was whirling. Was she telling the truth? Maybe I'd suspected Greg was seeing other women—but Joan? Was I crazy or was she? I sat rooted in my chair, clutching the arms.

She was still talking. 'So, Lana dear, why don't you be a good little girl and tell him you're finished—that you know the truth now, and it's over . . . Make it easier on yourself. He doesn't want to hurt you.'

'Thank you, Joan,' I said, as calmly as I could. All I wanted was to get the hell out of there. I was starting to tremble with anger, against her, against Greg. And the incredible hurt . . . I was damned if I'd let her see it.

The minute I got home I confronted Greg. He strongly denied it. Had she made it all up? I wanted desperately to believe him.

43

Maybe she was jealous of me, or she'd gotten herself into some kind of hysterical state . . .

I grew more and more confused, I spent evenings agonizing over where Greg was, who he was with. Then I'd see him and start to believe all over again. I constantly swung from love to hurt to rage to humiliation.

It's funny what you remember. 'Deep Purple' was a popular song then, and many times I had danced with Greg to the romantic melody. During that period of doubting Greg, with all my girlish heartbreak, I recall that I couldn't bear to hear that song. In fact I couldn't stand it—or the color purple for years.

I buried myself in my work. In *These Glamour Girls* I was billed as costar with Lew Ayres. There were so many girls in the picture that the studio had just slapped up some flats as our dressing rooms. As soon as I saw them I got Mr. Mayer on the phone. I could hear someone on the set whispering, 'Uh-oh, she's going to get in trouble.' But I went ahead and told him directly, 'I want a dressing room of my own.' And I got it.

Emily Torchia, a publicist, once said about it, 'If there was ever a point at which the studio recognized her as an important star, that might be it. Or was it when a special salad named for her was put on the commissary menu? It was called Lanallure Salad.'

Maybe that was it. I got top billing in my next picture. It was *Dancing Co-ed*, featuring Artie Shaw and his band. Artie was twenty-eight when he arrived in Hollywood, at the height of the swing-band fever. A fine piano and clarinet player, he'd found radio jobs in New York at an early age. He had rivaled Benny Goodman as the King of Swing with such arrangements as 'The Back Bay Shuffle,' 'Copenhagen,' and 'Begin the Beguine.' Even so, he claimed to hate leading the band, and once he'd quit to write a novel based on the life of Bix Beiderbecke. It was never published. His own band members called him an intellectual snob.

Although he was one of the most popular band leaders in the country, Artie was despised on the set because of his arrogance. He never missed a chance to complain that it was beneath him to appear in a Hollywood movie. The crew plotted to drop an arc light on his head. I hated him too, and I even told the press that I thought he was the most egotistical person I'd ever met.

He was complaining in print, too: 'The film business reeks to high heaven. I got a lot of bad publicity. I don't care. I was supposed to play Artie Shaw, but they wanted me to say, "Hi-ho, lads and lassies." That's a mixture of Rudy Vallee and Ben Bernie. I refused.'

After he finished the film, Artie went to Mexico for a while. When he got back to Hollywood, Phil Silvers, hoping to needle him, brought him to the set of my new picture, *Two Girls on Broadway*. If Silvers wanted to see a fight, he was disappointed.

It wasn't that I had forgotten Artie's behavior on *Dancing Co-ed*, but after six months, my bad feelings had evaporated. Chatting to Artie that day, I found him surprisingly pleasant. My free evenings were reserved for Greg, so when Artie mentioned having dinner sometime, I said we should make it lunch. I gave him my phone number.

I had just passed my nineteenth birthday. My mother's birthday was February 12, four days later, and Greg had invited us both to dinner to celebrate. Around six-thirty, when we were both dressed and ready, Greg phoned to cancel, pleading a bad stomach ache. Furious, I banged down the phone. A minute or two later it rang again. I was sure it was Greg calling to apologize.

But it wasn't Greg. It was Artie.

I suppose that if Artie hadn't called just then, I'd have stayed home like a faithful puppy and forgiven Greg once more. But when Artie suggested dinner, I said, 'Fine.' I was so furious at Greg that I did something I'd never done before—I took off his engagement ring and put it in my change purse. I've since wondered about that. If Artie had seen my engagement ring, would the evening have turned out differently?

We drove toward the ocean along Sunset Boulevard, and Artie did most of the talking—about how tired he was of the big-band business, about the concert orchestra he was planning that would make people take jazz music seriously, about how he wanted to write music and someday write books. He talked about Nietzsche and Schopenhauer. (I'd never heard of them, and when I tried to read them later, I didn't get far.) He said he was sick of jitterbugs and autograph hounds. What he wanted now were the basic things—a good, solid marriage, a home, and children.

Those were the things I had wanted with Greg. When he'd slipped that little gold and diamond ring on my third finger, left hand, he'd said to me, 'Now you're my girl.' I'd believed it with all my heart. Yet Greg had never painted a picture of marriage for me. And I wanted to be married, to have babies. I love children. Although my career was beginning to blossom, it wasn't so important to me then as it became later, when I fell in love with acting. Then I was very young, and to me acting was work. It meant getting up at horrendous hours, reporting to a studio and to bosses. I'd have given it up in a snap to be someone's wife, a mother,

Artie built me a romantic dream, with a white picket fence around it. His eloquence stirred me, and the evening took on a glow as we parked in a spot overlooking the ocean. We forgot about eating. We didn't kiss, but as we talked we held hands. Artie was right. I'd had my taste of fame and prosperity. Now it was time for more serious things. I told Artie that I didn't care if I never made another picture. And at the moment I meant it, or thought I did.

It wasn't that I fell in love with Artie that night. I wasn't even physically attracted. But here was a wonderfully intelligent man, far more talented and famous than Greg would ever be, who took me seriously. And underneath it all I can see, looking back, was the desire to get even with Greg.

So when Artie asked, 'Do you mean what you're saying?' I said, 'With all my heart.'

'Suppose I were to call up right now and charter a plane? Would you come with me?'

'Yes, I would.'

'Swell,' Artie said. 'Let's go.'

We didn't even kiss on it. He simply squeezed my hand and started the car. We drove to his house on Summit Ridge, where he called Paul Mantz, who had a charter plane service out of Burbank. When he hung up we drove straight to the airport. It wasn't until we were seated in the plane, side by side, that Artie kissed me shyly. We smiled at each other.

Looking down on the lights of Los Angeles, I thought, 'How my life is going to change! But it seems so right, and it will be. It was destined to happen like this . . .'

In Las Vegas a taxi met our plane, and the driver found us a justice of the peace. George E. Marshall married us in his bathrobe and pajamas. When it was time to place the ring on my finger, Artie took off his own, a blue star sapphire set in platinum. Of course it didn't fit, but it made me his wife.

After the ceremony we went out to an all-night diner for coffee. Suddenly I realized that my mother had no idea where I was. The taxi drove us to the telegraph office, and I wrote out a message: GOT MARRIED IN LAS VEGAS. CALL YOU LATER. LOVE, LANA.

Maybe it was subconscious, but I didn't mention who it was I'd married.

My mother couldn't imagine that I would run off with Artie, so she called Greg's number. When she read him the telegram he was as astounded as she was. Utterly bewildered, he told her he would try to find out what had happened. How he found out I don't know, but he called her back within an hour and told her that I had eloped with Artie. She said his voice shook as he added, 'I've lost her.'

We flew back to Burbank, not suspecting that the newspaper people were already after us. Near the top of Summit Ridge Drive we found the narrow street lined with cars. Several carloads of reporters and photographers had followed us up the hill, so we couldn't turn around. All at once questions were hurtled at us, cameras were thrust in our faces. I prayed that Artie would be polite. But he was fuming, almost purple in the face, screaming obscenities at the press. I had never heard cursing like that before. Yanking my arm, he tugged me through the crowd.

'I'm sorry, I'm sorry,' I cried to the reporters, with a helpless gesture of my free arm. 'I can't talk now. I'm sorry.' Artie's behavior frightened me. I could understand why the elopement was considered news. It wasn't all that long ago that I had freely, publicly aired my low opinion of the man who was now my husband—and who was now dragging me up the walk. He double-locked both front and back doors, closed and locked all the windows, pulled down the blinds and closed the drapes as though fending off a siege. A siege was what it turned out to be.

We heard banging and then the crash of breaking glass from one of the windows. I ran to a phone and called Howard Strickling, who was MGM's head of publicity. I told him where I was and begged him to help us. 'The press is here, a whole mob, and they're breaking windows!'

'My God,' he said. 'Get Artie to talk to them.'

'He won't.'

'Then you've got to talk to them.'

'He won't let me.'

Howard dispatched some people to placate the reporters, but they couldn't shake them all. Artie was beside himself. He screamed out the broken windows while I cowered in the bedroom. I did

47

manage to phone my poor shocked mother from there, to try to explain the night's events. It was close to midnight before the last cars had driven away and we felt safe enough to sneak out through the shrubbery to Artie's car. His friend Edgar Selwyn, who'd produced *Dancing Co-ed*, had offered us his guestroom and had bought me a wedding ring on Artie's instructions.

I'd been wearing the same damn clothes for more than twenty-four hours, a little navy blue dress trimmed in red, with a jacket and suede shoes to match, under some kind of cloth coat. I felt dirty and rumpled and weary.

And I was still shaken by seeing the violent side of Artie; it was worse than he'd ever been on the set. His rage at the reporters, his screaming and cursing . . . You were always on your best behavior with the press; you might be seething inside, but, boy, you didn't show it. Artie had shown it, and then some.

It was about midnight now, and Edgar showed us to the guestroom, which he'd filled with flowers from his own garden. He kissed me gently and then he said, 'Well, I'll leave you two alone now.'

And there I was alone beside a man I didn't know at all. I'd never been with any man but Greg, who was always romantic and considerate. But this man was a stranger, and I had to keep looking at the ring on my finger to remind myself that I was married. None of it seemed real.

Artie seemed tired, and I was exhausted. I hoped he wouldn't try anything. Maybe we could just sleep. And in fact, once we were in bed, I thought nothing was going to happen.

Artie asked, 'Are you all right?'

'I'm awfully tired. Aren't you?'

'Yeah, exhausted.' And he kissed me, a sweet little kiss, and turned off the light.

But then I felt his hand on me. I said softly, 'No, please don't,' but I was too shy to say more, and Artie became aroused.

He was clumsy and fumbling and I didn't help at all, and when we finally got into position . . . well, it was horrible. Meaningless and over in a minute. He just went limp, and he was so quiet about it. As for me, I experienced nothing but a question—what am I doing underneath this man? I don't even know him. It doesn't feel good. I began to feel as if I'd betrayed Greg. Yet at the same time I also felt committed to Artie. I was his wife for the rest of my life. And maybe it would get better if I could just get some rest.

But there had been no kissing and no cuddling, either before or afterward, and I had to fight hard to keep Greg out of my thoughts.

I read someplace that Judy Garland, then seventeen, had had a serious crush on Artie. She had gone out with him days before I did and hoped he was getting serious. The morning after we eloped, she was eating breakfast in bed when she saw the headlines, and immediately burst into tears.

Later that day Phil Silvers got an angry phone call from Betty Grable, who was in love with Artie and getting a divorce. 'That son of a bitch,' she told Phil, 'who does he think he is?'

That morning Edgar Selwyn gave us a champagne breakfast, and then we went back to Artie's house. I was still wearing the same clothes. I hadn't even brought my eyebrow pencil. The photographers were lurking, and Metro's publicity people had arranged for an interview. Quickly I sketched in some eyebrows with an ordinary lead pencil. I know it looked just terrible.

Once the press had gone I phoned Mr. Mayer at the studio. He said, 'You've really gone and done it this time.'

'Yes,' I answered, 'but I'm very happy.'

'That's good,' he said, 'but you do remember you're making a film, don't you? We can't stop production.'

'Can't they work around me for a while?'

'Not for long,' he barked. 'You can have three days.'

If I'd wondered how he felt about the marriage, I certainly knew now.

Next I went home for some clothes, and to see my mother for the first time since the marriage. We had moved from the house in Laurel Canyon to a big Spanish-style one on Beverly Glen Boulevard. She didn't criticize but simply asked me, 'Why did you do it?'

'Because I think I'm going to be very happy,' I told her. What else could I say?

I'd driven Artie's car, and when I got back I tooted the horn. Before he came out he checked to make sure that another siege hadn't begun. From then on he never came to the door without first looking outside for reporters. He stared in amazement at the number of outfits I'd brought, although it was only a small sampling, and his eyebrows shot up when he saw my assortment of shoes. I moved everything into an unfurnished room in the house. In our room there was only a three-quarters-size bed. I would discover that Artie couldn't bear to sleep by the wall. I had to sleep on that side, and I hated it.

After I'd put my things away, he suddenly asked, 'What are you all dressed up for?'

I was wearing a new dress, and I told him I always dressed that way, but it was no use. What he wanted me to wear was a blouse and skirt, with loafers. Mystified, I changed my clothes. 'Now, that's better,' he said. 'That's the way I want you to look. Except for one thing. Take off your lipstick.'

After I'd blotted it off, wondering if he was out of his mind, he said, 'Perfect! Stay that way all the time.'

I started to laugh, but he was deadly serious. 'When you're with me, that's the way you're to look.' So to avoid arguments I obeyed—once I was out of the house and on my way to the studio, I would stop and put on lipstick. Years later I would hear that Artie had given Ava Gardner the same treatment. Was he trying to strip away what he considered the outer shell to reveal the 'real' person underneath? If he wanted a drab, dowdy wife, why did he keep marrying beautiful, glamorous women?

I soon learned that he also wanted a wife who could cook and keep house. I had started working so young that I hadn't learned to cook, but Artie insisted that I try. And my mind also needed improvement. I had to read books. He pushed them at me so fast that I couldn't have kept up if I had been working for an advanced degree.

I suppose we must have had occasional good times together. I admired Artie's talents as a musician, but it seemed impossible for me to cope with the temperament of a genius, if that's what he had. When we argued—which was often—he would twist the discussion into a philosophical harangue from which I generally retreated in tears. It became clear that he had a distinct image of the wife of Artie Shaw, and that there was no way I could match it. 'MGM means more to you than I do,' he would accuse me. It's true, I still took my work seriously. But I raced home afterward every day because he wanted me to be there waiting for him. When I was late there were ugly scenes.

By the third day of our marriage I knew I was in trouble, but how could I get out of it? And besides, to me marriage meant forever. Although I came from a broken home, my parents had only separated, never divorced. I'd still like to think that, if my father hadn't been killed, they might have gotten back together. My mother never had another man, nor my father another woman. Marriage meant permanence to me, but with Artie, I began to realize, it was no marriage. It was hell.

We lived in the little cottage of my fantasy, but without two loving people inside it. Artie never planned things with me. We never sat down and discussed anything or imagined a future together, the way husbands and wives do. I just lived from day to day, trying to get through one day and one night at a time.

One day in the second month of our marriage, Artie let something slip. 'Well, my other wife did such and so . . .'

'Your *other* wife? What other wife?'

'Uh, my second wife . . .'

'*Second* wife?' I couldn't believe my ears.

'I was married only briefly to the first one.'

After that I'd walk around saying to myself, 'I'm this guy's third wife!' And I felt very gullible.

Right after *Two Girls on Broadway*, I plunged into a new film, *We Who Are Young*. No fancy wardrobes this time. I had the straight dramatic role of a young newlywed with a lot of problems. When the first call came Artie hit the roof. He'd planned to take me to New York to show me its cultural advantages. To keep the peace, I called the studio to explain that Artie insisted on the trip because we hadn't really had a honeymoon yet. I knew I was risking suspension, and sure enough, the studio threatened just that. My agent, Johnny Hyde, managed to get the shooting delayed for a few weeks, while the studio told the press I'd been granted a vacation as 'a bonus for excellent work.' It was my first time off in two years. Artie won that round; he also wangled an agreement that I wouldn't have to give interviews in New York.

Autograph hunters plagued us throughout our stay, and Artie reacted in his usual explosive way. As we left the Sherry Netherland for our first dinner date at Reuben's, fans began to press us. Artie started running, pulling me along with my coat flapping and my hair coming undone, shouting insults over his shoulder. We arrived breathless and disheveled. The columnist Leonard Lyons and his wife Sylvia, who were friends of Artie's, were waiting there. As I started to describe the chase, I burst out laughing. How ludicrous we must have looked! But all Artie could do was fume, 'This idiot here kept saying, "I'm sorry, I'm sorry." What the hell is there to be sorry about?'

I never knew why, but Artie didn't want me to meet his mother. But I noticed her number on a pad by the phone, and one day I decided to call her. A voice with a thick Jewish accent answered. When I told her who I was, she begged me to come and see her. 'Oh, please, please come now. Don't wait for Artie. I want to meet his wife.'

I called the limousine, and the driver took me to an apartment building somewhere outside Manhattan. Mrs. Arshawasky (Artie's real last name) had a small, beautifully kept apartment. She was warm and effusive, and obviously thrilled to meet me. When she asked, 'Why doesn't Artie come?' I explained that he was very busy, but that I was sure he would see her. After she had fussed over me and served tea, she wanted to bring over her neighbors to meet me. I said that I couldn't stay long, that Artie would soon be expecting me, and all at once an uncomfortable silence fell. With an odd look, she asked, 'Does my son know you are here?'

I told her the truth, as one woman to another, 'I somehow think he doesn't want me to meet you.'

Then Artie's mother began to cry. 'I'm so sorry,' I protested. 'I didn't mean to hurt you. I came here because I wanted to know you and love you. You're my one and only mother-in-law, and you're important to me.' She dried her eyes and begged me to have Artie bring me back before we left. I said that I would. We kissed and said good-bye. I never saw her again.

It was a few days before I found Artie in a pleasant enough mood to tell him about my visit.

'What!' he shouted. 'How dare you go behind my back? What are you, some kind of spy?'

My heart sank, but I guess I wasn't surprised. All in all, that New York trip—our honeymoon—was a disaster.

Artie wasn't always surly. Sometimes he actually enjoyed life. One night there was an MGM bash at Earl Carroll's, a nightclub on Sunset Boulevard. Artie played the clarinet in the show, and I performed a dance number from *Two Girls on Broadway*. Phil

Silvers did a comedy turn, and since he had no date, he tagged along with us after the show.

At Artie's insistence, we headed home. I made drinks and went off to change. When I came back Artie and Phil were smoking what they called 'reefers.' I'd heard of marijuana, of course, but I'd never seen it before. It was associated mainly with jazz musicians. Artie and Phil offered me some, and I said no.

'You watch Phil,' Artie said. 'Pretty soon I can tell him the house is on fire, and he'll start laughing.'

I lit my own ordinary cigarette and sat down. Before long, sure enough, they were both laughing at remarks that struck me as dull or idiotic. Feeling out of it, I asked Artie what was going on, and he said, 'Oh, the world is beautiful, and you're the most beautiful creature on earth. I love you so much.'

So maybe I should have kept him on the stuff.

After a while Phil announced that he was hungry, and we all went into the kitchen and began rummaging through the cabinets. Phil found a can of beans and began eating them with a spoon, straight from the can. Artie opened string beans, peach halves, pineapple slices, and pickles. They got out a loaf of bread and a box of crackers, and crammed all sorts of mixtures into their mouths like ravenous little boys. I'd seen enough. I went into the bedroom, took the pins out of my hair, and came back in a house-coat. By then they were absolutely silent. Artie stared at me with sleepy eyes, as Phil carefully daubed his nails with some polish that I'd left on an end table. He held up his hand. 'Isn't that beautiful?' he said.

'Hey, Phil,' Artie said. 'That looks great.'

I could see that there was no place for me in their scene, so I headed off to bed. But the incident stands out in my memory. Seeing Artie have fun was so rare.

One day I came home from the studio to find Artie and two friends waiting for dinner. There wasn't much in the house, so I made spaghetti. When I brought it to the table Artie took one sniff and said, 'What is this crap?' Then he slammed the bowl to the floor. 'Clean up that mess,' he ordered.

He kept making scenes like that, bullying, frightening displays, until one night I became hysterical. I couldn't stop screaming and shaking and crying. Artie tried to calm me down, and then he called a doctor, who injected me with something that knocked me out on the spot.

I came to briefly as I was being lifted from an ambulance. Artie put a towel over my face so no one would recognize me. The next morning I woke up in a strange bed.

'Where am I?' I asked, just like in the movies. But it was certainly a natural question.

The nurse told me the name of the hospital, and added, 'But you're doing well, Mrs. Johnson.'

'Who?'

'Mrs. Mildred Johnson. That's who you are.' She must have thought I was crazy.

My head felt dull and heavy. My tongue was thick from the sedative. Suddenly, in a flood, I remembered the night before— the argument, the hysteria, the needle, the towel over my face. There was no sign of Artie. The nurse and I were alone.

I telephoned my mother to tell her what had happened.

'Oh, my God!' she screamed. 'My baby. How are you? Where's Artie?'

I had to confess that I didn't know.

She came down right away. The nurse didn't want to release me until the doctor checked me out, so when she went to call him I got dressed. I was still unsteady from the strong drug, but my mother helped me. We just walked out the main door and got into her car.

I couldn't seem to think straight. 'What shall I do?' I asked over and over again.

'You could come back home with me,' my mother said, and we both shrugged a little. 'I don't know what to tell you, honey, but I think that maybe you'd better go back to Artie.'

Go back to him for what? Another fight? Another hysterical scene? Another needle in my arm? But, sadly, I knew she was right. I was overdue at the studio, and the last thing I needed now was a rumor that I'd left my husband and had a nervous breakdown.

Artie and I didn't discuss the incident, and for a short time our life was fairly quiet. Artie seemed brooding and pensive, and I kept my distance for the sake of peace. Slowly, though, our regular pattern reemerged.

One morning Artie was in the bedroom, and he asked me to bring him some orange juice. As an afterthought, he threw in, 'And when you go out, take my shoes to be shined.'

'I can't today, Artie. I'll be on the set all day.'

54

'Goddamn it, this is more important,' he yelled back.

When I brought him the juice, I couldn't get the door open.

'Pull it hard,' he shouted. 'It's not locked.'

We both kicked and shoved and pulled the door, but it wouldn't budge. Artie grew angrier still. 'What did you do to the damned door? I'm kicking it down!' he bellowed.

All of a sudden, I started laughing uncontrollably. I could imagine Artie behind the door, red-faced and steaming. With a few furious kicks he smashed it in and came charging out like a wounded bull. Ignoring the orange juice, he stormed out of the house, half dressed, trailing a towel behind him. 'You be sure to have those shoes shined,' he called back.

That trivial incident was the last straw. I went straight to the telephone and called Greg Bautzer, the only lawyer I knew I could trust. Though he hadn't been very good at keeping our dates, this time he came through. 'Get your things together,' he said. 'I'll have you out of there today.'

4

ARTIE TOOK the divorce suit calmly enough. Benton Cole, his band manager at the time, came home with Artie the day I left and later described what happened. In his haste Artie had forgotten his house keys, and he had to smash a window to get in. When he saw I wasn't there he roamed from room to room in a daze. After he'd seen the empty closets and opened my drawers and found them empty, too, he said with resignation to Ben, 'Well, I guess she isn't kidding.'

Do you know, Artie wouldn't give me the baby grand piano that was a wedding present? When my people came to get it, he refused to let it out of the house. Oh, it was a beautiful piano, a rich, dark mahogany, and it was an expensive gift. But what gets me is not the fact that the wedding presents by tradition belong to the bride. What gets me is that *this* wedding present came from *my* mother! I'll *never* forgive him for that!

We'd been living apart for a few weeks when he phoned to ask for a favor. He was recording at a radio station, and he had promised them a picture of the two of us. Would I come down and pose with him? I agreed because I didn't want any gossip, and so far the press was in the dark.

For the pictures Artie put his arm around me and kept giving me lovey-dovey squeezes. I tried to seem natural, but inside I recoiled from his touch. Then a reporter mentioned that there was a rumor we were splitting up and asked me to comment. I saw my chance for freedom—and grabbed it.

I took Artie's hand and firmly removed it from my waist. 'That is correct,' I said. 'We're really through.'

Then, smiling nicely at Artie, who looked astonished, I strode out of the room with my head held high.

After completing *We Who Are Young*, I felt drained and in need of a rest. I went to Mr. Mayer and asked for a few weeks off. As there would be problems if I traveled alone, I wanted the publicist Betty Asher to go with me. Not at all unhappy that the marriage was ending, he agreed to both requests. Betty and I booked a cruise

56

to Honolulu. On board we met a group of college boys, and one of them asked me to dance. I danced my way through the rest of the voyage, having the time of my life.

While we were in Waikiki, soaking up sun on the beaches, I noticed that I had missed my period. I told Betty Asher, who was worried and found a doctor to give me a pregnancy test. The test came back positive.

The divorce wasn't final, so I telephoned Artie on the mainland.

'What is it?' he asked brusquely.

'Well, I just found out that I'm pregnant.'

He was silent for a second. He cleared his throat. Then he said, 'So what?'

'So what? What do you mean, "so what"?' I shot back. 'My God, it's your baby!'

'How do I know that?'

I couldn't believe my ears, and I exploded with anger. 'What the hell do you mean by that crack? You know I've never played around. This is *your* baby!'

And again he said, 'But how do I know that?'

That did it! 'You no-good, rotten son of a bitch!' I screamed into the phone. 'You are the dirtiest, the lowest—I can't even call you a man! You're a creep! I hate you, I hate you, I hate you!' I slammed the phone down and burst into tears. And that for me was the end of Artie Shaw.

Still, when I got back I tried him again. He had left town, with no forwarding address. I explained my predicament to my mother. She suggested that we consult Johnny Hyde. I wanted the baby badly, and when I told him so, he said that I would have to go back to Artie.

'I'll never go back to Artie!' I said. 'I hate him, I can't stand him . . .'

Now both my mother and Johnny sat me down and told me, very seriously, that I must either go back to Artie, since the divorce action was still proceeding, or have an abortion.

What a hideous choice! I couldn't sleep for days. How could I find Artie if I wanted to? I went for long drives alone, trying to think the situation through. Johnny, of course, was thinking mainly of my career, and finally he laid it all out for me. He reminded me of the studio's strict taboos—one of them being no children outside of marriage. It was yes or no—did I or did I not want to continue my career? Reluctantly I said that the answer was yes. Emotionally overwrought as I was, I knew that my mother and Johnny were probably right.

I went by myself. I didn't want anyone with me. The abortion took place in a dirty, dingy private house downtown. It was a terrible place.

I was expecting knives or something like that, but the abortionist didn't scrape me. Instead he injected a fluid up into my cervix, so that I would abort later, safely away from his premises. I didn't even get fully undressed, just raised my skirt and pulled off my panties. I felt a tube enter, but I had no idea what was going on. He didn't explain anything to me. At last he was finished.

'Now you just lie there for an hour, and then you can go home.'

'But what about . . . the baby?'

'The fetus,' he said grimly. 'You'll pass it.'

So I went home, anxious and confused. All that afternoon nothing more happened. Toward six, I began to have cramps, just minor ones, and I figured this was it.

My mother got home around then and came up to my bedroom right away.

'How are you, darling? Is it all over?'

'Evidently not. I'm supposed to "pass it" tonight.' And then the pain really hit me and I doubled up. Wave after wave of cramps smashed at my body. But nothing happened.

I telephoned the abortionist. He asked me, 'Have you been walking?'

'No, I've been sitting. With these cramps, I can't walk.'

'Get up and walk. And drink lots of coffee,' he ordered.

I tried to walk, holding on to my belly, but the pain got so bad I kept dropping to my knees in agony. My mother walked with me and held me throughout the entire night. And I kept sobbing, 'I'm going to die. Something is wrong, and I'm going to die.' My mother would start to cry with me, but then she'd pull herself together. All I can remember is the pain, and the walking—endless walking. I remember saying, 'I'm getting tired of this floor, let's walk some-where else,' so we'd turn into the hallway. We continued for hours, walking and walking and crying and crying.

We telephoned the abortionist again. All he said was, 'If you haven't passed it by morning, call me.'

By the time morning came, the pain had worn me out. I just collapsed. I couldn't walk another step.

My mother phoned him angrily. 'I don't know what you've done to my daughter,' she said, 'but you'd better get here fast.'

So this creature came and laid me on my back and asked for some towels. Then, without an anesthetic, without even an aspirin, he went in and scraped me out. My mother had to sit behind me on the bed and hold her hand over my mouth to stifle the screams.

Excruciating pain! I had to bite on a washcloth, and the towels were drenched in my blood. It seemed to go on forever, and I didn't even know what he was doing to me. Was he taking my insides out? It felt like it. Finally, mercifully, I blacked out, but not completely, because I could faintly hear him saying to my mother, 'She'll be all right now. I got it all.'

All? What did he mean by *all*? I was too weak to ask.

He warned us not to call our own doctor, which was more for his own sake than for mine. And that butcher had the nerve to charge $500. That was a fortune in those days.

Even though I was very young and strong, it took me a long time to recover. Later someone reported to me that when Artie heard about the abortion—and who told him, I have no idea—he said, 'I think I should have been consulted.'

Consulted! This from the man who'd told a nineteen-year-old girl 'so what'!

Work rescued me. In *Ziegfeld Girl* I had my best part yet. The production was as opulent as *The Great Ziegfeld*, with the same director, Robert Z. Leonard. It had a cast of stars: Jimmy Stewart, Dan Dailey, Jackie Cooper, Judy Garland, and Hedy Lamarr. I played Sheila Regan, a girl from Brooklyn, who is discovered working in a department store and becomes a Follies queen. Sheila leaves her boyfriend (Jimmy Stewart) to become a rich man's mistress and then slides downhill into alcoholism. In the dramatic closing scene she leaves her sickbed against a doctor's advice to attend the premiere of a new Follies show. From her balcony seat, she staggers downstairs in a daze, imagining that she is once more descending the grand staircase of the Follies set at the height of her career. She falls and is carried backstage, where the picture ends ambiguously. Does she die or does she recover? Audiences could have it either way.

Developing the role of Sheila, I discovered how much I *liked* acting. I had recently suffered my own emotional baptism, and now

59

I found it possible to use those feelings and absorb them into my work. Few films have offered me the same dramatic possibilities, and I am disappointed that they came so seldom.

I was still so green that I didn't realize what it meant when they kept handing me new pages to learn. Added pages, and new scenes. I didn't know that 'Pop' Leonard, the director, had gone upstairs to tell them my part should be expanded. They continued to build up the role, and the more they asked of me, the more I gave.

I'm blessed with a good memory, so I never had to sweat over my lines. I've always looked to my director to guide me. To me, he would always be the captain of the ship, and that was true even later in my career. And Leonard was a wonderful, helpful director, always kind, never impatient or brusque. He was a big, red-headed darling of a man, and I worshipped him.

I'd never been drunk in my life, and now I was being asked to play a drunk, a girl who hits her peak and begins to disintegrate. I'd never been around drunks, either, so I had to use my imagination. All I knew was that drunken women are pretty unattractive. I had to create my own kind of alcoholism, not slobbering but definitely unsteady. And Pop guided me. I'd beg him, 'Don't let me go too far.' And he didn't.

I realized that I was gaining respect because I played my scenes well. Respect not only from the director, but from my hairdresser, my makeup man, my stand-in, members of the crew—my colleagues. It was a wonderful feeling, and the first time I understood the meaning of working together. We all had jobs to do; we were all crucially important. By working harmoniously we could create an object of pride.

For the final tumble down the stairs, Pop put me through a few rehearsals of the beginning of the descent, but avoided doing the actual fall. Then he sent the crew out for coffee and guided me through the action, stage by stage: 'Go as far as the newel post, counting the steps, then stop. At the newel post you feel a twinge in your heart. Now let yourself go very, very slowly. Let your knees hit the next step, then your bottom the next one, then your shoulders, then your head. Hold on to the post for a bit as you go through it.'

When I'd tried it, he asked if it hurt. I told him no, it just felt strange. 'But let's do it,' I said.

'A take? Now?'

'Yes.'

We did one walkthrough for a lighting rehearsal. While my stand-in, Alyce May, took my place for lighting and camera adjustments, I took a few moments to remember my feelings as Sheila at the top of the stage staircase, as a brilliantly sequined Ziegfeld girl. I wanted to recapture the thrill of it, not the drudgery of getting it right. Feathers fell off, hoop skirts got tangled, and Busby Berkeley—who directed the musical numbers—shrieked, 'Cut, cut, cut!' whenever something went wrong.

There's one little moment in that scene that I still like to see. Blink, and you miss it. It's when I tentatively start to reach for the banister, as though to steady myself, and then pull my hand back. This wasn't as we'd rehearsed it. Later Pop, who had caught it, asked what made me do it. Maybe I thought that Sheila wanted to fall. Then, at the precise moment, I took a deep breath and, as though I were a feather falling, let myself go. I hit each spot, with every light on me. I've read that Pop had to put me through 'twenty-six bone-bruising takes' to get the scene right. But that's not how it was.

Lillian Burns, the acting coach at MGM, once told someone that I deserved an Academy nomination for *Ziegfeld Girl*. But the studio didn't push it. They wanted a flashier image for me, more like Jean Harlow's. Plum roles went to 'actress' types, usually unglamorous women. How would my career have been if my talents had been used differently?

By my twentieth birthday I was the 'sweetheart' of forty fraternities around the country, or so Howard Strickling told me. I'd been elected Queen of the Dartmouth Winter Carnival, and sailors on some battleship had voted me the most desirable companion on a desert island. The most touching honor of all was the gift of some German shell fragments that members of the British Air Force sent me for my birthday.

But someone else's birthday made that winter memorable for me. Along with other Hollywood stars, I attended one of the President's birthday balls, held to raise money to fight infantile paralysis. The highlight of the trip was meeting Franklin Roosevelt himself.

I wore a full-length white fox coat and a silky white lace dress over a nude-colored slip. Before the ball a limousine drove us to the

White House, and we filed into the room where Roosevelt delivered his Fireside Chats to the nation. The President sat behind a desk and greeted each person in turn. Fascinated, I studied his lined, handsome face and the marvelous grin I knew from the newsreels. As I approached I saw a look of recognition in his eyes. He didn't wait for an aide's introduction. He just extended his hand and said, 'You are Miss Lana Turner.'

All I could say was, 'Yes, Mr President.' He gave me a long look that seemed to take in everything. What made me do it, I don't know, but I pulled back my coat so that he could see the lovely dress I was wearing.

'My,' he said, 'you are a beautiful young woman.'

'Thank you, Mr. President.'

'I understand you are all going dancing.'

'I believe so, sir.'

As he smiled, his eyes twinkled at me. Then he said, 'Oh, how I wish I could go with you.'

I felt my knees go weak, but I smiled back and choked down my tears as I thought about his semiparalyzed condition. Quietly I wished him a happy birthday. Here I was, barely more than a starlet, in the presence of the world's most powerful leader.

Outside the White House gates, where limousines were waiting, a thousand hands began to clutch at me. My coat was stripped from my shoulders. 'Please don't rip it!' I screamed. But when the guards got it back, it was torn. That coat was my prize possession, and worse, it wasn't fully paid for yet. Of course the national press reported that my fur had been 'ripped to shreds' by hysterical fans. But for me the real story of the night was the one I'd seen in the White House, in the eyes of the brave President who would have loved to dance at his own birthday party.

After *Ziegfeld Girl* I began to appear in the studio's major productions, paired with its most important male stars. One of these films was a new version of *Dr. Jekyll and Mr. Hyde*, with Spencer Tracy in the two roles. I'd heard I was slated for the role of Ivy, a barmaid and semiprostitute. When I read the script I recognized the range of emotions the part required. I wasn't sure I had the strength to play it.

Then Mr. Mayer called me in to talk about the script. I told him I liked it, that I was thrilled to be working with Spencer, but . . .

'But what?'

'If you want me for Ivy, I don't think I can do it. I'm too young, and, well . . . I'm afraid. That role is so deep, I don't know if I could trust a director enough to let me try to reach those emotions,' I began, taking a deep breath.

'All right then, you won't play Ivy.'

Now I became anxious. 'But what about the picture?'

'What about Beatrix? A nice, well-bred Victorian girl. Do you think you can manage playing Dr. Jekyll's fiancée?'

'Oh, yes.'

'Don't worry, my darling. I'll see to it that you play Beatrix. You *will* play Beatrix.'

Later I heard through the grapevine that Benny Thau, Eddie Mannix, and the director Victor Fleming had assumed that I would play Ivy and were upset about getting a replacement. The replacement turned out to be Ingrid Bergman.

It seems that Ingrid wanted to play Ivy because it would help her career in this country. She wanted to break out of the 'good girl' mold, she has said, so she went directly to Fleming to ask for the role. In her autobiography she wrote that she made a secret test with Fleming to show Louis B. Mayer. But when I went to see Mr. Mayer, Ingrid was never mentioned. They didn't hire her until I begged out of the part. At that time she was under contract to David O. Selznick, and MGM would have had to increase the picture's budget to get her services. Now that I know how much she wanted the role, I'm pleased for her sake that I withdrew.

Certainly she was magnificent as the barmaid who had the misfortune to encounter Mr. Hyde. The part of Beatrix was much less showy. I worked with Ingrid only once while we were shooting. That was during the strange dream sequence when Jekyll is transforming himself into Hyde. Spencer was shown fiendishly whipping two spirited horses whose heads turn into those of Ivy and Beatrix. Creating the scene was hellishly uncomfortable. We had to sit astride mechanical horses, which bucked worse than live ones, while machines drove gale-force winds through our long hair. That sequence is often cut out when the picture is replayed on television—I suppose because it is too suggestive.

My most demanding moments came toward the end of the film, when Spencer, as Jekyll, tells Beatrix that they must abandon their plans to marry. I was supposed to break down and cry. The dialogue gave me no trouble, but I was in a happy mood that day and I just couldn't force tears into my eyes.

Victor Fleming was as important at Metro as Pop Leonard, but his methods were quite different. A 'man's director,' he could be rough on female players. We did several takes of the scene, and I still couldn't cry. Losing patience with me, he called for the 'crystals.'

These were camphor crystals, inside a thin tube, which would be blown at my eyes through a cheesecloth. The crystals could be dangerous. I knew they had been used on Joan Blondell during a picture I made with her. The cloth had slipped, some of the crystals had gone into her eyes, and she had been rushed to a hospital, barely escaping serious injury.

I begged, 'Please don't blow anything into my eyes.'

'Well,' Fleming said, 'you're going to cry, and we can't keep doing this all day.'

Spencer had been standing near us, and he angrily told Fleming that he was being too harsh. After an exchange of strong words, Spencer stalked to his dressing room and slammed the door.

'May I have another chance at it?' I asked Fleming. He nodded, and sent an assistant to get Spencer, who came back glowering. I thought of every sad thing I could, but when the camera rolled my eyes still stayed dry.

Fleming, losing patience completely, called, 'Cut!' And then, 'Okay, makeup, hair, line it up for another take.'

My makeup man and the hairdresser fluttered around me. I'd just gotten a new puppy, and I visualized her running out to greet me and being run over by a car. Still no tears came. 'Cut!' Fleming yelled. Then he rushed over to me, grabbed my arm, and twisted it sharply behind my back, where he held it for so long I feared he would break it. 'Stop it!' I screamed. 'You're hurting me!' And tears rolled down my face.

Out of either pain or sheer fury, I not only started crying but went on crying so hard and so long that my nose was red and my eyes were swollen. Makeup didn't do any good. They could only shoot Spencer for the rest of the day, while I gave him my lines off-camera. I heard later that Spencer had wanted to take a poke at Fleming for being so rough with me.

Around the middle of 1941 I signed a new contract at MGM that paid me $1,500 a week. What a heady sum for a twenty-year-old!

In Wallace, Idaho, at age five (LEFT), and an early performance,
five years later. BELOW: I'm wearing my Catholic school uniform, and (RIGHT),
as a fifteen-year-old student, posing in front of Hollywood High.

ABOVE: With my mother
on Mother's Day.
On the set at Warner's, at sixteen.
After the walk in my first film,
Mervyn LeRoy's *They Won't Forget*,
the Sweater Girl tag would
haunt me for years.

All the young contract players at
the studio had to pose for publicity photos.
See how much older and sophisticated
they made me look?

More publicity shots, 1937:
With my mother at
the preview of *The Great
Garrick* (RIGHT), and with
the fellow who grew up
to become president (BELOW).

I left Warner's for MGM
in 1938 and co-starred with
Mickey Rooney in my
first film there,
Love Finds Andy Hardy.
I was the girl who
liked kissing boys.
BELOW: Along with Mickey
and Judy Garland, I finished
my schooling on the lot.

ABOVE: My mother and I
shortly after I came
to MGM. RIGHT: A year
later with my first love,
Greg Bautzer. He had,
well, other interests,
and broke my heart.

Then it was Artie Shaw. I was the third in his long succession of marriages.
Tough going for a nineteen-year-old.

Hah! – *this* was the 1940 bathing suit style. The next year I starred in my first dramatic role as a spangled Ziegfeld girl (OPPOSITE), who would become an alcoholic and suffer a spectacular fall down a staircase (RIGHT) in the final scene.

As part of the Hollywood contingent at President Roosevelt's birthday ball in 1941. Some of the others posing with the First Lady: Jean Hersholt, Sterling Hayden, Glenn Ford, Lauritz Melchior, George Raft, Wallace Beery, Red Skelton, Deanna Durbin, and Maureen O'Hara. The silky white lace gown I wore to the ball (BOTTOM LEFT) won the approval of FDR himself. BOTTOM RIGHT: Dancing at a Hollywood party with one of the most important men in my life, Louis B. Mayer, my boss at MGM. OPPOSITE PAGE: I got to keep Clark Gable in *Honky Tonk*. But only in the movie.

OPPOSITE: Between scenes of *Honky Tonk*. ABOVE: Ill-starred lovers in *Johnny Eager*, 1942. Producer Norman Lear recently nominated my scenes with Robert Taylor as the screen's sexiest.

I didn't know that
Stephan Crane's divorce
wasn't final when
I married him in 1942.
Pregnant with Cheryl,
I married him again,
legally. Cheryl was born
in July 1943.

While my marital problems with Stephan made news, I returned to the screen in the ironically titled *Marriage is a Private Affair.*

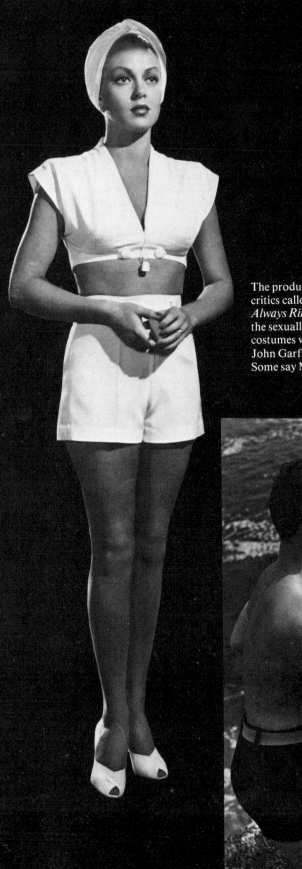

The production code notwithstanding, critics called my version of *The Postman Always Rings Twice* a lot steamier than the sexually explicit 1981 remake. All my costumes were white. BELOW: With John Garfield on location for *Postman*. Some say Marilyn Monroe copied this look.

And if I needed more proof that I was now considered a major star, the studio offered a role opposite the great Clark Gable himself.

The picture was *Honky Tonk*, a rollicking Western that had some serious moments as well. I revered Gable, who by then could almost write his own ticket at the studio. He could even choose his directors. Luckily we developed a pleasant working relationship, though not a close friendship. He had married Carole Lombard not many months before, after a long love affair and a divorce from his previous wife. I doubt that Carole believed the rampant press speculations about 'fireworks' on the set between the two 'powerful sex symbols' Gable and I were supposed to be. But one day I was playing a scene with Clark, and when I turned to look toward Jack Conway, the director, what I saw instead was the beautiful face of Mrs. Gable. Why, I'm not sure, but my knees went watery and I became so flustered that I excused myself and fled to my dressing trailer. I stayed there, trying to collect myself, until a knock came on the door.

'They're ready to shoot, Miss Turner,' a voice said. When I peeked out, there was no sign of Carole Lombard. I assume that Gable must have asked her to leave, saying that the kid was nervous. When I apologized to him, pretending that I'd forgotten something and had to run to the trailer for it, that famous smile lit up his face. He said simply, 'I understand.'

After *Honky Tonk*, I starred opposite Rober Taylor in *Johnny Eager*. This time I was fortunate to have Mervyn LeRoy as director. Bob played a supposedly reformed mob boss, and I was a society girl who falls in love with him. Bob had the kind of looks I could fall for, and we were attracted to each other from the beginning. I'll admit I flirted with him—but for me it was no more than that, since he was married to Barbara Stanwyck. Certainly our mutual attraction didn't harm our love scenes. Not long ago I came across a newspaper quote from Norman Lear, the producer, who had been asked to name the sexiest woman in the world. He had answered, 'Lana Turner, as she was held in the arms of Robert Taylor in the terrace scene in *Johnny Eager*.'

I still had bitter memories of the pain Joan Crawford had caused me. So when Bob confided that he wasn't happy at home and that he loved me, I felt a pang of fear. I would never be responsible for breaking up a marriage, however unhappy it was. I wasn't in love with Bob, not really. Oh, we'd exchanged kisses, romantic, passionate kisses, but we'd never been to bed together. Our eyes had, but not our bodies.

Bob said he wanted to tell Barbara about us, and I strongly discouraged him. 'I care for you,' I said, 'but don't make me the solution to your marital problems. Don't tell Barbara anything about us. As far as I'm concerned, there is nothing to tell.'

But he did tell her, and Barbara took it badly. She disappeared for four days and nobody could find her. Later I heard that she had hidden out in her maid's house to pull herself together. Bob had asked her for a divorce so he could marry me. Once I heard that, there was no more flirting with Robert Taylor. The situation cooled down eventually, but I fear it may have irreparably damaged their marriage. Years later, when both Barbara and I were at the opening of a hotel in Lake Tahoe, I called her room to invite her to stop by my suite for a drink. Her response was negative and her tone of voice icy cold. Obviously she held a grudge, but that didn't bother me a bit because I'd done what I could to discourage Bob's feelings for me—which, I believe, faded quickly enough.

With the increase in my earnings I was now able to buy my first house, a large cottage on a hilltop in the Westwood area, north of Sunset Boulevard and west of the UCLA campus. Westwood then was a lush, green community with attractive white Moderne-style homes and apartments nestled in the curves and dips of hills amid the eucalyptus and cypress trees. I furnished and decorated the house in the same colours as my landscaped garden—green, coral, and yellow, against the white walls. The shades I chose for the first house were rich and true, sunshine yellow, brilliant green.

Once I finished the decorating I began to entertain. I brought in a white piano, and because many of my friends were musicians, jazz and swing music often filled the house. One particular Sunday the guests included Tommy Dorsey, Buddy Rich, and Frank Sinatra, along with two of my favorite girl friends, Linda Darnell and Susan Hayward. The party began in the early afternoon and was still going strong that evening when my mother returned from a visit with some friends in San Francisco. She seemed astonished at all the noise.

'It's just a party, Mother,' I said.

'You mean you haven't heard? Pearl Harbor has been bombed. Turn on the radio, for heaven's sake.' During that whole fun-filled afternoon we hadn't had an inkling that the country was about to go to war. I got the musicians quieted down and turned on the news.

As we listened I looked around at the stunned young men in my living room, and thought how drastically our lives were going to change.

Stars signed on for railroad tours across the country to help sell bonds for defense. I played my own small part. When I had time between pictures I boarded that long train that rolled into cities where munitions plants were located. At every stop we were greeted by wildly cheering crowds, often mostly women. That sea of female faces—you knew the men had gone to war.

I wrote my own little speech to deliver at those rallies, and I added a special touch. When there were men in the crowd, I promised a sweet kiss to anyone who bought a $50,000 bond. And I kept that promise—hundreds of times. I'm told I increased the defence budget by several million dollars.

I appeared in so many cities that they're all blurred together in my mind, but I do remember a stopover in Chicago, where I ran into Johnny Meyer, a sort of right-hand man to Howard Hughes. He told me that Hughes had enjoyed my pictures and was eager to meet me. So I wasn't exactly surprised when, not long afterward, Howard Hughes called me and asked me out to dinner.

After the breakup with Artie and a sober period of hard work, I had begun to date again. Of course the gossip columnists inflated any casual new friendship into something torrid. I was spotted in Las Vegas, wearing dark glasses. Was I marrying again, as they reported? No, I was simply there as a witness to a friend's wedding.

I did go out a lot, and with many different escorts. Tony Martin, the singer—he taught me to play golf. Victor Mature—I saw once, I think. Gene Krupa—I was known to be attracted to musicians— but he was tangled up in divorce proceedings. Not that I was growing cynical, but I wasn't shopping for a husband then.

I remember a party that Robert Stack gave at his family's home in Rossmore. I was showing off my very nice tan in a bathing suit with a halter. When I dove into the pool, the strap broke. As I struggled to stay decent and afloat, Bob gallantly rescued me, holding me up while I held the suit in place. That incident began a pleasant friendship, which the press inflated into a breathless love affair.

As for Howard Hughes, I found him likable enough but not especially stimulating. In our most personal conversations, he confessed his preference for oral sex. I wasn't interested, but that didn't seem to bother him. I saw him from time to time, and

67

occasionally he'd come to the house just to sit and talk to my mother. She liked him and sympathized with his partial deafness. Of course it wasn't long before gossips were writing that I'd 'set my cap' for Howard and that I'd had my towels embroidered with the initials L.H. in anticipation. Howard was embarrassed, and I was furious.

Even in those days Howard dressed strangely. He always seemed to wear the same pair of worn, gray slacks and a white shirt, usually missing buttons. He sported a battered gray hat and scuffed black shoes without socks, and I never once saw him when he didn't seem to need a shave. He'd offered to teach me to fly; and he kept his word. A couple of times we even flew all the way to New York and back in his small plane.

One evening he phoned from the airport to ask me to dinner. He arrived looking even more slovenly than usual. When I invited him in to sit down, he said, 'No, I'll just stand.' I thought this was just an example of Howard's peculiar sense of humor.

A few minutes later my mother came into the living room and offered to make him a drink.

'No,' he said. 'I really just stopped by to say hello. I'm due someplace else.'

I wondered what had happened to his dinner invitation. And why did he keep standing in one place? When we encouraged him to stay for a while, he looked sheepish and murmured, 'I can't sit down. There's a rip in my trousers.'

'Well, just take them off,' my mother laughed, 'and I'll fix them.'

'Can't,' he said.

'Come on, no one is going to harm you, Howard.'

He finally confessed, 'Mildred, I don't wear shorts.'

'What?' I howled. 'You go around with those dirty slacks next to your body, with no shorts?'

'Well,' he said, defensively, 'I don't like 'em.'

'Hush, Lana,' my mother said, and sent Howard into the bathroom to take off his pants and wrap himself in a towel. She got a needle and thread, and she repaired the rip. Maybe that's how the towel-embroidery story originated. Howard was clearly brilliant, but in all honesty I found him boring. It was obvious to me that it wasn't my mind he was after.

5

EARLY IN 1942 the studio paired me with Clark Gable again. This time the film was *Somewhere I'll Find You*, and we both played newspaper reporters in wartime. We had been working for only a few weeks when production was suddenly halted. Carole Lombard, Gable's wife, was dead.

She was on her way home from a war-bond selling tour, and her plane had crashed outside Las Vegas. Afterward I heard a dreadful rumor that she had been scheduled to take the train, but decided to fly instead—the reason, the story had it, was her uneasiness over my working with Clark.

Clark was devastated by her death. The whole studio was in a state of shock. A pall settled over everyone connected with the picture. For all we knew, the filming had shut down for good; we hardly expected him to come back at all.

At the studio I found a message that Mr. Mayer wished to see me. When I went to his office he told me that things were going to be very trying for Clark and for everyone else. 'Now, Lana,' he said, 'here's where you come in. You're going to be very patient with him. If his mind should wander, don't be upset, you just be ready at all times. If he wants to come in earlier, you be there before him. If he wants to work through lunch, do it. A lot of the pressure of this picture is going to be riding on your shoulders. We're trying to arrange for people to go home with him for dinner. If he should ask you, go. Agreed?'

'But I don't know him that well,' I said.

'Never mind. Just do as I say.'

'I'll try with all my heart,' I promised him.

One night Clark did invite me for dinner. A studio limousine delivered me to the house he had shared with Carole. His male servant served the meal. As we ate I chattered brightly, trying to ease the sorrow that lined his handsome face. But he never mentioned it. He was courtly and cordial, and far too private for that.

After dinner Clark showed me his gun collection. He had been polishing some of the pieces—a cherished hobby, I thought, that

69

gave him comfort now. Then the studio limousine arrived to take me home.

After that evening my esteem for him grew even greater. That was the first and only social occasion I ever shared with him, though we made two more pictures together and got along well. His willingness to finish the film at all showed his decency. And although some say they could see a difference in the way he performed before and after the tragedy, I for one was not able to detect it. He was the consummate professional. No wonder they called him the King.

Once the film was completed the studio sent me on another war-bond tour, and I took my mother with me. The itinerary had been arranged so I could visit my birthplace, Wallace, Idaho. All those little towns, with their little frame houses and quiet main streets, each with a barbershop, a luncheonette. Even the cities— factory towns near the munitions plants, filled with row on row of shingle-faced homes—were so different from the extravagant Los Angeles that was now my home. Riding through the mountains I had a spell of homesickness, I remember, thinking of the vast blue California sky. But as we approached Wallace I saw a splendid rainbow spanning the road ahead. It was like a sign of welcome to the town I'd left when I was six.

We checked into our hotel, and we were told that the Mayor had declared a holiday in my honor. A banner stretched across the street read, in large letters, WELCOME HOME, LANA. We'd been in our rooms only a few moments when people who claimed to have known us when we lived in Wallace began knocking on the door. Their names were strange to me. My mother said later that she remembered only a few of them, but she played her part graciously.

Later, when we stood on the platform with all eyes fixed on us—if I'd stayed there, I'd have been among them—I thought of how much my life had changed since my parents swept me off to the Golden Gate. Then I realized that it was only five years since I had first walked down a studio street, wearing a tight-fitting sweater. During those short years I had appeared in some fifteen pictures, had been married and divorced, and had become America's glamour queen. Only five years before I had been wrapping Christmas packages after school for $12 per week. And today the bank and the schools were closed because I was back in town. The movies could do all this. What power they had to fire the public imagination!

70

What was the elusive quality that separated me from the young Wallace, Idaho, girls straining to get a glimpse of me, that quality that made me a star?

By the day's end my mother and I were both worn out. As we had dinner in our rooms she was silent. I knew why. More than anything else, the visit must have brought back vivid memories of my father.

I was glad to get back to Los Angeles. But the studio had no new picture ready for me and I was getting restless. One night Johnny Meyer invited me to join a group he was taking to dinner. The company was pleasant, but they talked about nothing but business. I was feeling rather bored and plotting my escape when a young man came over to our table.

His looks and manner charmed me instantly. Johnny introduced him as Steve Crane. Later I learned his full name, Joseph Stephan Crane III, and I always called him Stephan. He mentioned nonchalantly that he was in the tobacco business, in a way that suggested that any kind of business bored him. Certainly it seemed that he had no money worries. We chatted for hours, and by the time he took me home, I was ready to fall in love. With my weakness for a certain kind of good looks, coupled with witty charm, I took him at face value. In no time we were a pair. Only three weeks later he asked me to marry him.

I did wonder vaguely why he was in such a rush. Like me, he had been married before. But when he proposed eloping to Las Vegas, though my inner voices were telling me to delay, I didn't want to listen. An amazing man, handsome and cultivated and clever, loved me. And I passionately wanted him, too.

Linda Darnell and Alan Gordon, a publicist who was a good friend of Stephan's, flew with us to Las Vegas. Again Las Vegas! All four of us were giddy with excitement. Linda and I giggled as we pinned on our orchids. Then suddenly my eyes filled with tears. 'Oh, Linda,' I wailed, clutching her, 'I'm going to be so happy.'

The ceremony was simple and brief. Stephan kissed me sweetly, as the justice and our witnesses clapped and laughed. It was a different justice of the peace this time, contrary to legend. Then we all went out for a champagne brunch before returning to Los Angeles and to the reception my mother had organized at our house on McCullough Drive.

71

That was in July. The first five months of our marriage were blissfully happy. Stephan had rented an apartment for us, but I didn't like it and so we moved back into my house. We had agreed to share the household expenses, though Stephan didn't seem to be doing any regular work and I still had no real idea of how he made his money. But his not working meant that he had more time for me. To add to my happiness, I discovered that I was pregnant.

Meanwhile the studio had cast me in a new picture with Robert Young, called *Slightly Dangerous*. It was only when shooting wrapped up in December that I let it be known that I was expecting a child, and the publicity department went to work recasting me as a glamorous wartime mother-to-be.

Then came the blow.

One day Stephan told me to sit down, that he had some bad news for me. It was about his divorce in Indianapolis. 'I got this paper,' he told me. 'I thought it meant I was free, but it appears I wasn't.' There had been an interlocutory decree, with a one-year waiting period before he could re-marry. That year wasn't up even now.

I stiffened with shock. I tried to control my rising nausea. To this day I've never been sure whether or not Stephan knew about the waiting period. 'Please understand,' he said. 'It's just an awful mistake, but it's probably going to cost us some money.'

I said, 'You mean you want to give her money—my money? Do you think I'd pay to have her lie?'

'It wouldn't come to that,' he said, trying to soothe me. 'It can be handled.'

I shook my head, and said, 'Let me see a copy of that decree.'

It turned out that he didn't have it. 'I hardly looked at it. I don't even know what's happened to it.'

'But *she* has it'

'Yes.'

My anger and my pregnancy combined to make me ill. I felt sick and faint and defeated. I wasn't legally married. Here I was expecting the child of a man who wasn't my husband. My head started spinning and I just made it to the bathroom, where I leaned over the sink for a long time.

By the time I went back to the living room, I had made up my mind. 'Listen,' I said to Stephan, 'I want to meet her. I want to hear the whole truth.'

72

The next evening we drove to her apartment. She was a small pretty brunette. I managed to stay calm as she outlined essentially what Stephan had told me. But the last straw was the slight smile that crossed her face when she said that Stephan wouldn't be free to marry for a couple of months.

I blew up. I accused her of knowing all along that Stephan had no right to marry and of waiting until I announced my pregnancy to make waves. But no matter what I said to her, my marriage was still illegal. Where did that leave me? What about my baby? Why, why, I kept asking myself, did these things happen to me?

Stephan was abject, but I was too hurt and angry even to listen to his apologies. My attorney advised that unless I sued for an immediate annulment I could be charged with bigamy. I ordered Stephan out of the house. In court my attorney testified that I had made a clean break with Stephan and requested custody of the child when it was born. Of course the reporters were on hand, and there were more headlines. This time they were accurate. The annulment was granted.

A few days later I suddenly felt faint and weak, and everything went black. My mother found me on the floor and rushed me to a hospital. I passed ten days there in semiconsciousness. What had happened to me? My body ached, and my eyes hurt so badly I couldn't stand the light. Then, in a darkened room, doctors were telling me that my white blood count was dangerously high and that I'd become extremely anemic. That was all they knew. I'd almost miscarried, and they recommended a therapeutic abortion. They didn't think I could carry the child to term.

How could I save my baby? I loved that child before it was even formed. Every small sensation, every tiny spasm thrilled me, as I imagined the cells coming together. A tiny hand, a tiny ear, an arm, a heart, a tiny perfect human being.

The doctors warned that whatever they tried would be dangerous for me. I would probably lose the baby anyway. I told them stubbornly, 'Go ahead. I'm going to keep this child.'

Devastated by the annulment, Stephan kept calling, begging me to marry him again. Now his divorce was final, so it would be legal. 'Please,' he pleaded. 'You're carrying my child. Don't deny me the right to be a father.'

Angrily I rebuffed him. He had dashed my cherished dreams of a family and a comfortable home. Disillusionment, despair, the ugly glare of publicity—that's all his love had given me. I needed him,

73

yes, to see me through this difficult and painful pregnancy, but I distrusted him far too much to accept his support.

Finally I agreed to see him in an out-of-the-way place. He courted me and charmed me, and I wavered. But when he took me home I told him my answer was no.

A few nights later I was startled from sleep by a loud crash outside the house. Stephan's car was perched on the edge of the hilltop, buried in the shrubbery. Shaken but unhurt, he claimed his tire had hit a rock and he had lost control of the car. The papers wrote it up as a suicide attempt. Then a few days later the hospital called. Stephan had overdosed on sleeping pills. When I phoned he explained that he had been distraught, and a friend had committed him to calm him down. All these efforts to make me feel guilty only angered me more.

But then Stephan's draft number came up, and he had to report for his physical. My stomach was expanding, and still feeling ill, I was confined to the house, but his siege continued. Heavy and weary and lonely, I began to listen to Stephan. The baby would need a father. I wanted someone there when it was born, to share those first intimate months of life. Slowly Stephan's pleas wore me down.

On Valentine's Day, 1943, we drove down to Tijuana. Just over the border billboards advertising marriage and divorce services cluttered the roads leading into the squalid town. The weather was sultry and oppressive. We chose a small office on a side street, and Stephan found a Mexican man outside whom he persuaded to serve as our witness. I am not sure he even spoke English. In a few minutes the ceremony was over, and I was Stephan's wife once more.

The next day he had his Army physical, and he was placed on limited, noncombatant duty because of an old knee injury. The Army deferred his induction, so we resumed living together—but not in the same spirit as before. For me the love was no longer there. I suppose it was in an effort to brighten our relationship that he brought home an eight-week-old lion cub as a pet! With a baby coming, having a lion around the house seemed too risky to me. We had a fight over that, but I won. The next day I called MGM and asked if I could donate it to the studio. They agreed, but what they did with it I don't know.

Stephan planned to apply for officer training, but his injury made him ineligible. So he was sent to Fort MacArthur, hardly an hour's

74

drive from the house, for six weeks of basic training. Then the Army assigned him to Special Services at the same military post. With weekends off and his overnight passes, he slept at home as often as he did at the camp. At first he hitched rides to and from the post, but when I could no longer drive he began using my car. Soon he started bringing home a field-grade officer or two in my baby-blue Lincoln convertible, and urged me to invite friends to dinner, so the officers could meet the movie stars they had always admired on the screen. Stephan's celebrity connections surely enhanced his standing at Fort MacArthur.

In my seventh month I had early contractions. Back to the hospital, where I lay for twelve hours on a table with a needle in my spine. As the fluid dripped in, hour by hour, my labour pains subsided. If I had delivered then the baby would have died.

Then one lovely, balmy evening in July, my mother and I went out for a walk. All of a sudden I realized I was all wet. My water had broken, right there on the street. Calmly my mother walked me back to the house. Luckily the car was there, not parked outside the Army post, and Stephan drove me to the hospital. I was in labor for eighteen hard hours. Bored with waiting around, Stephan went off to watch a boxing match, and that's where he was when I gave birth.

I had only a spinal anesthetic, so I was wide awake when my baby was born. I was exhausted but exultant. 'It's a her! It's a her!' I kept repeating proudly. We named her then, Cheryl. She had a mass of black curly hair and beautiful skin, a delicate ivory color.

I didn't realize that something was wrong, not knowing that babies are usually born dark red. Dr. Thompson, who delivered her, ordered blood transfusions and rushed her to the Los Angeles Children's Hospital. She was actually dying of erythroblastosis.

Miraculously, Dr. Madeleine Fallon, an expert on Rh-negative births, was on duty that night. She had actually worked with the old-world rhesus monkeys that gave the Rh factor its name. During my pregnancy Cheryl's Rh-positive blood cells had entered my circulatory system, and my body had produced antibodies to destroy them. In effect, I was killing Cheryl even while I was struggling to give her life.

Soon after Dr. Fallon saw Cheryl, she called for a complete

blood exchange. Every drop of Cheryl's blood was pumped out and new blood pumped in. It saved Cheryl's life.

I was so anemic myself that I was hospitalized for nine days. I produced so much milk that my chest swelled all he way up to my neck. Absorbent pads were placed on my breasts, but even so, the milk ran down my sides and over my now-flat stomach. At feeding time, I could hear the other babies crying, but I couldn't even give milk to my baby. I could hear the other doors open, and then the peaceful silence as the babies nursed. But my arms were empty, and no nurse ever wheeled a tiny crib into my room. Even after all these years a heavy lump comes into my throat when I remember that time. Not seeing my baby, not touching her! Aching to hold her, knowing she was gravely ill. It was driving me crazy.

My mother came to visit every day, after she went to see Cheryl. I bombarded her with idiotic questions, just yearning to know every detail about my daughter. 'Mother, does she have all her fingers? Does she have long hands? Are they chubby? Does she have fingernails? All of her toes? Did you count her eyelashes?'

And the more serious questions. 'Tell me, Mother, does she have rosy cheeks?'

'No, Lana.' My mother shook her head sadly. 'Not yet.'

The agony, the waiting, became unbearable.

'My God!' I begged my doctor. 'I *cannot* live through any more of this! I must see my baby. Please, please, may I go and see her?'

They had been giving me glucose to build me up because I was so anemic, and they still wouldn't let me leave the hospital. Finally, I received grudging permission to see my little girl. I gladly traveled the three blocks between hospitals by wheelchair. A nurse pushed the chair, and my mother came with me.

We rolled down a long corridor, and the nurse pushed open the door, and there was the crib, at the far end of the room. And such a tiny baby, lying on her tummy with her face pressed against the mattress, and with her little fists clenched. She wore a tiny dress of some kind with a hospital stamp on the back. As they wheeled me closer I put my head to one side, so I could see her face as well as possible.

'Is she mine? Really mine? Is she breathing? Please, may I hold her?'

The nurses just looked at each other and shook their heads.

76

Tears filled my eyes. 'Please!' I begged. 'I won't move, I promise, if you'll just put her in my lap, in my arms. Please! I really can't live another minute without touching my baby!'

The nurses murmured sympathetically. Then one of them picked up Cheryl very gently and brought her over to my wheelchair. I held out my arms, and she laid the baby into them. Oh, the feeling! I can't find words to describe the intense joy I felt when I first held my little girl. She weighed almost nothing. She was so fragile, so delicate. Looking on, my mother said, 'Why don't you hold her properly?'

'How, Mom?'

'Well, put her on your lap. Support her head and neck. Now lift her up gently.'

As I brought her close to my face, instinct took over and I cradled her in my arms naturally. Her eyes were closed. Her eyelashes were so amazingly long and silky and thick.

My mother said softly, 'I think that's enough, Lana.'

'Mom, please! Can't I hold her a little more?' I was begging like a child.

But my mother knew how frail Cheryl still was, and she signaled to the nurse, who took her from me. As I left the room I turned back to look at the sleeping baby. It was a moment I'll never forget, no matter how long I live.

Cheryl was in the hospital for two interminable months. Later they told me that the wonderful Dr. Fallon sat by Cheryl's crib, day in and day out, for weeks. What a woman! I am so grateful that my child had her devoted care.

I was taking forever to recover. I left home only to visit Cheryl. I'd have to lie down in the back of the car because I was too weak to sit up. At the hospital they'd have a wheelchair waiting for me, and they'd roll me down to the nursery to look at my child through the glassed-in sides of her crib.

But the day finally came when I did drive myself to the hospital, along with my mother. I was stronger and more confident.

The hospital had told me to call ahead before I paid Cheryl a visit, but nobody told me why. One day I neglected to telephone. On my way to the usual room I surprised a nurse who was carrying Cheryl in her arms, and what I saw made me scream. The baby was completely covered with blood. Someone led me off to a room and explained that Cheryl's blood transfusions were administered through dozens of tiny needle tubes. They had to use every vein in her feet and legs and even her head, because the tiny veins would collapse. My poor darling. When they removed the tubes she would have blood all over her.

My mother's mother died in childbirth, and my mother herself was a sickly baby. She was also Rh negative. It's one of life's bitter ironies that I, who wanted a big family, could bear only one child. Eventually I lost three babies, two boys and a girl. Today most mothers are tested for the Rh factor, and science has learned to control its damaging effects. But in my day it almost took a miracle just to save my baby's life.

Finally, I brought Cheryl home on a beautiful late-summer day. Her room had been ready for ages, and as I carried her in, the sunlight streamed through the windows. Stephan touched her tentatively, lovingly, as we smoothed her tiny blanket. Amazing to think that we had created this fledgling life.

I had hired a highly praised nurse to care for Cheryl when I went back to work. She was an elderly Scottish woman named Margaret MacDonald. Kindly, capable, and energetic, she loved my little girl dearly and became part of our family.

Soon I would have to return to work. My hospital expenses and the long months of illness had badly strained my resources—and I had some unexpected expenses as well. Stephan found that the regulation Army garb chafed his sensitive skin, so he'd been having his uniforms custom-tailored of fine light gabardine. His caps were made to order, too, and I footed the bills. My husband was probably the best-dressed private the U.S. Army has ever seen.

The fastest way to pick up cash was on radio shows. The Philip Morris Playhouse paid $5,000 or more in those days. Cheryl hadn't been home two weeks when the studio booked me on a radio series in New York, and Stephan wangled a leave to come along.

Ever since we had reconciled, Stephan had wanted to show me the town where he grew up, Crawfordsville, Indiana. We could stop off there on the train ride back from New York. I knew how much the trip meant to him when, before we left, he ordered three new uniforms from the tailor. He had arranged for a limousine to pick us up from the station. In this grand style

Private Stephan Joseph Crane III came home with his movie-star wife.

Now, it must seem odd to you that I knew so little of his background. Nonetheless, I had no more than the impression that he came from a fairly well-off family who had a tobacco business and perhaps other holdings, with an ancestral home where he had been born and raised. Now, as the chauffeur drove us through the town, following Stephan's directions, I kept looking for a handsome family residence. But we appeared to be passing through a working-class section. Women in faded housedresses, men in work clothes, children running around in the street. My own ancestors were hardly blue-bloods, so it wasn't just snobbery that led me to expect a better neighborhood.

'Just ahead, two more houses,' Stephan said, and then we were stopping in front of a weather-beaten old two-story house with a front porch, like a million others, down to the rocking chairs. Stephan's mother and grandmother were waiting on the porch to greet us. I liked his mother, and I admired the proud way she hid an infirmity. One of her legs was shorter than the other, yet you hardly noticed it from the way she walked.

The trip had tired me, and I wanted to rest. But the neighbors came pouring in, all supposedly to see 'Joe,' until the crowd overflowed into the living room. I inched my way to Stephan and told him I couldn't stand having to talk to so many strangers. He had his mother take me upstairs, and after a while she managed to shoo everyone out. Then we enjoyed a quiet drink and a light supper together. After dinner they brought out the photograph albums and pointed out pictures of Stephan as a boy. What sweet, comfortable, down-to-earth people. They did their best to make me feel at home. But the whole time it was clear that it was not my home. They regarded me as a curiosity, not a member of the family but someone from another world.

The next morning the chauffeur picked us up for a tour of Crawfordsville. Stephan showed me the schools he'd attended and the local college where he'd earned his degree. As we went down a street lined with little stores, Stephan stopped the driver at a storefront marked BEER, TOBACCO, POOL.

'Why are we stopping here?' I asked.

'I need cigarettes,' he said. He went inside and returned a few moments later, saying, 'Let's go in. There's someone I want you to meet.'

It was only then that I realized that *this* was the tobacco business Stephan had mentioned so casually when I first met him. His father had died, and now someone else ran the place. From then on I couldn't help seeing Stephan with different eyes. Why had he felt it necessary to imply he was something he wasn't? Later on he would prove that he could become a success in his own right. Meanwhile, I was headed for trouble—and it wouldn't be for the last time, either—because of the way money passed from my purse to his pockets.

The studio had been preparing a new picture for me, *Marriage Is a Private Affair*, costarring John Hodiak and James Craig. I was thankful that Pop Leonard, my favorite, would direct—especially because I'd be onscreen for most of the two-hour film.

During my early days at Metro I had dreamed of costumes created by the gifted Adrian. I got my wish with *Ziegfeld Girl*, and then Adrian was replaced as head designer. His successor, Irene, planned a stunning series for *Marriage Is a Private Affair*. I had twenty costumes, including a wedding gown of shimmering satin and tulle. I've had some creative, inspired designers over the years: Jean Louis, Moss Mabry, Nolan Miller, and Helen Rose, besides Adrian and Irene.

People don't realize the hard work it takes to dress a star. In those days the studio kept eight or ten mannequins made to the exact measurements of each of us. They reflected every tiny imperfection—for example, my left shoulder and hip are higher than my right—that the designer would have to accommodate. Each mannequin was labeled with the name of the star: *Greer Garson, Judy Garland, Hedy Lamarr*. My hip mannequin was the smallest in the entire studio. Greer Garson's was largest, but she is a tall woman.

Although the mannequins saved us hours of standing for fittings, costuming was still a tedious process. I took longer to fit because I was a perfectionist, highly critical of the way I looked. I knew instinctively when a gown wasn't right for me, and I never met a designer who forced me to wear something that was wrong. But after hours of consultations and fittings I'd be sick of the costume by the time we started shooting. 'If I have to put that damn thing on again,' I would say, 'I'll scream.'

I should also mention the corps of seamstresses in the golden days at MGM. There were at least a hundred—more than at any other studio—most of them old ladies with gnarled fingers. They had one of Hollywood's strongest craft unions, and young people could rarely break in because of the rigid seniority rules. But what beautiful work they did! That aspect of Hollywood is long gone. Today no studio employs its own seamstresses; instead, costume houses usually outfit each picture.

For *Marriage Is a Private Affair* I wasn't exactly up to looking glamorous. I was still anemic, and I'd tried to put on weight without success. Problems at home, in my marriage, always seemed to show on my face. Nervousness made me gulp air, so they'd have to pat my back like a baby's. In short I hardly looked like the radiant bride I played. To help my appearance, I got a special makeup man, Del Armstrong, who would become a trusted friend in later years.

When it came time for the wedding close-up, I knew I looked much too pale. I just couldn't do the take until Del touched up my makeup. But he was working on another sound stage, and I'd have to wait until he was free. When word went out that shooting was delayed Eddie Mannix rushed down to investigate. He was the tough-guy executive, Mayer's hatchetman.

'So,' he asked, 'whatsamatter with my baby?'

'What's the matter? Just look at me!'

'Yeah, you look like hell. Where's the makeup man?'

'He isn't here,' I said and started to cry.

He demanded to know where Del was, and they said he was on Greer Garson's set.

'Fuck Garson,' he said. 'Get him back here. This little girl is more important.'

Del hurried back, and from then on, whenever I was filming, Del stayed beside me constantly. He was there for the next twenty years.

I was forming my own little entourage: Del; my hairdresser, Helen Young; and my stand-in, Alyce May. More than anything else, having them always with me represented stardom. And the truth is I needed them. Another privilege I enjoyed was a record player on the set, to help me relax while the crew was setting up shots. A special girl maintained my record collection. The crews on my pictures enjoyed the music too.

But Pop Leonard ran pretty relaxed sets anyway. They were the scenes for some outlandish practical jokes. Once John Hodiak jumped into his twin bed and found a gigantic, ice-cold fish under the covers. And as I who played his sweet little wife lay in the other bed, I looked up to the ceiling on cue and saw a water bag descending toward me!

But if my marriage onscreen was idyllic, at home it was exactly the opposite. After we returned to Los Angeles Stephan was placed on inactive duty. He applied for a Navy commission but flunked the physical. That was the end of his war career. Stephan was relieved to be out of the Army but seemed to have no desire to go to work. So now I managed all the expenses, with a mother, a child, and household help to support.

He liked to gamble. Often he disappeared in the evening and returned as I was leaving for an early studio call. 'Well, good morning,' I would say as I passed him in the hall. When I came home tired from the set, I would usually find him slouched in an armchair, wearing elegant silk pajamas, drinking coffee. He was really rubbing it in. My respect for him declined daily, and love was dwindling with it. I guess it's not easy for an unemployed man to be married to a star.

One evening I made up my mind that it was time for a serious talk. I told Stephan that I couldn't take it anymore, that the marriage was over and I wanted a divorce. He slammed out of the house in a rage. When he came back he said that he refused to let me divorce him. We were stalemated for a while because he wouldn't move out. Once he locked our bedroom door and grabbed me by the arms, threatening to shake some sense into me. He kept shouting that I couldn't divorce him, that I had to think of our child.

I rarely lie, but this time I did. I made up a story on the spot, though I was shocked to think of it afterward. I told Stephan that I was in love with another man. 'Who?' he asked, but I said it didn't matter. When he persisted I came up with a name. A second bold lie, the handiest name I could think of. 'It's John Hodiak,' I said.

Stephan couldn't believe it, but I convinced him with details. I spun out a whole fictitious affair. Finally he agreed to the divorce, but he threatened to countersue, naming John as the corespondent. I eventually talked him out of that plan. But then I knew I had to tell John how I'd used his name.

He was utterly shocked—and worried. 'Suppose he comes gunning for me?'

I assured him that Stephan was not dangerous, and in April 1944 I got the divorce.

Now that I'm older and possibly wiser I can understand better what went wrong between Stephan and me. Just as I hated his dependency, I am sure he resented being in that position. My career was thriving. His hadn't begun; he wasn't even sure of the direction he wanted to take. Eventually he found his calling in the restaurant business. He married other wives, and he retired a rich and successful man.

6

O N NEW year's day, 1945, I became one of the most highly paid actresses in the world. My new contract paid me $4,000 a week, and by Hollywood ritual that meant it was time to buy a new home. I looked for a place in Bel-Air, a gracious section with handsome estates enclosed by Spanish-style adobe walls or ornate wrought-iron fences and sculptured hedges, and I found a lovely house hidden in the woods overlooking the ninth green of the Bel-Air Country Club. Sometimes golf balls smacked the windows or flew into the pool. Whenever I retrieved one I would fine the player a quarter for going out of bounds. It gives me a chuckle to remember those startled faces.

Now I was dating again. First it was Turhan Bey, an exotic-ally handsome Turkish-Viennese actor. But when things turned serious, he introduced me to his mother, who seemed to dislike me on sight.

Once when I was dancing with Turhan at a party in Beverly Hills, Stephan appeared and tried to cut in. When I glanced at Turhan meaningfully he gallantly stepped aside to let Stephan take his place. I still wore Stephan's engagement ring, a three-carat diamond, which I'd had reset to my taste. Now Stephan told me he wanted it back.

'But it's been reset,' I protested.

'I don't care. Give it back!'

He snatched my hand and yanked off the ring, then strode quickly away.

When Turhan saw me standing there, he asked me what had happened. I told him, then excused myself to recover. When I got back from the ladies' room, Turhan wasn't there, but everyone was rushing to the garden.

In the center of a knot of people were Turhan and Stephan, scuffling on the ground. The other guests pulled them apart before they could hurt each other. Thank goodness! But Stephan had dropped the ring and was searching frantically through the shrubbery.

The next day Anita May, who had given the party, called to say that her gardener had found the ring. I recovered it, but the story made the papers. The gossips inflated my connection with Turhan to the level of a grand passion. Those same busybodies linked my name to Rory Calhoun, Robert Hutton, and Frank Sinatra—the mention of Frank's name in this connection showed how little the gossips really knew about any of us. Yes, Frank had been a good friend for years, and I was close to his wife, Nancy. But the closest things to dates Frank and I enjoyed were a few box lunches at MGM. Despite our later differences of opinion about his relationship with Ava Gardner, I always found him warm and especially kind to me.

But I did go out a lot. The war had just ended, and the city was booming again. Affluence was in the air. Developers had bought up acres of land and dotted them with row upon row of small, brightly colored tract homes for returning servicemen. Almost overnight the orange groves and open spaces disappeared under the spreading blanket of suburbs, and the city got its first whiff of smog. But in Beverly Hills, Brentwood, Bel-Air, Holmby Hills set high in the Santa Monica Mountains, prewar glamour and opulence were reborn, with a modern flair. The magnificent homes were palaces of glass that let the light stream in, not the tile-floored haciendas or Tudor manors of the past. Light—that's my strongest impression of that post-war time. After the long years of blackouts and conservation, the city was adazzle with blazing bulbs, brilliant and glittering and fun.

And the men were home. They seemed to catch your eye everywhere you went, like the first greening after a thaw. How I'd love to dress up and go dancing with a handsome dark man. Ciro's was a favorite haunt. I'd walk up the steps and through the glass door, and pass the velvet rope that barred the less-fortunates. And the headwaiter would spring forward—'Ah, Miss Turner . . .' and escort me in.

I had a special table right by the stairs so I could watch the comings and goings. I'd head straight there, never glancing right or left. And then, when I was seated, I'd give the room a long casing, bowing to this one or blowing that one a kiss. Silly, I guess, but fun.

Ciro's was designed for dramatic entrances and exits because a long flight of stairs led down to the tables and dance floor. And at the top of the stairs—that's where the stars stopped, to let everyone see them come in. It was all part of the game. Everyone would stare, and you knew you were making an *Entrance*.

I'd usually be dressed in something clingy, black or white, sometimes gold, occasionally red. I'd wear diamonds and a fur of some kind draped over one shoulder. Often white fur, my favorite. Maybe ermine or silver fox, the fashionable furs at that time. Or sable. I had beautiful sables. I'd have jewels in my hair, or flowers, and every hair in place.

But talk about an Entrance! Hedy Lamarr holds the record for that. One Entrance she made at Ciro's is a vision I'll never forget.

Hedy was at the height of her beauty, with thick, wavy, jet-black hair. With that stunning widow's peak, her face was magnificent. We all looked up and there she was at the top of those stairs. She wore a cape of some kind up to her chin, and it swept down to the floor. I can't even remember the color of the cape, because all I saw was that incredible face, the magnificent hair—and a huge diamond. The most fabulous solitaire diamond on her forehead, just at the tip of her widow's peak. She was enough to make strong men faint.

How the hell did she keep that diamond on her forehead? Was it pasted on? You couldn't tell. Later, Sidney Guilaroff told me that he had taken jet-black wire, very fine, and woven it into Hedy's hair. He anchored it with a little spot of glue. But that diamond was absolutely real. It was breathtaking.

The first picture I did after my divorce was *Keep Your Powder Dry*, a light comedy in which I played a WAC. Once again my designer was Irene. Filming was due to start and my costumes weren't ready, and some of the blame fell on me. But it was Irene who kept missing appointments. When she did appear she would usually hold a handkerchief to her face, saying she had a bad cold and warning me not to come too close. When I received a memo of reprimand, I went directly to Mr. Mayer. 'I *have* kept my wardrobe appointments,' I told him. 'I don't think I should be blamed!'

He sat back in his chair. 'I know you're not missing them, Lana. You see, Irene is having a very hard time.'

He explained that both Irene and her husband were alcoholics. Although the studio knew it they bore with her because of her marvelous abilities.

86

The more I heard about Irene, the more sympathy I had for her. One day her sad life ended when she jumped from the window of a suite in the Knickerbocker Hotel on Hollywood Boulevard. She didn't hit the pavement but landed on the awning, dead, and they didn't find her for two days.

I had come a long way since the time I'd turned down the role of Ivy because I was afraid. Finally the part I had been hoping for did come my way—Cora in *The Postman Always Rings Twice*. MGM had held an option on the story for years, but fear of the censors had kept it off the screen. But now they finally had a screenplay that retained the flavor of the book and also satisfied the Production Code.

Reading the script, I knew I could play the young woman who had married an older man for security, then conspired with a younger lover to murder him and inherit his property. And it pleased me to be working with John Garfield, in the part of Cora's lover.

The director, Tay Garnett, wanted to film in as many natural locations as possible. And he came up with a brilliant costuming idea that was executed by Irene. As he later explained it, 'There was a problem getting a story with that much sex past the censors. We figured that dressing Lana in white somehow made everything she did less sensuous. It was also attractive as hell . . . They didn't have "hot pants" then, but you couldn't tell it by looking at hers.'

The reviewers loved it. My costumes stimulated as much discussion as the film itself. Jeanine Basinger, who called my entrance a 'great film moment,' described it better than I can: 'The searching camera follows her dropped lipstick as it rolls across the floor, over to her white, open-toed high heels and up her perfectly proportioned figure to her insolent face framed in a white turban. This image of the tanned and beautiful Lana Turner, dressed in white shorts and halter top, is one of the most famous in screen history. When she applied her lipstick, preening herself in front of John Garfield merely to show him plenty of what it is he can't have, an entire generation remembered the image.'

What the public never knew was that we almost couldn't finish the film. Tay Garnett once had a drinking problem. He'd been on the wagon for three years when we went down to Laguna for the beach footage. A fog rolled in, and we had to stop shooting until it lifted.

Each day we'd go down to the beach and sit there in the dense mist, waiting and hoping. After several hours the production people would give up and send us back to our lodgings.

Hoping the weather might be better at a new location, we packed up and moved to San Clemente. But we found ourselves socked in there, too. Then we got a report that the weather was about to clear at Laguna, so back we went to the starting point. But the fog still hung over the beach for days and days, and costs kept mounting. The studio's budget people were frantic. Tay Garnett kept begging for a little more time, but the fog didn't lift and days stretched into weeks. That's when Tay fell off the wagon.

Nobody could control him. He was a roaring, mean, furniture-smashing drunk. The girl friend he'd brought along stayed for a while, then gave up.

The studio sent nurses, but even they couldn't help. Rumors flew like sparks—Tay Garnett would be replaced, or the production would shut down. That was when John Garfield and I got together to discuss the situation. I respected John as an actor, and we had developed a certain steamy chemistry as we performed together. His private habits were his own concern—he had a penchant for picking up girls, sometimes two at a time, and a reputation as a demon lover. He died young, in bed, which was understandable.

Since Tay had been drawing good performances from us, John and I both hoped that he wouldn't be replaced. So we decided to go and see him. John went first. He forced his way past the nurses, who were there not only to care for Tay but also to protect his visitors. When John came back, he said, 'It's terrible, Lana. He didn't know who I was. When I tried to talk to him he'd say, "Sure, Johnny boy, whatever you think." But a moment later he'd start shouting, "Who the hell are you? Get out of my room." Then he came at me with the cane he always carries. I don't know how much longer we can hold out, Lana, and if he goes or they shut down the picture, we're both burned.'

'Maybe,' I said, 'if I went to see him . . .'

John didn't think I should. But I called one of the nurses and asked her if I could stop by for just a few moments. First they had to quiet him down, she told me, but eventually they let me in the room. The nurses had managed to take his cane away, and what I found was a besotted man who regretted what he'd done. I did my best to comfort him, and he sniffled and begged my forgiveness.

Now he was rational enough to be sent back to Los Angeles for treatment. By the time he returned a week later the fog had obligingly lifted, and we were able to complete the film.

Otherwise I loved making *Postman*. I adored Cecil Kellaway, who played Nick, the elderly husband—so much so that I hated having to help kill him on camera. A nice moment came when James M. Cain, author of the controversial novel, took me to lunch at Romanoff's and said he'd often imagined me as the perfect Cora.

When they remade *Postman* in 1981, with Jessica Lange as the star, they didn't have to worry about the censors. I'd had to project a rather intense sexual presence, but always with my clothes on. I was amused to read that Vincent Canby considered the remake a pale, rather sexless imitation of my version. It always amazes me that when Hollywood makes a really good movie, and some producer gets the bright idea to remake it, he comes up with something inferior to the original.

When I had finished *Postman*, I took Cheryl to Palm Springs so that we could have an uninterrupted month together. She had become a lovely, active child, with such energy that our walks together wore me out. She was now two and a half. I was twenty-five. I had been twice married and divorced. And my mother was still living with me.

Since I'd given her that first $50 check she had never worked another day. That had been my wish, of course. But it wasn't altogether good for either of us. I felt smothered. She was living her life through mine. The time had come—though it seems a strange thing to say—for me to separate from her.

For example, when a date brought me home, I would often invite him in for a nightcap. The bar was in my library, which was lighted only by a fire glowing in the fireplace. But when I turned on the lamp, there would be Mother, sitting in a chair with her arms crossed, saying, 'Well, good morning.'

How embarrassing it was for me, a divorced woman in her mid-twenties, to have my mother waiting up for me to come home. After my date had left, I'd say, 'Mother, please, can't you stay in your own room after midnight?' But it did no good. No matter what time I got in—and when I was between pictures it might be one or two in the morning—there she would be. It was during this

89

time that I came closest to hating my mother. Not only was she living vicariously through me, but she was taking over Cheryl as well.

I made up my mind that something drastic had to be done. I had planned a trip of several weeks through South America, and before I left I went to see Greg Bautzer. I explained why my mother had to move, which meant that I wouldn't need as large a house. 'The only way to have her leave,' I told him, 'is to sell the house. So I want you to do it while I'm away.'

'You've talked to your mother about it?'

'No. I want it to happen while I'm gone. And I'd like you to make other arrangements for her.'

Seeing how unhappy I had become, he said he was sure he could arrange everything, and that he would talk to my mother and work it all out. When he asked about the furnishings, I said, 'Sell them all—or if you can't, put them in storage.'

So I left it all to Greg. My mother knew only that I was leaving on a long trip. She wasn't exactly happy about it, but there was the consolation of having Cheryl all to herself. Of course Cheryl also had her Nana, whom she adored.

My companion on the trip to South America was Sara Hamilton, a magazine writer whose company I enjoyed. She claimed to be devoted to me, and as usual I took her at face value. I needed a friend I could trust. More than once, when she complained about being short of money, I would slip bills into her purse or help out with a gift of clothing. Once I gave her a valuable fur. Later I was told that she had used our friendship to feed items to fan magazines and gossip columns. Then, in order to have her company, I paid for her trip as well as my own.

I had notified the studio of my itinerary, not realizing how they would use it. At every stop, there would be an MGM publicist to greet me, with an buzzing group in tow. And not only press people. Latins, I quickly learned, love blondes, blonde movie stars above all. So there were hundreds of fans crushed at the airport gate as we deplaned.

Our most hectic and frightening arrival was at Buenos Aires. Just reaching customs was an enormous struggle, even with an MGM representative and a police escort to move us through the crowd. Sara was white with fright. We clung to each other, with flashbulbs popping in our faces. When we finally reached customs the officials made a point of rifling our hand luggage in full view of everyone,

90

as if to show the eager fans what an American movie star carried with her. They even opened my jewel case in public, which was imprudent, as it placed us in danger of thieves. In those days I carried a lot of jewelry when I traveled, emeralds and sapphires, diamonds and pearls.

Finally—though the damned MGM man didn't speak Spanish— I managed to convince the customs officials that we needed a private room. Even so, an amazing number of customs and airport personnel happened to be on hand while they inspected my luggage, piece by piece. They especially enjoyed handling my underwear. Grrh!

After customs there was another ordeal. Our car waited outside the terminal and so did a huge crowd of yelling, screaming fans. They broke through the ranks of the police who were trying to hold them back. Sara was shoved through an open door of the car and landed face down on the floor. Hands grabbed the flowers on the big hat I wore. Fingers snaked out and closed on my choker string of pearls, but I managed to knock the hand away. Then I too was pushed into the car on top of Sara. The chauffeur went roaring off, and people went flying off the fenders. 'Be careful!' I screamed to the chauffeur, who naturally spoke no English and was in a panic besides. I heard thumps as we parted the crowd—it was as if none of them cared about the danger. And I was in tears, less for myself than for those people risking their limbs for a glimpse of a movie star.

There was never a chance for quiet sightseeing on that vacation. We had to take the limousine everywhere, for lunch, dinner, and shopping. Always shadowing us was a maroon sedan carrying four men who could have been extras in a gangster film. Our MGM man swore that the men were not a studio protection team. Later we learned they were following us on the instructions of Madame Eva Perón.

A good friend, Betty Dodaro, threw a huge party to welcome us to Argentina. Madame Perón was there. She sat in a corner of the room while I went around being introduced. When we reached Evita I felt I was expected to curtsy, and when I didn't she extended a hand and murmured a few words of greeting. What a handsome woman! But it struck me that she had gone blond; her hair was then the same pale color as mine. Her hairdo resembled mine, too. As I mingled with the guests I could feel her eyes trained on me. Those eyes were like narrow slits, and they fixed on me all night. I was relieved when she quietly slipped away from the party. Later Betty told me that she often dressed like me. She copied my hair-styles exactly, and she couldn't get enough pictures of me. How strange!

At that same party I met a famous horse trainer, Horatio Luro, who had come south to buy horses for Alfred Gwynne Vanderbilt, I believe, and some other American breeders and owners. He invited me and Sara to visit a ranch with him. While he was examining horses for his clients I asked him to pick one for me. He chose a handsome filly that I named Cheryba, for Cheryl and Buenos Aires. Cheryba was shipped to Belmont Park in New York, and about a year later I saw her race there. She won one purse, and then I sold her in a claiming race.

While I was in Buenos Aires I got a call from Greg Bautzer. 'Guess what,' he said. 'Your house is sold. You've got your price, and they want everything in it—furniture, draperies, bedding, linens.'

'What about my mother?'

'Don't worry. I'm working it out.'

Good old Greg. I almost forgave him for his infidelities during our engagement.

Our next stop was Rio, where we planned to arrive at Carnival time. I wasn't sorry to leave Buenos Aires. Argentina was torn by political strife. It was election time, and there were rough political rallies right in the plaza under our balcony. The Peronista guards would sweep into the crowd with their sabers drawn. It terrified and sickened me to see their battered victims, with blood streaming down their heads. Once, at three in the morning, someone threw a bomb into a service entrance of our hotel. The blast almost shook me and Sara out of our beds. For the rest of the night we sat up, terrified and shaking, in the living room of our suite.

In Rio social life was far more pleasant. I had acquaintances there, who invited me to several posh parties. During Carnival the whole city throbbed with the seductive samba beat. We danced long and late. One night someone said, 'Let's go into the street!' Out there we were simply swept off into the crowds. Now it's forbidden, but at that time the men put a little perfumed ether on their handkerchiefs, which would be vapourized by the heat of their bodies. The air was sweet with intoxicating ether fumes. With that and the blaring wild music you just seemed to float on and on. In a seductive black satin halter dress, with flowers in my hair, I danced until dawn.

Back at the hotel I made the mistake of hanging my evening dress in the closet with my other clothes. Soon everything reeked of ether. As a result of overheating and overexertion, I caught a cold that threatened to turn into pneumonia. The doctor who treated me advised against traveling on, so friends arranged to send me to Quinadita, a mountain resort. Ten days later when I returned to Rio, the odor of ether still clung to all my clothes. I should have had the sense to burn that satin dress. Or would it have exploded?

We continued up the east coast of South America, then flew to Miami for a two-week rest. Still not at all anxious to return to Los Angeles, we went on to New York for another three weeks, and two months had passed by the time I returned home. My mother, Cheryl, and Nana had moved into a smaller house on Crown Drive in Brentwood. Greg had handled it all. Now, after we talked over our differences, my mother agreed to move into an apartment. She never lived with me again, but she was always nearby, and it was remarkable how our relationship improved.

It was fine to have money. I spent it on clothes, jewelry, furnishings for my home, cars, vacations, and on the comfort of my daughter and mother. I gave gifts to everyone I loved and contributed to charities until I had pretty much used it up. I left the details of my contracts to my agents; my business managers paid my bills and balanced my books. Two or three hundred thousand dollars a year then went about as far as a million today, but though I was rich in earnings my income rested on the shaky base of my box-office standing.

But more important to me than money was, as always, the love I longed for. And finally I found it, if only for a moment. The man was Tyrone Power. I had always been attracted to him but I kept my distance because he was married. Then he and his wife Annabella separated, and one night he invited me over for drinks. What an evening! All we did was talk and listen to music, but for hours on end. We discovered we had similar thoughts and feelings, much the same values and tastes. Before he took me home he held me in his arms and kissed me, and my heart started beating faster. This was a man I could love.

I believed then, and I believe now, that if Tyrone could have settled his divorce quickly, we would have married. All our friends expected it. No, we were never formally engaged. But the gossips assumed we were—an electric current flowed between us. You only had to look at us to know we were in love. And we made a breathtaking couple, racing down a beach hand-in-hand, or sitting knee-to-knee in an intimate restaurant.

Why did I love him? He was the most gentlemanly, enchanting man I have ever known. He loved music and books. His tastes were worldly yet he had a certain innocence, a love of life, a sense of romance. He had always wanted to film *The Little Prince*, by Antoine de Saint-Exupéry, because something in that magical children's book touched him deeply. When he asked me to read it I could understand what he saw. It was a kind of bond between us.

Another film we talked about making was based on *Forever*, a sweet, otherworldly love story by Mildred Cram. Janet Gaynor bought it first; later MGM acquired it for Norma Shearer. But the studio held on to it, and to this day it hasn't been filmed. If Tyrone and I could have starred in it together, it could have become my favorite picture.

Why we couldn't do it I never learned. Tyrone represented at Fox what Gable did at Metro, top box office. But neither Fox nor MGM wanted us to star together, although nothing was ever said to us directly. For some reason the studios frowned on our relationship. We heard rumors that Zanuck and Mayer actually conferred about it, and I believe those stories are true.

Whatever Zanuck thought, he and his wife, Virginia, treated us well and invited us to Palm Springs nearly every other weekend. They lived on a large estate, and sometimes they'd entertain as many as fifty guests. Croquet was a big fad then. The men seemed to play from dawn to dawn, for Darryl had installed lights over the court, and heavy betting accompanied the games. One movie tycoon almost lost his studio, and I heard that Sam Spiegel once ran out of cash during a game and put up some scripts as collateral. I thought they were all crazy.

Tyrone and I would wander off for walks or take long, lazy drives. Although we had separate rooms, sometimes at night he'd sneak into mine. But he'd have to leave before daybreak because that's when they all got up to play croquet. That damned game!

But what glorious times. It was a different kind of love for me, richer and more mature. And Tyrone was always warm and fatherly with Cheryl, who was almost three and knew him only as 'my friend.' Our future was unclouded, except by Annabella, who still refused to give him a divorce.

What we shared was, to me, far more important than the physical side of our love. I might as well confess that I was not a great companion in bed. Sex was never, with any man, the first thing on my mind, and if I didn't make love for weeks I was content. No, I wasn't frigid. But I hated the public notion that I was constantly picking up men. Sex was so much what I symbolized, so much of my image, that I closed myself off to the pleasures of the act. Holding hands, cuddling, being close together in bed, all those intimacies I enjoyed more than the actual sex. Tyrone never pressured me. His gentleness was part of the reason I loved him. Later I heard rumors of a homosexual element in his nature, but I never saw it.

Like me, Tyrone was a prisoner of the romantic appearance that had made him a screen idol. I sympathized with his need to prove himself in roles of greater depth, especially when he campaigned for a grim and unusual film called *Nightmare Alley*. My loyal support of the project didn't endear me to Zanuck. But Tyrone eventually won. He succeeded in creating a role unlike any of his others, and he earned the critics' respect.

After *Nightmare Alley* Tyrone had to go back to the swash-buckling roles that Zanuck demanded. Next Tyrone starred in *Captain from Castile*, which was to be shot in Mexico, while I was filming *Green Dolphin Street*, another costume epic, on location in Oregon. There the producers had built an entire river community. In the grand climactic scene the river rose and swept the town away. My entire household was to wash away in the flood, including a maid played by Linda Christian. Later Linda wrote that I mistreated her on the set, but I certainly don't remember that. Stick around, there's more to come about Linda Christian.

When the New Year's weekend came I had three days off, and I longed to see Tyrone. He was still on location in the mountain village of Morelia. Three days was enough, I decided, to fly to Mexico City, find his set, and return in time for my work. So I bought gifts for him and Cesar Romero, his close friend, who was also in the cast. I planned to make the trip a surprise. But once I was in the plane I began to have qualms, so I called him from Mexico City.

95

'Good Lord,' he said. 'What are you doing here?'

'Since we missed Christmas dinner, I thought I'd help you celebrate New Year's.'

'But, Lana,' he said, 'there's no train and no bus, and all the roads are terrible. I'll have to dig up a plane somehow. Wait there, and I'll get back to you.'

I waited in the lobby of the Hotel Reforma, hiding my face in a newspaper. Tyrone hadn't sounded overjoyed to hear I was in Mexico. But he called back to say he had found a plane; my spirits rose. When he met me at the tiny airport, he seemed delighted to see me, and I began to feel I had done the right thing. It was 1947, a New Year's Eve I will never forget.

That night, we had a very late dinner in a little restaurant on the town square. At twelve o'clock the church bells began to ring. Midnight! Tyrone and I looked at each other, and I think the same thought popped into both our heads at the same instant. Without a word, we leaped from our chairs and ran across the tiny town square, racing for the church, determined to make it up the steps and onto the steeple balcony before the bells finished chiming . . . I really can't remember why. Maybe we thought it would mean good luck for us both, maybe it was inspired by wine, but we just did it, like a pair of kids. Tyrone held my hand as we ran, and I struggled not to fall in my long dress and high heels. Eight, nine, ten—and we made it! Laughing, we reached the church balcony just as the last two peals of midnight sounded. Then, I remember, we turned to each other and the laughter stopped. Solemnly, we made our silent wishes for the New Year, and we embraced. That long kiss was among the most heartfelt I've ever given or received. I wanted it to go on and on, and I wished with all my heart that that magical night would never come to an end.

But we couldn't stay up on the balcony forever, for all our wistful longing. Strains of music wafted up from the little square below. Morelia was awake and the New Year's revels were reaching high key. So hand-in-hand we descended into the warm, winter night.

In my memory we will always be an especially beautiful couple. I say this, I think, without vanity. Tyrone, so stunningly handsome, was majestic, and I wanted so to be his equal—I like to think that on that night I succeeded. I wore white satin brocade, cut in the Chinese fashion, with a high mandarin collar and slits up the long, tight skirt. The sides and the sleeves of my gown were heavily beaded with seed pearls and rhinestones that gleamed like the stars in the Mexican skies. I'd even brought jewels with me. I like to think of that Mexican night glittering off the jewels I wore in my hair. Oh, I think we *were* beautiful. But more than that, there was such an aura of love about us that we would have shone just as brightly even without the diamonds and the pearls.

When we got back down some spirited musicians were playing on the bandstand in the center of the little square. We paused a moment to listen to a trumpeter in the front row, who couldn't take his eyes off us. As he played he leaned over the railing, trying to keep us in sight as we passed. In fact, he was so enthralled that he kept leaning and leaning until he tumbled right over the railing, down to the ground.

He wasn't hurt, thank God, he just picked himself up and signaled to the band that he was okay. The funniest thing was that he was still staring at us, with the biggest grin on his face. So we blew him some kisses, and he blew kisses back at us. Then suddenly the whole band was blowing us kisses and clapping and laughing. It was so damn beautiful he had me laughing and crying at the same time. That funny little man!

A storm seemed to be brewing so we went off to join the cast and continue to ring in the New Year; we celebrated until morning. But the bells, and the church, our secret wishes for each other, and the little trumpeter—those were the special, private joys. Those belonged to Tyrone and me alone.

I planned to fly home early the next day to make my studio call, but the planes were grounded because of the weather. I had to get back. They couldn't shoot the scheduled scenes around me, and my absence would cost time and lots of money.

'I'll have to go by car, then,' I declared.

But Tyrone and the others shook their heads.

'A car can't make it. The roads are out.'

Stuck in Morelia, I watched it rain and rain. I was scared stiff. I was due back on the set, and if it hadn't been raining, I would have been back on time, and nobody would ever have known I was gone. Now it looked as though I'd be holding up production, and I'd be in big trouble when I finally got back. Finally the weather cleared enough for take-off, and after a bumpy, scary flight, I was back in Los Angeles on the third of January. I had missed almost two full days of filming. I headed straight to the studio and went at once to my dressing room. Something seemed peculiar on the set.

Strangely, no one mentioned the fact that I was late. Mr. Mayer's dreaded reprimand didn't come. So, I thought, I was going to get the silent treatment. All I could do was brazen it out.

I had brought back a large colorful serape. I draped it over my shoulders, stuck a rose between my teeth, and walked out on the sound stage. Not only was it dark, but no one seemed to be there. Standing there alone with that rose between my teeth, I felt like a perfect idiot.

Suddenly the lights blazed and the whole cast, along with the director, Victor Saville, came out from behind the flats, all of them wearing Mexican hats. Someone had a guitar, and everyone began singing 'South of the Border.' The joke was on me! I was lucky. My contract required me to be in Los Angeles whenever we were filming. Leaving for Mexico had been a serious breach. I could have been heavily fined even though the weather had trapped me there. Thank goodness Saville had protected me by shooting around me as much as possible, so as to minimize the delays. I escaped an official reprimand, although later I noticed that two days were docked from my pay.

We finished most of the shooting on *Green Dolphin Street*, and then I started my new picture, *Cass Timberlane*. My old champion, Spencer Tracy, was the costar. Production had just begun when the studio called for retakes on *Green Dolphin Street*. I would have to divide my days between the sets.

For *Green Dolphin Street* I had long dark hair, styled thirty-four different ways, because I matured in the course of the story. But for *Cass Timberlane* my hair was cut short and dyed back to its usual blond. How could I do those retakes with short blond hair? Helen Young came up with the answer. She assembled thirty-four hair-pieces in the appropriate styles. Every afternoon she would spray my hair with vegetable dye and then weave in the false hair. After the retake she'd strip out the dye so I would be a blond the next morning.

Marianne, my character in *Green Dolphin Street*, was British-born, so I'd developed a kind of mid-Atlantic accent. Not quite English, but not quite American either. But in *Cass Timberlane* I played a thoroughly American girl. I struggled to keep the accents straight, but sometimes my Marianne voice came out. 'My, my,' Spencer would say, 'aren't we British this morning?'

By now Tyrone was back in Los Angeles, and for a while we resumed our affair openly. Annabella had half agreed to the

98

divorce, but they were fighting the property battles—those ugly scenes that lawyers take endless hours to get straight. Perhaps, having made *Nightmare Alley*, he'd begun to rethink his career. Maybe he was questioning the prospect of life with me. Whatever his reasons, and with studio pressure, he began planning a flying press junket, combined with a long vacation, alone.

7

THE MONTH before his departure my period was late. I'd never been all that regular. But after two weeks passed, then three, I went for a pregnancy test. Sure enough, it came back positive.

My doctor, who knew who the father was, asked just what I was wondering, 'Lana, what are you going to do?'

Well, what indeed? Of course I wanted the baby. I loved Tyrone deeply, and I was thrilled to think it was his. I allowed myself a moment of joy, of deep secret satisfaction. Then I had to face facts. Tyrone was legally separated but he was still married, and we were both very much in the public eye. I could picture the headlines already. And Tyrone was leaving town, and I didn't know why, although he assured me that he loved me . . . No, this wouldn't be easy.

Still, he had to be told. For three anguished days I postponed it. He noticed my pensive mood, and one night as we sat together on the sofa, he asked me what was wrong. His dark eyes searched mine anxiously. I knew this was the moment.

'I'm pregnant.' How else could I put it?

'Oh,' he said softly, and that was all. He just sat back. And suddenly the most beautiful smile broke out over his face, a real ear-to-ear grin that said more than any words could. That smile was enough to bring out every single thing I was feeling. I leaned forward and threw my arms around him. And he hugged me back, very tightly. We didn't say a word, we didn't even kiss. We just held on to each other for dear life, hugging and gently rocking.

Then finally he held me away from him, at arm's length, and looked into my eyes and said, 'Well! Let's have a drink!'

But when he brought the drinks back his face was serious. 'This puts a different light on things, doesn't it?'

I couldn't deny that.

'Well, Lana, what are we going to do?' He'd said *we*, what are *we* going to do, so I was still feeling that everything might turn out all right. 'How do you feel about it?'

'How do *I* feel about it? I have mixed emotions, Tyrone. I want

100

this baby so much because I love you so much. But I know that there are problems.'

'Yes, there are problems. I don't know when the hell I can get a divorce.'

I leaned forward eagerly. 'Do you think if you told her the situation and she realized how serious it is that she would give you a divorce?'

God, I can't believe I was so naïve. For the first time I noticed that Tyrone was hemming and hawing. He didn't come right out and say. 'That's a good idea,' or 'No, it's impossible.' Instead he just kep frowning and saying, 'Well . . .'

I guess it was my fault, though. I was so happy, so exhilarated and so damned *sure* that there would be a happy ending that I never let him finish a sentence. Maybe if I had kept my mouth shut, he'd have come right out and said, 'We can't do it.' I don't know. But the more I tried to talk him into my own state of jubilation, the more somber and silent he became.

Finally I did shut up. Obviously he was going through mental and emotional turmoil. I'd already been through mine in those three days when I'd carried our secret by myself. So finally I said softly, 'Let's not talk about it any more right now.' And that's the way we left it. Undecided.

Two careers were on the line here, two big careers. In those days you didn't make babies just because you were deeply in love. Nobody got away with it then. Even years later, when Ingrid Bergman tried, they put her through hell for it. And Tyrone was still married, at least in name. Oh, maybe he could get off lightly in the eyes of the world. After all, he was the man, and the double standard was applied with a vengeance then. But I'd be publicly branded a whore, and I'd probably never work again.

But even while thinking realistically, the other part of my mind was saying, *No! Nobody's going to take this baby away from me.* I fantasized that I'd go away to an island and have the baby and say I'd adopted it. Now I can laugh at myself. How the hell could Lana Turner go away to an island and come back with a baby that looked exactly like Tyrone Power and get away with it? But then I half convinced myself that I could.

Of course we talked about it again in a few days.

'You know this trip is coming up,' he reminded me.

I nodded; I hardly needed reminding. 'Well, what do you want me to do?' I asked. 'Have it or not have it?'

There was no smile in his face or his eyes. 'I can't tell you that,' he said in a low voice.

There was no *we* anymore. Just *I* and *you*.

'Then you're leaving it up to me,' I said unhappily.

'I'd like you to have a talk with Mrs. X,' he urged, naming the wife of a powerful film executive.

'Why her?'

'Because she loves us both, and because I trust her.'

But I wouldn't promise.

Days passed and we didn't discuss it again, but the now-painful subject hung between us. I couldn't delay the decision too much longer, and Tyrone was preparing to leave for Europe. He would be gone a long time, and this certainly wasn't a subject we could discuss with the overseas operator listening. But he kept telling me, 'I want you to talk to Mrs. X and then you have to let me know. I want to know what you decide.'

So we devised a code. If I decided to abort our baby I'd say, 'I found the house today.' If I decided to keep it I'd say, 'I haven't found the house today.'

When I saw Tyrone off at the airfield I promised I'd do as he asked. I remember standing there watching until the plane was out of sight. I couldn't help crying, wondering what would happen to the two of us when he came back.

When I went to visit Mrs. X, she laid it right on the line for me. 'I believe that you want it, and I believe that Tyrone does, too. But you two don't stand a chance.'

It didn't matter that I had all the dreams in the world of having this baby; there was no way it could happen. Two major careers were at stake. If I wasn't concerned with mine, I owed it to Tyrone not to destroy his.

I had known what she was going to say, and I'm sure Tyrone knew too. Looking back, I believe she gave me the best advice she could. I'm convinced she loved Tyrone and me and wished us well. But she was on the spot, too—married to one of the most important men in Hollywood, a man who had a financial stake in Tyrone's career. Her words dashed my silly illusions to pieces.

So I made the arrangements, and again I went alone. This time I was luckier. I had a woman doctor, not a butcher, who was capable, sympathetic, and warm. I had a clean hospital bed and anesthesia. There were no complications. But that abortion took more than a fetus from me. It took some part of my heart, a living symbol of the happiest time in my life. I believed that Tyrone would come back to me and that we'd go on as before until Annabella relented about the divorce. I thought we'd eventually marry and try to have other children. Oh, my beautiful dreams.

On a prearranged evening a group of us went to see a friend of Tyrone's who had a ham radio. Tyrone was waiting somewhere in Europe—funny, I've blocked out where—and we called him over the shortwave and said hello. And when it was my turn I said, 'Tyrone, I found the house today.'

Clark Gable and I again costarred in *Homecoming*, directed by Mervyn LeRoy. In any love story made then, the challenge was to suggest the passion that the censors kept off the screen. So Mervyn shot close-ups of several fervent kisses. To keep my mouth fresh for those clinches I chewed gum, and during takes I would poke the wad up next to my teeth. But once Clark kissed me too forcefully. When he drew back we were attached by a ribbon of sticky gum! I shrieked with laughter as Clark glumly picked the gum from his teeth. From then on I gargled instead.

Soon Tyrone and I would celebrate our own homecoming. When I finished filming the picture I flew to New York to wait for his return. Frank Sinatra was also in town, appearing at the Capitol Theater. We spent some pleasant evenings drinking and dancing and chatting about friends and our careers. Of course it made the papers as a budding romance, and someone passed on the information to Tyrone in Rome.

The bearer of bad news, I later heard, was my dear friend Sara Hamilton! She knew very well that Frank and I were only friends and had never been anything else. What possessed her to mention to Tyrone that I was 'dating' Frank? That strange tale she told eventually broke up our friendship for good.

I waited in New York for two and half weeks, and then Tyrone finally phoned—from Palm Springs.

I was bewildered. 'But you were to pick me up *here*.'

'Well, Zanuck called me in Rome and told me not to stop in New York.'

'Didn't you tell him of *our* plan?'

'I didn't get the chance to.'

'Tyrone, I don't understand this,' I said. 'Do you want me to come back? I can get a plane to Los Angeles right away.'

103

'Well,' he said, 'if you're having fun there . . .'

That was the first real clue I had that something had gone wrong between us.

'Do you mean . . . with *Frank?* Tyrone, you can't possibly believe that stupid gossip—'

'Well . . .' he said.

The irony was that Frank knew very well that I was in love with Tyrone. We'd spent many hours in New York discussing him! So I called Frank right away to ask him what I should do.

'Get on the first plane out there,' he said. 'I'll arrange it.'

First thing in the morning I hopped a plane for Burbank, an endless, agonizing trip. Before I left I called Tyrone to tell him I was coming home. I asked him to meet me at the airport, and he said he would be there.

But when I arrived, he wasn't. So I sat alone on one of those uncomfortable benches for over an hour, all the time wondering and wondering. But still no Tyrone. Finally in walked, of all people, Sara Hamilton.

'What are *you* doing here?' I demanded. 'Where's Tyrone?'

'He's in the car. We're parked at the curb.'

I noticed that she was walking strangely, and her eyes were glassy. That struck me as odd, because Sara never drank much. But I picked up my bag and followed her, and sure enough, there was Tyrone sitting at the wheel of his car.

'Uh, sorry to be late,' he said.

'I have a little bag here. Would it be too much trouble for you to put it in the trunk?'

'Gee, sorry. What was I thinking of?' And he climbed out and put my case away, then got back in the car without even bothering to kiss me. Not so much as the peck on the cheek you'd give an old friend. I slid in next to him, and Sara sat by the door. Tyrone smelled strangely of liquor, too, of something heavy like brandy.

We drove to Sara's apartment, to drop her off, Tyrone said. But then he urged me to come up to Sara's place for drinks.

It was pretty obvious that he was putting off the moment when the two of us would be alone, but I couldn't yet figure out why. Wasn't he glad to see me? And why had he been drinking with Sara? I was getting madder by the minute. The hell with this!

'Tyrone, I'm sorry,' I told him stiffly. 'I want to go home.'

'Oh, not yet.'

But I insisted. On the way to my house he was silent, except to answer my questions as briefly as possible. I was so frustrated I wanted to scream. Something was wrong—very wrong. I had to get home and find out what.

As soon as we arrived I went upstairs to change into a robe. Not a negligee or anything sexy, more like a housecoat. When I came down he'd made us two drinks, and he held his up and said, 'Welcome home.' But he wasn't smiling as though he really meant it.

We sat down together on the window seat, and a feeling of dread overcame me. I knew there were questions I had to ask, and I was afraid of the answers. I drew a deep breath.

'All right, Tyrone, what is it? There's something going on, isn't there? Something I don't know about.'

Now he looked straight at me, and his expression told the story. 'Yes, Lana, there is.'

'Is it another woman?' The dreaded question.

The dreaded answer. 'Yes.'

Looking back now, I suppose he expected me to ask who and how and why. But that one word *yes* deflated me completely. It took everything out of me—my heart, my soul, my guts. I couldn't say a word. Here I'd given up the baby I'd wanted so much, believing that at least I'd have Tyrone and someday we would have children together. Now, a double blow, like in a bad movie; only it wasn't a movie. Later I learned who the other woman was. Linda Christian. She had just happened to be in Rome and had run into Tyrone at the Hotel Excelsior. Linda Christian, the girl I supposedly mistreated on the set of *Green Dolphin Street*. What a coincidence. Tyrone's whole trip may have been nothing but a setup to break the two of us apart. And it worked. I just couldn't believe it.

Now Tyrone was standing at the door, looking at me mournfully. 'This doesn't have to be the end for us,' he said. 'You know I care for you, so we can be friends, can't we?'

'No.' I shook my head, calm on the outside, inside churning with pain, rage, humiliation.

He smiled at me, a charming, winning smile. 'I don't understand why we can't have a drink now and then, or go to dinner.'

'Tyrone, will you please leave?' My control was slipping fast, but I was damned if I'd lose my dignity in front of him.

His face sobered up completely, and he reached automatically for the doorknob. He kept staring hard at me as though trying to read my face. I showed him nothing but pride. 'All right, I'll leave,' he said quietly and shut the door behind him.

There were no good-byes, nothing. Just a door shut between us forever. A simple click of the latch and everything ended.

I put my glass down on the little bar in the den, walked quickly upstairs, threw myself onto my bed, and wept until I was too exhausted to cry anymore.

I was, I remember, in Acapulco in November 1958. I had just come in from the beach, and the phone was ringing. It was Teddy Stauffer, who managed the hotel.

'Lana,' he said, 'Lana, are you all right?'

'Of course I'm all right; I've just been swimming. Why? What's going on?'

'Oh, my God, you don't know,' he wailed. 'That *I* should have to be the one to tell you!'

Now I was annoyed. 'Teddy, just say it. What is it?'

'Tyrone had a heart attack. He's dead.'

All I remember is going numb. I think my hand simply dropped, still clutching the phone. Although he had been gone from my life for so long—for roughly ten years—I wasn't prepared to hear something so definite, so final. Tyrone, that beautiful, sensitive man, so in love with life . . . I could hear Teddy screaming, 'Lanita, Lanita,' and I realized we were still connected.

I put the phone to my ear again.

'Do you want me to come over, Lana?'

I shook my head blindly, then remembered that Teddy couldn't hear that. 'No. No, I'm all right. Good-bye.'

I sat down on the edge of the bed, disbelieving, still numb. I didn't cry, not then, and not later when the numbness wore off and I realized it was true. Tyrone Power was dead. My tears had all been shed years before when that door closed. Now it was truly closed forever.

In my life I loved other men, but Tyrone was special. He was the one who broke my heart.

8

O NCE T YRONE walked out on me, I just couldn't bear to stay in California. Less than forty-eight hours after I'd arrived, I escaped to New York.

Throughout the gloomy flight I went round and round in my mind, trying to figure out what *I* had done wrong. Where had I failed? Or was the failure in Tyrone? I had devoted more than a year to him, but I had been only chasing another illusion of life with the ideal mate. What was the tragic flaw that made me, time and time again, choose and believe in the wrong person? Was I living in my fantasies rather than in reality?

As if to emphasize the fact that I had to get down to earth, the Internal Revenue Service came down hard on my tax returns. My business managers routinely took deductions for the essentials of a star's career—such things as clothes and furs, a limousine and driver, entertaining, gifts. Other stars wrote off the same expenses and they too were being severely scrutinized, but there was no denying I was a bit extravagant. Now the IRS was disallowing item after item, year by year. They assessed me so heavily that I couldn't possibly pay the back taxes I now owed. Never mind that my war-bond tours had added many millions to the Treasury.

Metro's legal department and my own lawyers bailed me out by arranging to deduct large amounts from my weekly checks and sending them straight to the IRS. I signed a new contract that raised my salary to the same level as Gable and Tracy. Time to sober up, I told myself. I would have to keep a more careful eye on income and outgo. Cash flow, as they call it today. But that could come later; once I was back in New York I indulged myself a little. I desperately craved activity to help me forget Tyrone. By day, the studio kept me busy with interviews and publicity stints surrounding the release of *Cass Timberlane*. After work I sought out my friends and plunged into the magnificent glittering night world of the city.

There was a man ready and waiting to show me the town. Many

months earlier, while I was filming *Cass Timberlane*, a flood of roses from a certain Henry J. Topping, Jr., had arrived to swamp my dressing room. After the flowers came a huge box of candy, which the crew enjoyed, and then a telephone call from the gentleman himself. I told him please to stop the nonsense, not to call me again, and he'd retreated gracefully.

Here I was at the Plaza, ready to have a good time, and Topping was trying again. Somehow he got through the switchboard. He said he'd heard I was in New York and that he was still anxious to meet me. Was I free, by any chance, that evening? By now I'd heard, among other things, that he was married to the actress Arline Judge. I brought that up. That was all finished, he assured me; they had separated. 'Oh, what the hell,' I thought. 'Why not see him?'

Later that day MGM's New York publicity head telephoned to ask a favor. That night they were premiering *The Bishop's Wife*, and Loretta Young was slated for a welcome speech to the invited audience. But she had been taken ill. Could I possibly substitute for her? I'd just have to read the greeting off the cards. Of course, I agreed to do it. I telephoned Topping to say I'd have to cancel our date; he countered by offering to escort me to the premiere.

When Topping picked me up at the Plaza he didn't exactly bowl me over. He was ordinary-looking and slightly overweight. He had the easy, friendly manner, though, of one born to wealth, and he seemed pleasant enough company for one evening. By the time the limousine came I hadn't learned much about him except that he was called Bob instead of Henry.

On the way to the premiere I had to review my speech, so I asked him to excuse me. I quickly scanned the cards, memorizing a few key lines. Then as I opened my purse to put them away, he dropped in something wrapped in tissue paper.

'What's that?' I asked.

'Unwrap it and find out,' he said with a smile.

I opened the ball of tissue to find a magnificent pair of diamond earrings. Now this was something new. No one had ever tossed diamonds at me before. I was stunned, hesitant, and shy.

'Haven't you noticed,' I asked him, 'that I'm wearing my own diamond earrings?'

'I thought you might like some new and different ones. I hope you'll wear them tonight. It would please me very much.'

108

I started to demur, 'No, no, I can't accept this, it's really too much. I don't even know you . . .' But we were almost there, and so I thought, 'Well, why offend him?' and I took off my own and put on his. So this was how millionaires treated their blind dates. And after all he could certainly afford it. His mother's father was the 'tin-plate king' Daniel J. Reid, who had amassed some $140 million in tin plate, steel, tobacco, banks, and railroads. His mother had died a few months before, leaving her estate to be divided among her three sons, Dan (who owned the New York Yankees), Bob, and Jack.

We had many more dates during my stay, and I learned he had a history of marrying quickly. First it was Jayne Shadduck, when he was twenty-one, right after her divorce from the playwright Jack Kirkland. When they divorced three years later he became engaged that same day to Gloria (Mimi) Baker, the famous café society glamour girl of 1937, the half-sister of George and Alfred Gwynne Vanderbilt. A few years and two children later, he divorced her and married Arline Judge, who had just divorced his brother Dan. Now he and Arline were splitting up, and she was pressing for a big settlement.

Toward the end of 1947 Bob invited me and my family to spend the holidays at his estate, Round Hill, in Greenwich, Connecticut. I had never met anyone like Bob before, and I had never encountered anything like Round Hill. The six-hundred-acre estate had its own lake and a vast Tudor-style mansion. The house had been assembled brick by brick, including the chimneys and even the marble fireplaces, from some sixteenth-century manors in England. It had four huge drawing rooms, and the servants' quarters alone took up twenty-one rooms. The master hall reminded me of something out of a Gothic romance film. I was *impressed*.

By this time Bob was asking to marry me. I was growing fond of him; I enjoyed his attentions and his sumptuous life-style, but I still had the deep hurt left over from Tyrone. When I told him, 'I don't love you, Bob,' he answered confidently, 'You will.'

My stay in the East had stretched to five weeks. It would soon be time for me to return to Los Angeles and the studio. I was scheduled to play the cunning Lady de Winter in a new version of *The Three Musketeers* directed by George Sidney, with a cast that included Gene Kelly, June Allyson, and Vincent Price. But Bob wanted me to stay on in New York. What an attractive but confusing proposition! I had tried love often enough, and it had failed. Bob was offering me security, the fulfillment of the same dream that had lured me to Las Vegas with Artie Shaw. A husband, a name, a respectable life, a loving environment for my daughter. And I would have time to mother her, for if I married Bob, I wouldn't have to work unless I wanted to.

Still undecided, I planned to go back to Los Angeles to mull things over at the studio. A few days before I left Bob and I spent an evening at '21.' And what were we doing? We were drinking. I didn't think of that as a problem then. I was drinking a bit but not the way Bob and his friends did. Bob was the kind of drinker who liked his companion to keep up with him, but I was shocked at the number of martinis he consumed. It didn't strike me then that he might be close to becoming an alcoholic.

While we were sitting there a messenger arrived, and Bob excused himself from the table. When he returned I didn't notice that he had dropped something into my martini. Eventually, I picked up the drink, and something flashed in the bottom. Believe me, it was not an onion or an olive.

'Fish it out,' he said.

What I fished out of the martini glass was a fifteen-carat marquise diamond ring! As I wiped it dry it flashed brilliant rays. It was the most beautiful diamond I had ever seen, with a luminous, intense fire. The messenger had brought it along with some others, from which Bob had made his selection.

For a few long minutes I was too amazed to speak. Finally I asked, 'What's this for?'

'I'm asking you to marry me.'

'But you know I don't love you. I've told you that. And you haven't gotten your divorce yet.'

'Don't think about that now,' he said. 'You'll learn how much I love you and how much I'll treasure you for the rest of our lives if you'll only tell me yes.' And he went on, making promises the way men in love do and assuring me that I'd learn to love him. He said it all so sweetly and dearly and sincerely that I really believed it might work. And I did want to be loved by someone who would shelter me in his arms and protect me, and help me get over the shattering loss of Tyrone.

I tried on the ring, on the engagement finger.

'Yes?' he asked.

110

'Yes,' I whispered. There's something awfully compelling about a large engagement ring.

'And you'll stay here?'

I shook my head. 'No.'

He said, 'Then I'll go back with you.'

Back home, when I read the script for *The Three Musketeers*, I found that Lady de Winter was not a starring role. Surprised that my agents had signed me for it, I went straight to Mr. Mayer and refused the part. With Bob in my future I felt strong, since I wouldn't have to depend on that weekly paycheck from the studio. We fenced a little. The wily Mr. Mayer said that the studio couldn't *force* me to honor the commitment, but that I would have to cover preproduction costs of several hundred thousand dollars.

'Sorry,' I said bravely, 'I still won't do that script.'

I soon found out that when your agents are empowered to make a deal, it's the same as doing it yourself. So now, for the first time ever, the studio suspended me. There were meetings and negotiations; they rewrote the script to give me more to do, and finally I agreed to make the picture.

Am I glad I did! I enjoyed the filming enormously. George Sidney flavored the story with humor and comic swordplay. He had Gene Kelly leaping all over the place. It was my first picture in Technicolor and my first chance to play a truly villainous lady. At the end I was beheaded.

My equal in villainy was Vincent Price as Cardinal Richelieu. He was a master of high camp. I had been playing Milady straight, but Vincent was stealing every scene. I studied him, and it challenged me, and I began to try things I never knew I could do. I found my own little touches—a certain sly look, the flap of a glove, a tilt of the head. I began to stylize the role. In my prison scene June Allyson replaced one of my regular guards, because a woman wouldn't fall for my feminine wiles. With lightning flashing outside the windows, I played cat-and-mouse with her and let my eyes go crazy. They were things I'd never been *allowed* to do before, things that were not in the pages of the script. June told me later that I terrified her.

I was supposed to have a beauty mark near my chin, and Del had found an assortment of moons, stars, and hearts. I would use different shapes for each shot or put the mark in different places.

111

The poor script girl. She had to make sure the details were the same in every shot. I know we drove her crazy.

When the reviews appeared I was singled out, and what a deliciously warm feeling that gave me. I hadn't wanted to do the picture, but I had made something of it and, thanks to Vincent, had found a new facet of my abilities.

One writer, Jeanine Basinger, liked one of my favorite parts, the carriage scene. 'Turner,' she wrote, 'was covered with jewels and costumed exquisitely. The drama of her first appearance on screen is heightened by the effect of having her sit in a darkened carriage, giving the audience a sense of an apparition beyond life, a mysterious creature in the dark. When Turner finally *does* lean slowly forward into the light—and the Technicolor—audiences were not jerked out of their mood and back to earth. She *was* unreal. A proper goddess.'

Unreal? I should say it was. It was pure Hollywood illusion. Nobody could have known that beneath the cloak and bodice of that 'proper goddess' were casual slacks and street shoes. It got so warm when we were filming that I couldn't stand my huge heavy skirt and petticoats.

Bob Topping was in constant attendance while I made that picture, and he attracted so much attention from the gossip mill that Arline Judge started sounding off to columnists like Earl Wilson. 'He won't get a divorce from me for *any* money,' she was quoted as saying. 'I'll ruin him first'—that kind of thing. Bob didn't take her threats seriously and neither did I. I'd met her a few times at parties, and I admired her spunky spirit and I think she liked me.

She and Bob had gotten married on a drinking spree, and they'd had some marvelous fights. Once I asked why he'd split up with Arline. He said only, 'She broke a bottle of champagne over my head. A great year, too.'

If I didn't really love Bob, then why was I marrying him? For his money? No. What I wanted was some security and peace. Everything I had, the kind of life I lived, had come through my own efforts, from hard, continual work under pressure. That pressure never seemed to let up. The studio had helped promote me by pairing me with important stars. Now I was being used to help build other stars—I was carrying pictures on my own shoulders. And the more I did, the greater the glare of publicity on me. The press was always nipping at my heels. Gossip about me escalated—some of it friendly, some of it vicious, all of it intrusive. There was no way I could protect myself from it.

With Bob I felt I could be myself, not just the glamorous image that my roles portrayed and the studio worked to enhance. But what I didn't realize was that, by taking the Topping name, I would only strengthen that image and become more of a target for unwanted attention.

Our plans progressed rapidly. Bob wanted to marry immediately after his divorce became final, in April 1948. Twice before I had missed out on a real honest-to-God wedding, a ceremony with all the trappings. This time I wanted a traditional wedding gown, flowers, a reception, and a perfect honeymoon. A beautiful celebration, with our good friends present.

My house on Crown Drive was too small for a reception, and I didn't want to marry at Round Hill. So Cubby Broccoli, Bob's good friend and a darling man, mentioned our problem to Billy Wilkerson. Billy immediately offered us his large house in Bel-Air, with its spacious grounds, for the wedding.

After finishing *The Three Musketeers* I had only three weeks to get ready. Don Loper created my wedding gown of champagne-colored Alençon lace over champagne satin, and he also designed a suit for my mother and a dress for Cheryl, who was almost five.

With lavish indulgence Bob filled Billy's house with hundreds of beautiful flowers: roses, delphiniums, gladioli, daisies, and gardenias. For the reception he ordered an extravagant feast, prepared by the chefs at L'Aiglon and LaRue's. As the French press described the fare, 'Picture for yourself a kind of Japanese garden placed among the most exotic delicacies designed naturally enough with rivers and lakes. In these little rivers and lakes there were swimming real tiny goldfish. The border was caviar, and salmon canapés were spread out through the countryside, and when you made a stab with your fork you didn't pick up a sole marguery but a live, little red fish . . .'

By the morning of the wedding my nerves were frayed. The wedding gown was late and got its final stitches only that morning. But the ceremony itself went nicely, with the retired pastor of the Hollywood Presbyterian Church officiating. Bob's best man was Billy Wilkerson, and Cheryl was my flower girl. I was given away by my good doctor, William Branch, while a string orchestra played the wedding music. Among the guests were Louis B. Mayer, Eddie Mannix, Greg Bautzer, George Sidney and his wife, Lillian

113

Burns, Ben Cole, Cubby and Nedra Broccoli, and of course my mother.

Only one news photographer had been invited to attend, and he was supposed to share his pictures with the rest. The studio sent bouncers to handle the press, and we didn't even know the Beverly Hills police would dispatch six uniformed men to keep out the public. But after the ceremony, pandemonium reigned as fans and newsmen broke down the barricades, trampling Billy's shrubbery to dust. Flashbulbs popped like fireworks as the newsmen shouted, 'Look this way Lana!' or 'Come on! Kiss each other.'

After the reception we escaped to a bungalow in the gardens of the Beverly Hills Hotel. But poor Billy! Thinking we were still there, an enormous crowd besieged his house until the wee hours of morning, when the police were finally able to disperse them.

The next morning the hotel left an elegant breakfast on our bungalow terrace. When we came out we found the intrepid Hedda Hopper already there with hat, pencil, and questions. She had just finished eating our meal, and she was helping herself to the last of the coffee. With no congratulations, even, she shooed us back into our room and began firing away. We tried to keep our good humor. Finally we managed to get her out—but not before she got enough to pass off as her 'exclusive' interview with us. 'Obtrusive' would be a better word for it.

Let's face it. Hedda Hopper and Louella Parsons dominated Hollywood. They took bribes and gifts and played favorites, and God help you if they ever got mad at you. The studio was forever begging me to go to Hedda's house for an interview because she found out I'd been to Louella's. Well, I'd had to go. Poor Louella, those last ten years or so of her life, was so drunk all the time she couldn't even leave the house. People had to come to her, and even then she was in a fog. Kowtowing, that's what it was, kowtowing, with the studios making the deepest bows.

Be nice to Louella, she's in a bad mood. Go be sweet to her, make her laugh. If you didn't do it, she'd get on your back in her column and never get off. Ginger Rogers made that mistake. I don't know what kind of falling-out they had, but for years Louella came close to ruining Ginger's career. That's the power she had.

Still, I liked Louella, and I understood her problems. The few times she printed something vicious, I phoned her and said, 'Louella, please, that simply wasn't true.' And I'd send her flowers, to kowtow a little. I would buy her gifts at Christmas until one year

114

I saw her tree. You couldn't even walk into the room. The gifts were heaped all over the floor, and the wrappings were from the most expensive stores and exclusive jewelers in Beverly Hills. And then she'd be flashing some new emerald bracelet or some enormous diamond brooch. Eventually, I sent her only fruit and flowers, because my gifts couldn't compare.

Hedda Hopper never liked me. She tore into me about Tyrone; later she was terrible about Fernando Lamas. She blasted my marriage with Bob Topping; she never let up on me, ever. So finally Howard Strickling persuaded me to agree to visit her. He phoned for an appointment and then called me back. 'Hedda doesn't believe it. She wants to hear it from you.'

'Does that mean *I* have to call her?'

'Yes, Lana,' sighed Howard. 'Will you, please?'

Now I was steamed, but I took her number. The secretary put me on hold, and finally Hedda came on the line.

'Hello, Miss Hopper,' I started politely. 'This is Lana Turner.'

'Oh, yes, Laaaannna,' she said, deliberately flattening the *a*— but she knew how to pronounce it. 'I hear you want to do an interview with me.'

I held on to my temper. 'No, I've been told that *you* want to do an interview with *me*.'

So we made a date, and her parting words were, 'Don't you dare be late.'

When I arrived at her house she gave me a cup of tea and then, I remember, she asked, 'Well, what's going on in your life?'

'Everything but what you print about me.'

She had the grace to look surprised.

'I know all about your leg people, Hedda, but you're getting the wrong information.'

'Well, what do you want me to print?'

'Only the truth, and when you have proof of what you're printing.'

'I can't just sit around waiting for that,' she protested. 'Besides, Louella's always writing about you.'

'That's different,' I said. 'Louella and I are friends.'

'Why can't *we* be friends?'

I looked her right in the eye and said, 'Because I don't like you.'

Hedda nearly fainted. 'How dare you speak to me like that!' she raged. Nobody had ever said that to her face before.

So I repeated it. 'I don't like you, Miss Hedda Hopper, and I really don't think I should stay here anymore.'

115

'You're right! Get out of my house!' she stormed.

So I picked up my purse and marched coolly out of there. But I wasn't as cool when I called Howard Strickling and told him about the interview. The consummate publicity man, he was aghast. 'Oh, my God,' he moaned into the phone. 'What do we do now?'

'I don't know,' I confessed. 'Wait and see, I suppose.'

Days and weeks went by, and she never printed one word about me, for or against. Nobody had ever had the nerve to stand up to her before, and it took her time to get over it. Later on, though, she and I made a truce, through the offices of Lex Barker. She adored Lex because he ass-kissed her to death. But now I'm getting ahead of my story.

9

M Y MARRIAGE to Bob Topping would generate publicity for months to come. Newspapers sermonized about stars changing spouses with 'disgraceful, careless abandon.' Goaded by the press, the Los Angeles presbytery formally rebuked our minister for performing the ceremony. And the fuss even reached the halls of Congress. Investigators criticized the Voice of America for broadcasting news of the wedding, calling the story a poor way to counter communist propaganda. Later someone suggested that the congressional censure was the first small wave of the coming tide of McCarthyism.

Bob and I planned a honeymoon in Europe, which would partly be a business trip for him. He and a friend, Burt Friedlob, had invested money in midget racing cars, and Bob hoped to promote the sport in England. A fierce band of newsmen pursued us aboard the S.S. *Mauretania* and raised a ruckus until the final whistle sounded. If I didn't know how many trunks I was taking, I read it in the papers once we landed.

When, oh when, would my orderly new existence, my peaceful married life begin? Well, not when I got to England. MGM had scheduled a press conference when we docked, and it was open season for questions. The first one came from a woman reporter, who asked, 'Is that your own hair?'

'Certainly,' I snapped. 'Isn't that yours?'

The next day more than one paper cited this evidence of my 'rudeness.'

Bob and his partner had arranged to demonstrate their little racers on a motorcycle track in a London stadium. They plastered notices on billboards around London, and someone foolishly printed on the posters that I would appear at the inaugural. Bob was in a bind because of the mistake so I loyally agreed to go. The Lord Mayor made a welcoming speech, though he didn't seem to know who I was, and I rode around the track in a convertible.

The racing venture was a disaster. The partners shipped twenty-three cars overseas, but they hadn't known that the tracks would be made of brick. The little cars needed a smoother surface so the brick was layered with cinders. Soon Bob discovered that the British didn't like Americans invading their scene. Somehow the cinders got mixed with stones, which flew up into the drivers' faces, and sand found its way into the gasoline tanks. Mysterious slits were discovered in tires so they quickly had to fly in replacements. Somebody even went so far as to plaster over the posters announcing the racing program. Eventually there was nothing to do but close up shop.

Huge bills piled up as the racing venture went under. On our last day in London Bob sat in our hotel room signing checks for more than $200,000. I actually wept as I watched him steadfastly meeting those commitments. He had loved those cars so.

On to Paris, where we stayed at the Hotel George V. One day I received a message that Aly Khan had telephoned. Since I had never met him I decided not to return his call. But as Bob and I were dressing to go out to dinner the hotel operator rang to say Aly Khan was back on the line. I told her to say we had left for the evening. The next day he telephoned a third time!

'Oh, take the call,' Bob said, laughing, 'and find out what it's about.'

'Miss Turner?' an intriguing voice, with just a trace of an accent, greeted me.

'I'm really Mrs. Topping,' I said.

'Yes, of course, forgive me. I have wanted to meet you for such a long time.'

'Thank you,' I said.

'And now that you're here in Paris, I would so like for you to have dinner with me.'

I gave Bob, who was sitting there listening, a glance with raised eyebrows.

'Mr. Khan, I must explain. I'm here on my honeymoon with my husband.'

'Of course, my dear, but that has nothing to do with your having dinner with me.'

'But I think it does.'

'Oh, I see. Of course. Well, he may come along.'

I looked at Bob and pointed to the mouthpiece, indicating that the conversation was getting nuttier. 'Well, that's very understanding of you, but I don't think that can be arranged.'

'Perhaps *you* don't understand,' Aly said. 'If your husband cares to come along, that will be all right.'

'No,' I said, 'I don't think it will be. So I suggest that you don't call me anymore. I'm very much in love with my husband, and I don't see anyone else.'

That ended that, but perhaps I gained a little insight into the international café society and the ways of Aly Khan. If that was the method he used to meet Rita Hayworth, it obviously succeeded some of the time.

We went on to the Riviera, where my mother, Cheryl, and Cheryl's Nana joined us. Bob had booked apartments for us at the Miramar Hotel in Cannes. He had a friend, Freddie McAvoy, a jolly sort of playboy, who was then involved in salvaging ancient wrecks from the sea bottom. Freddie helped Bob charter a large sailing vessel, which we used as our alternate headquarters. Then, for two of the most enjoyable months I've ever spent, we lived the life of the idle rich.

It was one big social occasion. We all went from boat to boat for lunch. We swam under the Mediterranean sun; we entertained and visited; we chatted about the troubles in the world, so far away from us. Bob bought some underwater tanks and gear, and he and Cheryl learned to use them. Under Freddie's guidance we'd set off in a little flotilla in search of treasure. A handsome young Mexican Olympic swimmer came along with us, and he dived for urns and other objects from an ancient Greek ship. In the evenings Bob's chef prepared marvelous meals and served them with fine French wines. What a glorious vacation! During this time I became pregnant, although I didn't find out until the summer was over and we had returned to the States.

A new script awaited me there. It was a flat, dull version of *Madame Bovary* and I didn't see how it could be successful. I notified the studio that I didn't like it and that anyway I was pregnant. When the studio threatened suspension I didn't budge. So they cut off my salary and my publicity, and I spent most of the year that followed out of the public eye. Even so, in a *Modern Screen* magazine poll, I was voted the year's Number 1 box-office star.

Bob and I were ecstatic about my pregnancy. We stayed at Round Hill for a while and made side trips to New York. It was the tail end of the baseball season, and since Bob's brother Dan owned the Yankees, we watched some of the games from his private box. There were clouds on our pleasant horizon, but I didn't know then that they were serious. The problem was that Bob, who had dried out on our honeymoon, was drinking heavily again. I had been drinking a bit myself, although once I got pregnant I stopped completely. But not Bob, and we began to argue about it.

'Bob,' I'd say, 'we're trying to have a baby.' He would control himself for a while but then start again.

Bob moved in another world, among people of a breed apart. They all had money, only it hadn't come from working but from inheritances and from family fortunes. They had no obligations and spent most of their time in idleness or in the pursuit of pleasure. Not that I envied them. I simply found them hard to understand.

At Round Hill the Toppings would throw parties for a hundred or even two hundred people. On weekends the house teemed with guests. There were twelve bedrooms; some of the couples who slept there were married, and some were not—it didn't seem to matter. Couples who were together in the evening would have changed partners by the next morning, when the ritual Bloody Marys were delivered to their rooms. A majordomo commanded a staff of butlers, all impeccably trained, I suppose, not to raise an eyebrow.

The life-style of Bob's circle didn't attract me at all; I had no desire to join in it. What I wanted desperately was that second child. Looking back on it now, I can see Bob and his friends were wasting their younger years, burning themselves out. At the time I was constantly amazed, but when I spoke of it to Bob, he merely said, 'Where have you been?'

'I guess I've been working too hard,' I answered.

At that time the brothers were dividing the valuable heirlooms their mother had left them. How they did it, I don't know. Maybe they flipped coins. From his share of the spoils Bob presented me with an exquisite pearl necklace and an antique emerald ring that deserved to be in a museum. He also gave me a diamond-encrusted watch that Mrs. Topping had worn around her neck on a long black satin cord. Once I put it on and found it stretched all the way down to my navel. I'd always had a weakness for shoes, but my feeling for beautiful jewelry amounted to a passion.

My mother, Cheryl, and Nana came for the holidays, and it was the first real Christmas I'd ever had. A tree fully thirty feet high reigned in the drawing room, and little Cheryl marveled at the decorations. For New Year's Eve there was a band for dancing, and champagne flowed. Round Hill actually *was* a hill, and people went skiing or sledding down the slope onto the ice-covered private lake.

That is all changed now, of course. Property taxes and upkeep grew too heavy for even the Toppings to manage. So the estate was sold.

One night that winter I went into premature labor, and Bob rushed me to Doctors Hospital in New York. It was the Rh factor again. How I longed for that baby! I was only six months pregnant, but I prayed desperately that the child would survive. With each contraction I closed my eyes and willed it life. But to my despair, after a full labor, I delivered a stillborn baby boy. Bob was heart-broken too. Grieving and despondent we returned to Round Hill, where I had to stay in bed for more than ten days. Burdened by our sorrow, we ate together in silence as the servants packed away the layette we'd set up in the next room.

A month passed, then six weeks, and Bob was growing restless. There was no reason to return to California since I was still suspended from the studio. Finally we decided to escape to the Caribbean, to the healing magic of sand and sun.

Each of the Topping brothers had his own boat moored in Miami. Bob's was a handsome custom-built model about fifty-eight feet long, outfitted with the latest in deep-sea fishing equipment. There was a luxurious master bedroom with an adjoining dressing room, which Arline Judge had redecorated with small pink baguette mirrors. A large mirror had been installed over one of the two beds in the bedroom. Bob wanted me to make love in it, but I said no. Some of his erotic inclinations were too sophisticated for me.

In the Caribbean we cruised and fished for long, lovely days, though nights were filled with parties and constant drinking. I quickly learned to handle the fishing gear and grew to love the sport. During a fishing tournament off the Florida Keys I hooked an immense tuna, which I fought for five backbreaking hours. I just knew I was going to win! It must have weighed 550 pounds! When I finally got it to the boat, the leader broke, and the fish flopped back into the water. I just burst into tears. I must have cried for an hour. My hands were scraped raw, even through my gloves. Every muscle and bone in my body had been strained beyond endurance. To be able almost to touch a fish you'd fought for five hours, then to watch it snap away . . .

121

But soon I hooked another fish. After an hour and a half of fighting I managed to get it aboard. It weighed 498 pounds, just 11 pounds under the first-prize fish. I had to settle for third place.

I didn't know it then, but that was the high point of my marriage to Bob Topping. The danger signs were clear, but I tried to close my eyes. The drinking, the parties, the dissipated life—yes, I'd begun to worry, but I hoped that things would smooth out when I got back to work.

My other nagging worry was Cheryl, and I feared that I couldn't be the mother she needed. Certainly I adored Cheryl, and yes, Bob was a loving stepfather. But the demands of my career and my marriage had been getting in the way. I was just beginning to realize how big a role my own mother had played in Cheryl's upbringing. I knew I couldn't be like the average American mother, and that recognition bothered me. I wanted to grow up with my daughter, to share secrets with her, to be close to her. As I worried about my marriage with Bob I also agonized about my life with Cheryl. Was I simply doomed to fail? Was I just a movie star? As I turned over those dark thoughts in my mind I could even remember well the first time I gave Cheryl a bath. She must have been close to a year old, past the age for being bathed in a Bathinette. Her Nana had shown me how to do it. It was a Sunday, Nana's day off. The house was empty, and it was the first time I had been absolutely alone with my baby. So I was surprised to read the romanticized account that appeared in *Photoplay* in December 1943, many months before I actually bathed Cheryl: 'I have navy blue eyes and black hair. I weigh ten pounds and thirteen ounces so far, and I was born on July 25 of this year. My name is Cheryl Christina Crane . . . What I wouldn't change is the life I lead. I lie all day long in the prettiest room you can imagine, which my mother designed herself. The walls are pale, pale blue with fleecy clouds painted on them—and pink cherubs pulling the clouds along, and riding them, and pushing them. My furniture is all pink and blue and white, too—and outside my room is a one-story white house on a hill overlooking the whole Pacific Ocean and the city of Los Angeles. A swarm of people live here—seven altogether. There's my grandmother, and Daddy and Mother, and two maids, and my nurse and me. Only I sometimes wonder what the nurse is for—because

122

Mother likes to do everything for me. She feeds and bathes me, very gently, and talking to me all the time . . .'

I had changed her diapers before and done other little tasks, but I had never given her a bath, and I was terrified. I must have communicated my anxiety to Cheryl, because the moment I put her in the tub, she turned into a little pixie. She defied me in every way a baby possibly could. If I reached for the soap she managed to grab it first, and then she'd throw it or try to hide it. Then she tried to climb out of the tub as I struggled to grip her squirming body. She tried to yank the facecloth away from me. She was playing games, while I was trying to be a serious mother.

'Cherry,' I said, '*stop* it.' And all at once we both began laughing—the first time I'd ever heard a baby give a real belly laugh. I finally managed to get everything away from her and to hold her under her arms at the same time—until suddenly I gasped, because my hands had slipped and I was clutching her by the throat! She had stopped laughing; her eyes were wide open. I dropped her on a side table and, though she was sopping wet, pulled her up close to me, saying, 'Cherry, Cherry, I didn't mean it.' Almost like a grown-up, she pulled away from me, then looked me straight in the face and laughed. I hugged her and the two of us ended up sitting on the floor in a tangle of towels. After powdering, diapering, and dressing her I sank into a chair exhausted, feeling as though I had been through a contest of some kind.

Later events raised harsh questions about Cheryl's upbringing. Once she was out of the hospital Cheryl had all the loving care that could be bestowed on her by me, by my doting mother, and by her capable Nana who, even though she was well into her seventies, still had enough energy to keep up with an active child. Nana handled her not only with great care but with great love, and Cheryl became attached to her. When Cheryl began to talk Nana told her charming stories and taught her little prayers. Cheryl showed high intelligence early and learned quickly. I adored her, but because I worked so often and late, she usually saw more of my mother and Nana than she did of me. Still, the times we had together were wonderful ones. I'm not a child psychologist. I did for Cheryl what my instincts told me was right, as any parent does.

Stephan visited Cheryl frequently after our breakup, but when he remarried he was free less often. During those crucial formative years I seized every relaxed moment I could to be with Cheryl. When she was two I took her for drives in the convertible with the top down, because she loved that—sitting in her baby's seat next to me, with the radio playing. She would beg and beg for the radio to be turned louder.

On one of our drives the music from the radio was suddenly interrupted. An announcer came on to say that the war had ended. I braked immediately and pulled over to the side of the road to listen for details. Cheryl said, 'Mu . . . mu . . .' wanting more music, but I said, 'No, Cherry, wait. The war is over.' Her eyes fastened on mine and, not knowing why I did so, I repeated for her slowly, 'The—war—is—over.' Again she just stared at me, and I thought how silly I was to say that to the child. I found some music for her and hurried home to share the wonderful news with my mother.

Around that time two men came to my door with credentials from the FBI. They wanted to know if I had received any threats to kidnap Cheryl. I listened with alarm as they told me they had learned of such a plot and that it seemed serious.

They installed plainclothesmen inside the house twenty-four hours a day, in shifts. The outdoor guards were dressed as gardeners, repairmen, deliverymen—anything that wouldn't excite suspicion. Finally the police caught the potential kidnapper, a cellmate of one of my mother's half-brothers. (Her father had married four times and had had several other children.) The half-brother had been jailed for some minor offense and had told a jailmate that he was my uncle. So the jailmate plotted to kidnap Cheryl. Yet another peril of the public attention paid me! You may be sure that from that day forward Cheryl was never left alone.

Very recently Cheryl asked me, 'Mother, was I ever kidnapped?' I wasn't aware that anyone had ever mentioned the incident to her. She must have heard it from my mother, who sometimes told Cheryl things I wished she hadn't. My mother had a strange love of fantasy and exaggeration. Once she told Cheryl that my father had been part of a vaudeville act, and when her own father took her to see the show, she had begged to meet him. No such thing ever happened, and I can only wonder how my mother imagined such a romantic meeting.

Of course I had the means to give Cheryl a very comfortable childhood. By her second birthday I was divorced from Stephan and living in the Bel-Air house, which had large enough grounds for a big party. I gathered together all the young children of parents I knew, many of them actors and actresses, and provided, besides a feast, riding ponies and monkeys who did little tricks. Each party after that had a different theme: a Hawaiian luau one year, a rodeo party the next. The other children looked forward to them as much as Cheryl did. Van Johnson's wife. Evie, brought her camera every year and photographed the events.

Cheryl's first school was St. Paul's, a parochial school in Westwood, where she stayed through the sixth grade. At the age of seven she was baptized Catholic, just as I had been and for much the same reason. Stephan objected, as my father had, but later in his life he converted and became a far more rigorous Catholic than Cheryl or I ever was.

She dressed very well, and why not? Yet during those first years she was never treated as a 'movie star's child.' Because I couldn't be with her all the time, I left the discipline to my mother and Nana. Soon the two of them began to compete over who was in charge of Cheryl. I settled that quickly. I told my mother that it was Nana who had the chief responsibility.

But Nana was growing older, and when she reached the age of eighty, she wanted to return to the British Isles. Because I was filming at the time, I left it to my mother and Nana herself to break the news to Cheryl as gently as possible. I was glad, at least, that Cheryl had started school. I hoped the new experience would lessen the great blow she was bound to feel.

But it didn't happen that way. Years later I learned that Cheryl had wandered into Nana's room, where some of Nana's friends had gathered to say good-bye. Cheryl saw the suitcases and began to guess what was happening. She fled to her own room in tears, and Nana followed her and comforted her. But Nana still didn't tell her that she would be going away the next morning.

The following day, still suspicious, Cheryl refused to go to school. I had already left for an early call at the studio. So my rather otherworldly mother, wanting to get Cheryl off to class, promised her that Nana would be waiting when she came home. At the end of the day my mother picked her up with her new governess, Irene Hulley. None of this did I know. It was only recently, when I began writing this book, that I found out the details.

When I came home that night I found Cheryl in tears, and my own mingled with hers as I tried to comfort her. Recently I learned that from then on she began to distrust me—and everyone, in fact, except my mother, whom she continued to cling to like a rock of security. None of her other governesses ever took the place of Nana.

125

There was something else that I took for granted—that Cheryl knew the kind of work I did. One day I happened to come home from shopping just as she got home from school. I put my things down in the foyer and was walking through a glassed-in room we called the lanai, when she came running up to me. 'What is it darling?' I asked.

She turned very quiet and looked out the window for a long, long time. Then she turned to me and said, "Hello, *Lana Turner*.'

'What?' I said.

Her seven-year-old face changed, as though she might have said something bad, and I thought she might burst into tears.

'What did you say, my dearest?' I asked again.

'I said, *Hello, Lana Turner*.'

'That's what I thought you said.'

'Is that wrong, Mommy?'

'No, it's not wrong,' I exclaimed, hugging her to my chest. I guessed what had happened. Some child at her school must have said, 'Your mother is Lana Turner,' and Cheryl then imagined me as being someone different when I was away from her.

So for the first time I tried to explain to her who Lana Turner was, and told her about the kind of work I did. That when you appeared on the screen people everywhere got to know who you were.

'Even so,' I reassured her, 'it means I am and always will be your mommy, and it doesn't matter what other people call me. Do you understand?'

She said she did. But from then on I feared that she thought my work made me different from other mothers. At least in the eyes of her schoolmates I was somehow strange because I was famous. Still one more curse of publicity. How I wish I could have spared her that.

10

M Y SUSPENSION finally ended when I agreed to return to work in a
film called *A Life of Her Own*, which was to be directed by George
Cukor. Having stood up to the studio for so many months, I was
starting to get a sense of my power to choose the films I would do.
And now the studio allowed me to participate in the casting process.
Dore Schary, who had replaced L. B. Mayer in a shakeup at MGM,
threw the names of some possible costars at me. I vetoed several
suggestions. Dore wanted to settle on Wendell Corey, but I felt he
wasn't right, either.

'Will you test with him?' Dore asked me.

'He doesn't look the part,' I insisted. 'I'm not testing with anyone.'

I had watched Corey in a few films, and I couldn't envision him as
the rich, suave married man who falls in love with the model I
would play. After we fought about it Dore used *his* power and hired
Corey. The starting date had been set but rewrites kept delaying
production. There hadn't been time to get the costumes right by
the time we began shooting. For the first scene my costume was a
red chiffon dress, but its seams were still unsewn. To speed things
up I offered to wear it anyway.

We basted it and pinned it, and then I went out for the master
shot. As I left the trailer I heard Corey say, as though talking to
someone nearby, 'It's interesting, you know. The wonderful
Barbara Stanwyck never keeps us waiting. Not even for one minute.'

When I whirled around I saw that he was alone. He was talking to
me, or rather, he had timed the remark for my benefit. The name
he chose to use made it all the more unpleasant, given Barbara's
misunderstanding about my relationship with Robert Taylor. I
didn't bother to answer him. Instead I went straight to the director,
who was seated next to the camera.

'Ready to go?' he asked.

'George,' I said, 'excuse me, but we're going to have one hell of a
long wait.'

'What's the matter, darling? The dress is fine for the master
shot.'

It wasn't the dress, I told him. There was going to have to be some recasting. When I walked past Corey to my trailer and closed the door behind me, I knew I was acting like a star for one of the very few times in my career. But I was shaking with anger when I picked up the phone and dialed Benny Thau.

'Benny,' I said, 'I'm stuck with this lousy picture, but if you want me to do it, you're going to have to recast.'

'Who do you mean?'

'I mean Corey, and you'd better get down here right away.'

Minutes later the MGM executives swarmed onto the set. I heard them talking to George as I sat fuming in the trailer. After a while I began to chuckle over the uproar I had created. I could be suspended, I might even be sued for the costs of production so far, but I didn't care. It might be absurd, but I'd stick to my guns no matter what.

Before long there was a knock at the door. It was Dore, the man who had annoyed me the most. 'Hello, sweetheart,' he said, reaching to take my hand.

'Get away from me,' I said, rather enjoying nursing my grudge.

'Tell me what's the problem. I'd like to hear it from you.'

'Dore, you're the problem. I told you from word one that I didn't want Corey. Then, behind my back, you went ahead and hired him anyway. Now I want him off the set.'

'He's already off the set,' Dore told me, soothingly. 'But where does that leave us? We haven't anyone else. You're leaving us in a very bad position.'

'You put yourself there. You can give me a call when you want me to report again. Either he goes or I go.'

I stayed home for two days, feeling very righteous. Production had been halted. Then Benny Thau called to ask, 'What do you think of Ray Milland?'

'He'd be great,' I said. 'You should have hired him in the first place.'

'This is going to cost us a bundle, Lana,' Benny told me. Understandably, the incident did not improve relations between me and Metro's new head of production. Wendell Corey didn't suffer at all, for he was paid $75,000 for his services without having to work. Ray Milland did very well, too. His agent, knowing the studio was under the gun, charged a fortune for him, $175,000. But if the studio paid through the nose, so did I. They got their revenge through the scripts I got stuck with next.

Holding Cheryl, age three –
only days after sharing
New Year's Eve with Tyrone Power
in Mexico. LEFT: Dancing
with the elusive Howard Hughes.
As you can see, he was
not fond of photographers.

TOP LEFT: 1946, with Frank Sinatra. A friend, never a lover.
BOTTOM LEFT: Striking out – but not for long – in *Cass Timberlane*. I married
Spencer Tracy in that one. BELOW: One of my many radio appearances in the 1940s,
this time as a guest star on the Edgar Bergen–Charlie McCarthy show.

Tyrone Power was my one
true love. RIGHT: As
Tyrone was about to
take off – alone – on
an international flying
trip. ABOVE: Our
last party together.
OPPOSITE: Playing the
villainous Lady de Winter
was a romp in *The
Three Musketeers*, 1948.

ABOVE LEFT: I married Bob Topping in 1948. ABOVE CENTER: Leaving the hospital after the 'accident', my attempted suicide. Fernando Lamas (ABOVE RIGHT) helped get me back on my feet, but then his Latin temperament – I mean temper – got in the way. LEFT: I was immortalized in cement outside Grauman's Chinese Theater in Hollywood on May 24, 1950.

TOP LEFT: With Ava Gardner on the set of *The Merry Widow.* My next film was
The Bad and the Beautiful (TOP RIGHT) with director Vincente Minnelli
and my longtime makeup man and close friend, Del Armstrong. A far less worthy effort was
The Prodigal, 1955 (BOTTOM), for which I redesigned the costumes. They had
wanted something sexy and they got it.

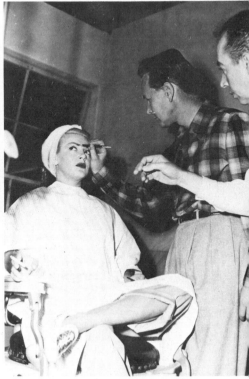

TOP: My fourth husband was Lex Barker, who had gone from Princeton and the Social Register to become Tarzan. BOTTOM: *Peyton Place,* with Diane Varsi, brought me an Oscar nomination as best actress.

OPPOSITE: Ronald Reagan and I chatting
at a Hollywood party in 1957.
In the spring of that year, the phone
calls and flowers from John Steele
(BELOW) started coming. By the time I
learned he was an underworld figure
named Johnny Stompanato, it was too late.

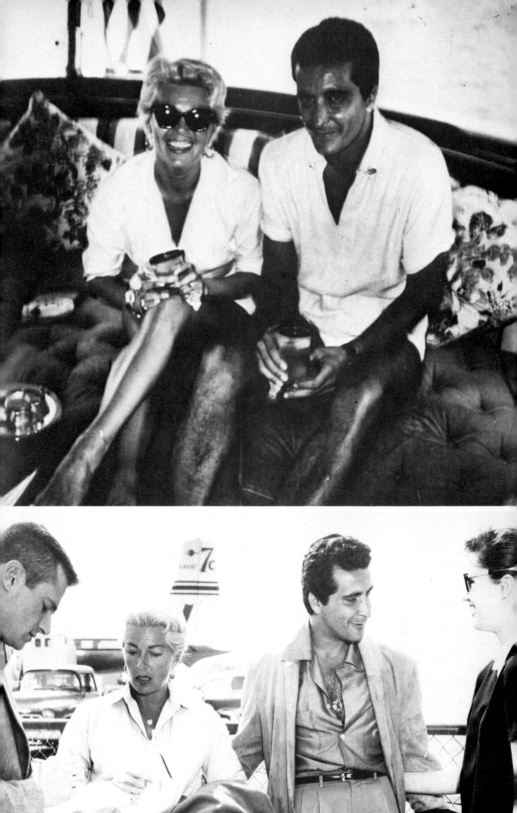

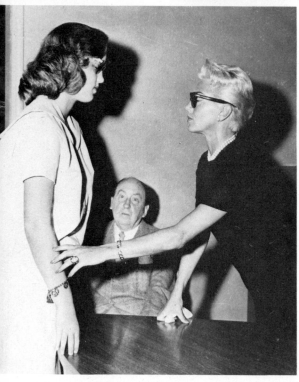

In Acapulco with John
in 1958 (OPPOSITE TOP).
John 'all smiles' with
Cheryl at the airport
(OPPOSITE BOTTOM). He
knew I was trying to
escape him. TOP LEFT: After
the 'happening '.
BOTTOM LEFT: With Cheryl
at her deposition;
attorney Jerry Geisler
is in the background.

1959, Cheryl and I (OPPOSITE) at *Imitation of Life* premiere.
That year Fred May (BOTTOM LEFT) became my fifth husband. TOP: In 1967
I went to the Far East with Bob Hope to entertain the troops;
Janis Paige and Jerry Colonna were part of our group. By then my marriage
to Fred had dissolved and I was married to Robert Eaton (BOTTOM RIGHT).

Madame X. I had to age twenty years during the film.

One was *Mr. Imperium*, costarring Ezio Pinza, who had just finished his run in the huge Broadway hit *South Pacific*. I thought the script was stupid. It was the story of a European prince who falls in love with an American nightclub singer. I fought against doing the picture, but I lost.

By then I was already three months into my second pregnancy with Bob. If I didn't make this movie, I'd be out of action for some time. A new doctor had prescribed a series of shots, one every week, that would help me keep the child. He warned me, though, 'Those shots are going to hurt like hell.' And they did. But I desperately wanted the baby, and I took them.

From the moment the picture started and I met Pinza, I knew I had another mismatch on my hands. After *South Pacific* I suppose he had good reason to admire himself, and the studio made much of his arrival. But that welcome soon wore off. The crew resented his lordly manner. Women ducked away from his florid attempts to charm them into his bed.

What bothered me most was his morning habit of eating cheese pastries and downing them with cups of espresso before taking his place on the set. It wasn't long before we dubbed him 'the man with the roquefort teeth.' I'm sorry if this disturbs any lingering worshipers, but the truth is that the odor of his breath was a trial. He did not clean his teeth after his morning food ritual and bits of cheese remained in the spaces between them. In my pregnant state I found it literally nauseating. Finally, I complained to our director, Don Hartman, but he was too timid to deal with the great Pinza— who, having failed to charm me, now turned his erotic attentions to my pretty stand-in, Alyce May. She quickly froze him out, and it was then the turn of Mary, who did my body makeup, a pretty young woman who had a husband and a small child. She was shy and rather retiring, and Pinza probably had no idea of her function on the set.

One day, just before we did a take, Don noticed that my neck needed more makeup. Instead of going to my trailer I sent Mary there to pick up her makeup kit. She was gone for so long that people began asking where she was. Del Armstrong, who did only my face makeup, volunteered to do my neck—but then we saw Mary coming out of the trailer in tears. A moment later Pinza sauntered out, adjusting his tie. Mary shoved her makeup kit at Del and then rushed off out of sight.

Very little stays secret among a close-knit crew, and later we learned what had happened. Pinza had followed Mary into my trailer, closed the door, and made a lunge for her while her back was turned. She had thrashed away from him but not before his hands had given her body a thorough going-over. That crude beast. From then on the crew made it clear to Pinza that they were keeping an eye on him, and he finished shooting in a fairly menacing atmosphere.

Some gossips have alleged that I would sometimes invite a good-looking stagehand into my trailer. If a lady is sexy on the screen, people presume she must be sexy offscreen as well. Although I've heard that some ladies now and then entertained a leading man after hours, I've never encountered anything like that on the set. Just think of all the people wandering around—dozens of crew members, the director, the assistant director, the script girl, the cast, the producer, the executives. How would it be possible? Where the scurrilous story about me came from I have no way of knowing. But I did get along well with crew members. I treated them nicely, and they were considerate of me.

Once I was back at the studio, Bob and I decided to settle in California. My mother, Cheryl, and Nana now occupied my house on Crown Drive. So Bob and I stayed in a suite at the Bel-Air Hotel, not far away, until we located a large, two-story Georgian-style house on Mapleton Drive in exclusive Holmby Hills. This new house was big enough for all of us; I was delighted to have a home again. The price was $97,000—a large amount then though hardly a twentieth of what it would cost today—and I was the one who made the down payment of $34,500. I had to borrow it from the William Morris Agency. Bob had invested in some outfit that manufactured fiberglass boats, so he was running through his capital at a pretty rapid rate.

As long as he had money Bob couldn't have been more generous. But his investments seldom panned out, and he often gambled and sometimes lost heavily. The monthly allowance from his trust fund wasn't large, and though he was certainly a millionaire on paper, there were times when his bills piled up.

The new house was on a three-and-a-half-acre corner lot, next to one that eventually became the home of Judy Garland and her husband, Sid Luft. Next to them lived Lauren Bacall and Humphrey Bogart. Since Bob and I had decided that this was going to be our home forever, at Christmastime we bought a live tree, roots and all, to plant after the holidays. Just before Christmas we were shopping for gifts in a jewelry store, and the jeweler brought out a beautiful diamond necklace. Bob had me try it on. 'So, that's what I'm getting for Christmas,' I thought eagerly. When I opened my package on Christmas morning I took a long time fussing with the paper and the ribbon, to make it seem like a surprise. And I was surprised. My gift was a small gold pin.

Cheryl had a little French poodle, a silver-colored miniature, whom she had named Tinkette. After Cheryl had oohed and aahed over her gifts, she began to call, 'Tinkette, Tinkette, come and get your presents.'

'I'll find her,' Bob said. He brought in Tinkette and dropped her at my feet. I saw that my mother and Cheryl were staring at me. As I reached down to pick up the little dog, glistening through her silvery fur I saw the diamond necklace. I screamed so loudly that I frightened the poor little creature. Oh, Bob, silly Bob. That was his way. If I wanted something he always gave it to me, but it was his idea of humor to make sure I suffered a little first.

Just as Bob had promised during our engagement, I had grown to love him. But now he was drinking very heavily. I know his financial reverses were part of the reason. Slowly I was coming to the realization that the husband I loved was an alcoholic.

I also realized that Bob couldn't guarantee me the security I'd expected. I would have to keep on working after all. The expensive life-style we maintained meant I'd have to protect my status as a star at a time when MGM, faced with the increasing threat of television, was already cutting back.

Luckily, I still had a high box-office standing. But large amounts of my salary were still being docked and sent to the IRS. Bob had borrowed against his inheritance and the estate had put him on an allowance of $1,000 a month. Well, hell, that man would go out and bet $2,000 on a golf putt! So what money he had he used for himself, and I was writing the checks for the gardener, the milkman, the telephone, the staff—you name it.

I remember one evening, when Bob was out playing cards, my mother stood watching as I went through a stack of checks my business manager had sent to be signed. I always made sure to look at every one of them, and that evening I kept mumbling, 'Oh, my God—what's this one?' Some of the bills were mine but most of them were Bob's. Halfway through the stack I put down the pen, lit a cigarette, and heaved a deep sigh. Quietly my mother said, 'Lana, may I speak honestly? Darling, you'll have to face it. You just can't afford to *keep* a millionaire.'

I broke out laughing, but I saw that her face was serious. 'You're right, Mother,' I said. 'I guess I'll have to do something about it.' Except that I didn't know what to do. I wanted my marriage to last. I was pregnant again, and I wanted the child I was carrying. I did not intend to face the hell of another separation and divorce.

When I confronted Bob about the expenses, his way of addressing the problem was to have a drink. When he was sober he was gentlemanly, with charm and a sense of fun. The first drink made him mellow. After the second he became a different man. Say the wrong word, even let your expression change, and he'd fly into a rage.

Once he suddenly picked up a crystal decanter and hurled it across the room, shattering it. Lamps went that way, too. He broke furniture. During one of our arguments I had happened to leave the bedroom door partly open, and little Tinkette wandered in. Bob, who not long before had fastened the diamond necklace around her neck, snatched her up and threw her clear out into the hall. Shocked by his sudden violence I hurried out to the hall to comfort the whimpering little dog. Luckily, she wasn't hurt. But what kind of man had I married, who took his anger out on an innocent animal?

Another time, after he had filled my glass with Scotch and caught me pouring it down the sink of the bar, he said in a cruel voice, 'Make another.'

'I've had enough,' I protested.

'I'll make it for you,' he snarled. 'And you'll sit right here and drink it with me.' When I objected, he added, 'You're putting me down. You're making me feel I drink too much.'

'Well,' I said, 'you do.'

It was the wrong thing to say. He picked up one bottle and hurtled it, and he went on throwing bottles until the mirror behind the bar was entirely smashed. The next day he couldn't believe what he had done. He promised he'd go on the wagon, that he'd see a doctor. But it did no good.

Throughout all this I kept on trying to maintain the image of a woman who had combined a satisfying marriage with a successful film career. Now I doubt that I ever really convinced anyone. A few of those close to me—my mother, my good friend Ben Cole—were aware of my bouts of depression. Then I lost our second child, again the victim of the Rh factor. Because Bob and I sometimes quarreled in public, the press began to take notice. So to maintain peace I began trying to keep up with him when he drank at home. But then came a new picture for me at the studio; my weight had to come down, which meant no drinking at all. When Bob no longer had me as a drinking companion his ugly moods grew more frequent. He would disappear from the house for long hours at a time. I heard rumors of wild stag parties and other women. Sick at heart, I hired a private investigator, who confirmed that the rumors of infidelity were true. The spoiled rich boy was out on the town again. When I confronted Bob with the evidence the ugliest scene we'd ever had ended with Bob's storming out of the house. I heard eventually that he had gone to Oregon on a fishing trip.

My anger wore off, and I was desolate. I wanted Bob back, to work it all out, somehow. But days passed with no word. Finally the announcement came from his lawyers in New York that Bob was planning to sue for a legal separation.

Again! Not again! The news slammed into me. Maybe I'd had deeper hurts before, deeper loves, deeper disappointments, but now I was overwhelmed by a sense of failure. Bob had loved me, I knew, but our marriage had dissolved in alcohol and I hadn't been able to stop it. I had been too blind at first, then too weak to keep Bob on the wagon. My love hadn't been enough . . . I was completely unlovable, I thought, I was a wholly unworthy human being . . .

As I recoiled from the news nothing seemed to matter anymore. My career was a hollow success, a tissue of fantasies on film. Cheryl loved my mother, and they were both comfortably endowed in my will. I had never before felt or believed I could be in such a dark hole mentally, physically, emotionally, and worst of all spiritually. All the good in my life—my mother, my child, my work, my friends—was blotted out by the dead feeling that nothing really mattered. I hadn't heard that suicide is a 'cry for help.' To me it meant putting a big *stop* to pain or anguish. There was none of that 'I'll show them. Boy, will they miss me when I'm gone' nonsense. I wasn't trying to hurt anyone. I was aware that everyone would go on and survive, but I knew that I definitely could not. I wanted *out*.

I planned everything. I had a bottle of sleeping pills. I sent Cheryl off to visit my mother one afternoon. Then, to compose myself, I sat down with a cigarette and a drink.

Suddenly the doorbell rang. My mother must have suspected

133

something because she asked Ben Cole to stop by. He chatted to me in the living room but I hardly heard his words. The talk became oppressive, an endless dull hum, unbearable. I escaped to the bathroom to shut it out and locked both doors.

When I caught sight of myself in the mirror I forgot Ben was in the living room. I grew entranced by my own image, thinking, 'This is the life that will be lost. It doesn't matter at all. There is nothing left to do.'—thinking calmly about myself like a different person, as if it were someone else's face that hung there in the mirror. In a trance I opened the cabinet and took out the bottle of pills. Methodically I downed them one by one. Then I thought I would take no chances of being revived. So I took out a razor blade. I didn't hesitate for an instant. With one sharp movement, I sliced across my wrist. There was no pain at all. I saw the blood spurt out and that was the last thing I knew.

I woke up in a darkened room at the hospital. Only one light was on, where somebody was working on my wrist. The pain was terrible.

I was vaguely aware sometime during the reviving process that they were interrupting, interfering with my big chance never to have to fight again, or know distrust, deceit, unfaithfulness—so many rotten feelings no one knew I had because I had kept them so deep within me. I heard myself yelling, 'It hurts. It hurts. Give me something.' And a voice (it was Dr. McDonald's) answering, 'Like hell I will. You've had enough.' He was sewing up my wrist. I had cut a tendon and the veins had retreated. He had to stretch them to join them together again. I listened as he scolded me, telling me how much I had to live for, how many people loved me. How my sufferings were terrible, yes, but other people suffered, too. I was lucky to have a beautiful daughter, I was blessed with talents and the means to support myself well. Slowly I began to feel ashamed. I cried quietly for what seemed like hours, and when I had exhausted my tears I felt a sense of hope, a stiffening of the spirit.

Always before in moments of crisis I called on that power we call God to help me through. This time, having lost faith in others and my faith in myself, I had lost my hope in God, too. Now that hope returned. I really believed that He hadn't wanted me to die.

Later I learned that Ben grew alarmed when I was upstairs so long, so he forced open the bathroom door. He found me lying in a pool of blood and made a hasty tourniquet out of a towel. Then he called my mother and Dr. McDonald, who lived only a few blocks away. The doctor arrived within minutes and raced me to the hospital in his own car.

To the reporters who saw us leaving hospital two days later—how do they manage to find out when someone is in trouble or in pain?—dear Ben smoothly explained that I had fainted in the shower and smashed the glass door with my arm. Dr. McDonald told them he had advised me to replace the door with a much stronger one. One of the reporters was still suspicious and asked me point-blank if I had attempted suicide. I told him that was utterly ridiculous, and that I planned to live to be the oldest woman in the country. Until now there have been only three people—Ben, my mother, and Dr. McDonald—who knew the truth.

For a long time I was busy with lawyers, both mine and Bob's. The newspapers reported that I was holding out for a large financial settlement. But I was fighting to keep the house because, after all, I had made most of the payments. What Bob wanted in turn were the heirloom jewels he had given me—the pearl necklace and the antique emerald ring. My business manager told me flat out, 'Look, Lana, you can buy your own pearls and jewels. Give them back.' And that, eventually, was the way we worked it out. He got the jewelry and I got the house, though I did keep the marquise diamond engagement ring I had fished out of my martini that day at '21' and all the other lovely presents he had given me.

11

VIEWERS OF The Merry Widow may have noticed that all during the picture I wore long gloves or a very wide bracelet, or I carried a fur piece on my wrist. Filming of the picture began only a few days after my suicide attempt, and my slashed wrist remained bandaged for most of the shooting. No one at MGM seemed to doubt that my injury was an accident. I was bouncing back quickly, partly because of my natural resiliency. But I also had help. His name was Fernando Lamas.

I hadn't liked the script at first and wasn't pleased to be cast in another costume picture. Why Schary kept assigning me to period films is still a mystery. And why an operetta? I could dance, but I was not a singer. So I had to mime the vocals, and later a 'real' singer's voice would be dubbed in. Some changes in the script had made my role more palatable, and the costumes created by the brilliant Helen Rose were gorgeous. But of all these improvements I was most satisfied with my new Argentine dancing partner.

Metro then had two 'Latin lover' types under contract. Ricardo Montalban was the one originally chosen to play Count Danilo. Later Metro reversed itself and gave the role to Lamas. I didn't care at the time. One Latin lover seemed as good as another. But from the moment we met on the set, Fernando and I were thrillingly in rapport.

He was separated from his Uruguayan wife, just as I was from Bob. There was nothing to hold us back—and nothing did. If ever I had needed someone new, it was at that moment. The publicity people at MGM appreciated the gossip we were generating, although we certainly tried to avoid it. We would escape—or think we had—to Palm Springs, only to be discovered by the press. Fan magazines speculated wildly over when we would be free to marry. But even though I was in love, as he was, I had no intention of marrying Fernando. He was handsome, he had charm, and, above all, he could be funny. After what I'd gone through I needed to laugh as well as to love. He could also be jealous. But since we were inseparable for most of a year, from late in 1951 until well into 1952, he had little chance to demonstrate that quality.

After *The Merry Widow* Metro scheduled the two of us for another picture, *Latin Lovers*. Toward the end of the summer of 1952 Marion Davies gave a huge party. Fernando and I were sitting with Ava Gardner and Esther Williams, watching the dancing, when a tall, handsome actor came over to our table. It was Lex Barker. I didn't really know him, but I'd heard that his marriage to Arlene Dahl was on the rocks. He asked me to dance, and I replied, 'I'd love to.'

From the cloud that darkened Fernando's face, I could see that I'd said the wrong thing. When Lex brought me back to the table and thanked me for the dance, I was stunned to hear Fernando saying something in a loud voice, something like, 'Why don't you take her out to the bushes and fuck her?'

Lex froze. Tears came into my eyes. Ava and Esther stared at Fernando in horror. Humiliated and embarrassed by the attention we were getting from the other tables, I said to him, 'Let's get out of here,' and hurried off to find my wrap.

In the car we were both silent. I felt numb, still hardly believing that he had used such words. For some time he had had a key to the house on Mapleton Drive. Now he used it to open the door. The minute we were inside, he began shouting, and the battle boiled over into a physical fight that I'd rather not describe. After I got him out of the house I was in such a condition that I dreaded being seen by anyone I knew. I drove immediately to Palm Springs, where I stayed for most of a week. But soon I was due to report for costume fittings for *Latin Lovers*, which was one long series of love scenes—with Fernando! Back at MGM the first thing I did was to see Benny Thau.

He took one look at my bruises and scratches and asked what had happened to me. I told him the truth, and he said, 'Oh, my God. The doctor must see this and write a full report.' Benny agreed that it would be impossible for me to do the picture with Fernando.

'And I hope you'll keep him away from me,' I told Benny.

'Yes,' he said, 'we'll take care of that.'

And he did. Fernando received the word that his part in *Latin Lovers* was cancelled, and almost immediately it was announced that the other Latin lover, Ricardo Montalban, would take the role. I found Ricardo a delightful costar. A rigorously devout

137

Catholic, utterly loyal to his wife, he played his role professionally but not privately.

Later I read somewhere that Fernando claimed he never found out why he was replaced. When the interviewer asked about our breakup, all Fernando would say was, 'I am an ordinary man, with ordinary defects, ordinary faults. I am human, thank God. I suffer. I love, and I can hate.' He concluded, 'About Lana I have nothing to say. Because there is nothing. It is over. You read a good book, a beautiful book. You come to the end. You close it. That's it. The *end*.'

In Hollywood we were like fish swimming around in an aquarium—always the same fish, but forming different combinations. When Lex Barker heard that I was no longer seeing Fernando, he called me and asked me out to dinner. Once Arlene Dahl was free of Lex Barker, Fernando called her and eventually he married her. After they divorced Fernando eventually married Esther Williams, the third of the women at the table when Lex had asked me to dance. And I eventually married Lex. All of which made for difficult seating at parties, quite aside from the gossip and the trouble at home.

One pair whose marriage generated both trouble and gossip was Frank Sinatra and Ava Gardner. Both were good friends of mine, and once I happened to stumble into some of their troubles when I went down to Palm Springs for a few quiet days.

It was so innocent. I bumped into Frank on the lot, and he said to me, 'What are you doing?'

'I'm going to Palm Springs. I'm looking to rent a house.'

'Why don't you take mine?' he offered.

I said, 'You mean you're not going to use it?'

'No. I'll be busy working.'

'Frank, that's wonderful! But let me pay you for it.'

Frank was always very generous, and he said, 'Come on, don't be silly.'

'But I want to stay a week.'

'That doesn't matter. The house is yours.' And he gave me the key.

Not sure that I wanted to be alone, I asked Ben Cole, who had saved my life, to come along. I had my cook prepare a big roasting pan full of fried chicken, spare ribs, and salads, and we brought along two bottles of liquor. We left Los Angeles early in the morning in order to enjoy the full day.

Frank had a three-bedroom house. I took the master bedroom, and Ben took one of the other bedrooms. Right away I hung up my clothes, put on a bathing suit, and went to get some sun. We were out sitting by the pool when the front door opened and in came Ava. I was all the more startled to see her because she and Frank were separated at the time. But she obviously still had her key. After we'd gaped at each other for a moment, I explained why we were there. Ben was a friend of Ava's, and she realized that his being with me had no special significance. Finally I apologized for the intrusion and said, 'Frank didn't mention you'd be around.'

'Oh, screw him,' said Ava. 'He doesn't know I'm here.'

'Do you want us to leave?' I asked.

'Oh, hell, no. There's room for all of us.'

We all settled down by the pool. When we began to feel hungry we trooped inside to Frank's beautiful kitchen and laid out the feast on the long countertop. Ava loves fried chicken. We hadn't yet started to eat when the back door burst open. There stood Frank.

And the first words out of his mouth were, 'I bet you two broads have really been cutting me up.' We couldn't say a word, and I just kept shaking my head no because we hadn't even discussed him! With that, he pointed at Ava and growled, 'You! Get in the bedroom. I want to talk to you.'

With a shrug, Ava headed for the bedroom I'd been using. Frank followed her, and before long, harsh words came from the bedroom, and a crash, as though a piece of furniture was being thrown.

'Ben,' I said nervously, 'let's get the hell out of here.'

He asked, 'But what about your clothes?' Of course they were in the bedroom where Frank and Ava were fighting.

'Forget them,' I said. I got my light summer coat from the closet in the entryway and my purse from the living room. After Ben had collected the bags from his bedroom, we left the house and got into my car and drove around for a while, considering what to do. I kept seeing Frank's red face and blazing eyes as he burst through the kitchen door, and I was worried about what he might do to Ava. Her car had been outside, and seeing it must have inflamed him— though why he had suddenly decided to come to Palm Springs I'll never know.

139

Ben and I stopped at a bar for a drink and wondered aloud whether there was a chance the storm had blown over. 'I wish I had that fried chicken now,' I joked.

Ben wanted to leave Palm Springs, but I had come down for a rest and didn't want to go back quite yet. So we found the home phone number of a realtor I'd heard of, and after a couple of calls he found us a house to rent for the week. All I had to wear were the clothes on my back. Ben persuaded me to go back for my things, hoping that life had quieted down at the Sinatras'.

It was dark when we arrived at Frank's place, and a strange sight greeted us. Police cars were drawn up in front of the house, with red lights blinking, radios squawking. The glare of spotlights illuminated the house. The sounds of battle inside, I learned later, had grown so loud that neighbors had called the police.

As Ben turned into the driveway, I wanted to get out of there right away. But Ben said no, he was worried about Ava. Just as we were getting out of the car, the front door opened and Frank and Ava came out, still fighting.

The police moved in to separate them. Ben managed to get close enough to Ava to let her know where we'd be—obviously she couldn't stay in the same house with Frank that night. We drove to the rented house, and after a while Ava's sister, who was also in town, brought her over. We did what we could to make Ava comfortable, and after a few drinks each of us went off to our separate bedrooms. Poor Ava. She was badly shaken, and after my own grim experience I could sympathize with her humiliation. But alone in my room, I was surprised that I also felt sorry for Frank. It was a bad time for him. His career had slipped badly, and he was losing Ava.

None of us ever referred to that evening again. It was as though it hadn't happened, except that a lot of sick rumors grew out of it. One particularly vile rumor had it that Ava had walked into the house and found Frank and me in bed together. Another one suggested that it was Frank who walked in to find Ava and me in bed. There was even a third version that Ava and I had gotten mad at Frank, picked up a strange man, and shared him between us—and Frank had walked in on that scene. The simple fact is that Ava, Ben, and I were about to eat chicken in the kitchen when Frank appeared at the door.

So much for Hollywood Babylon. Their marriage was a dreadful fiasco, and believe me, I did my best not to get involved in their domestic quarrels, whatever the consequences. I stayed fairly close to Ava in Hollywood, but after she moved to Europe I gradually lost touch with her.

After that horrible night at the Sinatras', followed by a restful week with Ben, I was eager to get back to work. The property I had my eye on was *The Bad and the Beautiful*. The top studio people didn't think much of its commercial prospects and had allotted it a skimpy budget. It was to be shot in black and white. As MGM's glamour star I wouldn't have had a chance at the dramatic role of Georgia Lorrison except that John Houseman and Vincente Minnelli, the film's producer and director, respectively, had asked for me. Word came down from on high that they could have me but for only four weeks of my contract time.

When the script reached me I knew right away that I understood the character—a film star who is seen at first as a soggy mess and then is resuscitated by an unscrupulous producer. I could believe in her. Moreover, the screenplay was a much better one than those I usually received. The atmosphere of the film was totally familiar to me. The sets were the very sound stages where I had spent so much of my working life. The conferences in executive offices, the nerve-racking sneak previews—all of them had a familiar ring. Even the Hollywood party scenes were true to life.

In the first scene, the most difficult except for one near the end, only my legs could be seen dangling through the railing of an upstairs balcony, down into a baronial living room. My speech had to show unmistakably that I was drunk. But it was not supposed to be funny or the mood would be lost. I had to convey what a wreck I'd become, and also my yearning for my father, who had been a famous actor. I've always been anxiety-ridden during the first day or two of filming, though once I'm into it I'm fine. But for this scene there were also bothersome technical problems with lighting and camera positions. I had to go through take after take until the director, Vincente Minnelli, was satisfied he had it right. It soon became clear that I would have to work longer than four weeks, but I hardly minded.

From then on everything went well. All of us felt we had in Minnelli a director who was in firm control. Each member of the cast—Kirk Douglas as the producer Jonathan Shields, Dick Powell, Gloria Grahame, Walter Pidgeon—performed to the utmost. Minnelli knew exactly what he wanted and he got it. The film gained nominations galore at Academy Awards time, and there was talk about why I had been overlooked. But that didn't surprise me or bother me. The studio had never regarded me as an *actress*, and they made no effort to 'sell' me to the Academy membership.

When production closed down, the scene I had thought most important to my role had not been shot. As Georgia, I took an emotional drive through a blinding rain after discovering that Jonathan, the man I loved, had betrayed me. Minnelli told me that the special effects for the scene were still being developed, so he would shoot it separately later on.

I had made reservations for a three-week vacation in Acapulco, and Minnelli told me to go ahead. When I returned I called the studio's production department, only to learn that the special effects still weren't ready. I couldn't imagine what was taking them so long. Were they planning to cut the car scene after all? I had worked hard to build my character and sustain her mood, but with so much time passing I'd be coming to the scene cold. After two more weeks I called Minnelli himself.

'Don't worry,' he said. 'The way we're setting it up you can do it in a day. We'll have everthing ready for you.'

Six more weeks were to pass, in fact, before the call came to report to the sound stage for the wrap-up of *The Bad and the Beautiful*. The script gave me almost no clue about how to play the scene. There was no dialogue. I was sure Minnelli would run the previous scene for me so I'd be able to pick up the mood again. But as it turned out, the rest of the film was in its final editing stages. Still I didn't fret. After makeup and hairdressing I got into costume and went to the sound stage. There the sight of what they'd been working on all those weeks sent me right through the floor. The chassis of a car, with its trunk and fenders missing, sat on gigantic springs on top of some planks. Standing around it was a group of men dressed in the heavy yellow slickers deep-sea fishermen wear. They had big buckets of water, huge sponges, and hoses with fine spray nozzles. Pipes hung from the rafters above the car.

'What the hell is that?' I said to Minnelli.

'Well,' he said, 'it starts to rain, you see.'

As I muttered anxiously he turned to an assistant director. 'Now that Miss Turner is here,' he said, 'let's show her how it's going to work.' He asked my stand-in, Alyce May, to get into the car while crew members alongside pushed the planks this way and that, making the chassis sway, or dipped sponges into the buckets and sprayed water on the windshield. I watched goggle-eyed, wondering how I was supposed to be able to act a scene in that contraption.

As they made the final adjustments I closed my eyes and tried to imagine Georgia's thoughts, getting into the car, turning the key in the ignition, driving off into the night. But every time I opened my eyes and saw the planks and springs and hoses, I lost my concentration. Finally I asked Minnelli, 'What do you want me to do?'

'Lana,' he said, 'I really don't know. You're a good enough actress for me to rely on you.'

'Vincente, you're going to send me out there on my own without discussing what you have in mind?'

'Yes, I want to do it that way. It's in your hands.'

I went to the set, climbed over the paraphernalia, and got into the chassis. I tried to re-create the shock of finding Jonathan with another woman, the scene I had filmed nearly three months earlier. I dug for it, dug deeper into my own feelings, into my own bitter experiences with love. God knows, I had enough by then to call upon. After a few minutes I decided I was ready and caught Vincente's eye.

The car moved and threw me from side to side. I concentrated on my hysteria, building with each movement of the car. *It's my big night, my premiere, and meanwhile he's with another woman . . .* Emotions welled up inside me and tears sprang to my eyes.

I don't like to cry but once I am in tears, the more I try to fight them, the more they come. They came gushing now and were echoed by the gush of water against the windshield.

'Cut!' Vincente called. He explained that they had to change lenses for a new set of camera angles. I told him I didn't think I could take any more.

'Yes, you can, darling,' he said.

Now they removed the door, and the camera came in closer. Water spattered the top of the car, and the men with the sponges kept splashing it onto the windshield. I had to concentrate on Georgia and not see them. I went through the scene again, and yet again. It took the whole day. After each time he said, 'Cut,' Vincente would come to me and take my hand and kiss it. Then another angle. The mike was pushed into the cab, and in my hysteria I sobbed and the mike picked up the sobs. The agony by then was genuine. Too much was coming back to me, too much of

143

my own life: the bitter marital disappointments, the babies I had fought to keep and had lost—and that crushing last meeting with Tyrone, the man I had loved most of all. When Vincente said, 'Cut. That's it,' for the last time, I was totally drained.

I had no idea that I had spent that difficult day making screen history. When the reviews came out my scene in the car was cited again and again. As one writer has described it: '. . . Turner emerges from the mansion, dazed, in white ermine, and drives away. Her sobs soon build to hysteria, and lights of cars send flashes across the windows as she reaches a moment of unbearable frenzy, releases the steering wheel entirely, and screams in emotional agony. Her foot presses the brake. One hears only her screams, the honking of passing auto horns, and, suddenly, it is raining. The car bumps along uncontrollably for a second, then comes to a standstill. Turner falls over the wheel, still sobbing uncontrollably as the sequence fades. It is superb theater, one of the great moments of human despair shown in cinematic terms, and a prime example of the coordination of actress, director, and cameraman which can create a perfect visual moment of dramatic poetry on the screen.'

But by the time the picture won its five Academy Awards, my personal life had become the center of my attention. You guessed it. I was swept up in another romance.

12

A T THE start it hadn't looked very promising. Lex Barker, who had inadvertently helped to cause my split with Fernando Lamas, called me to ask me to dinner. He picked me up at my house, we had a pleasant meal in a quiet restaurant—a dinner date like many other dinner dates.

When he brought me back to my house I asked him in for a nightcap. He said he would like a glass of brandy. As I remember, I poured some Remy Martin into two pony glasses. I took a sip from mine, then stared in surprise as he downed his drink in a single gulp. I politely offered him another and I filled it partway up, as you do with brandy. 'Cheers,' he said and he swallowed the second drink as quickly as the first. And then a third. And a fourth. And more.

I was wondering if I had another Bob Topping on my hands, except that Lex didn't *seem* drunk, and he'd had only one drink at dinner. But when he got off the barstool, one leg at a time, to stand up, he suddenly toppled over backward. It was as though somebody had yelled, 'Timber!' This big, good-looking hulk of a man just crashed to the floor. He lay there on my rug with his eyes closed.

I leaned over the top of the bar and called, not loudly, for I didn't want to wake Cheryl or the help in the house.

But he was out cold. I went around the bar and felt for his pulse. Thank God he was still alive.

Now my head began to whirl with visions of awful headlines: MOVIE TARZAN COLLAPSES IN HOME OF SEX GODDESS, FOUND LYING ON RUG IN BAR . . .

It was one in the morning, but I dialed the number of a strong friend named Bob. He said he'd dress right away and come over. It was a half-hour or more before he drove up in his car. He came in, looked at this huge, handsome man lying peacefully on the rug, and began to laugh.

'Shh,' I said. '*Do* something.'

He did what I had done—slapped Lex's face, called him by name, and felt his pulse. 'Good pulse,' he said.

145

'Then can we get him out of here?'

'Where?'

I remembered that during the evening Lex had told me where he lived, up a hill on a little street off Olympic Boulevard. He had described it as a kind of doll's house, small and pretty, with a flight of steps leading up to it. I said I thought we could find the house if we could get Lex into his own car. I didn't want it sitting in my driveway for everybody to see. Bob struggled to get Lex up off the floor and over his shoulder to carry him out to the car, where we propped him in the passenger seat. Then Bob got in beside him, while I got into my car to lead the way. Finally I saw a house that resembled his description, with at least fifty steps leading up to the front door. 'Oh no,' I said, laughing. 'Can you carry him up all those steps?'

'Guess I'll have to,' Bob shrugged. 'But how do we get him inside? We can't just leave him lying outside his door.'

'Look in his pockets,' I said.

Bob found the housekeys on a separate ring in Lex's pocket and handed them to me. I climbed the long flight of steps and tried the keys until I found one that fit the door. It opened. Finally! But relief turned to anxiety again: Would somebody on that quiet street look out a window and see Bob lugging a body up those fifty steps? Would the cops come, and with them the photographers? It didn't bear thinking about. Meanwhile Lex was getting heavier and heavier, Bob was moving more and more slowly, and the flight of steps kept expanding. Finally, Bob got Lex through the door and into the house. 'Where shall I put him?' he asked, like a furniture mover. And Lex was still as inanimate as a chest of drawers, and twice as bulky.

'Well, a bedroom,' I said.

To find a bedroom I had to climb yet another flight. Even so it was a very small house for such a large man. I guessed that Arlene Dahl had gotten a bigger one in the split-up. 'Up here,' I called to Bob.

He moaned when he saw more stairs but finally got him up to the top. We placed him faceup on the bed. 'Should I undress him?' Bob asked.

'No, let's get the hell *out* of here.'

We left the house, crept quietly down the steps to my car, and left Lex's parked at the curb. I drove the hero, Bob, back to my house, thanked him profusely, and after he left I went inside and

146

poured myself another brandy. By then, I *needed* it. I certainly hoped I'd never have another date like that one.

The next day a sheepish telephone call came from Lex. When I asked if he was all right, he said he wasn't quite sure. 'Listen,' he said, 'I hope I didn't misbehave or do anything out of the ordinary.'

'You don't remember?'

'No. No. I woke this morning and found myself still dressed. I don't even know how I got home.' When I told him the story, he laughed heartily. 'So that's what happened! I've been fighting off an infection, took some medication for it, and wasn't supposed to drink. You say I did?'

'One after the other,' I said.

'I don't know what got into me,' he said. 'How can I apologize? I don't suppose you'll want to see me again.'

I hesitated. I had pretty much made up my mind not to see him. But there was a reasonable explanation after all. 'I'll see you.' I said, 'but, *please*, let's not do that again!'

Flowers were delivered in the afternoon, and I began seeing Lex often. I discovered that this huge, handsome man had a fine mind and the kind of sense of humor that I appreciated. Our tastes in books and music seemed to match. He was in excellent physical shape, a fine golfer, and an expert swimmer. Soon he began occupying most of my free time. I fell in love again, slowly at first, but surely.

He was two years older than I was, and came from a Social Register family. In fact he was a direct descendant of Roger Williams, the founder of Providence, Rhode Island, and also of Sir William Henry Crichlow, the first governor-general of Barbados. Princeton-educated, a major in the Army during World War II, Lex had married for the first time shortly after the war began. He had two children by that wife. By the time I got to know him he had made six Tarzan films and had decided that was enough. Meanwhile he had received an attractive offer in Italy, which was fast developing its postwar film industry, and had decided to accept it. Then there were tax advantages in living abroad if you stayed for eighteen months or more. So I began to consider making the move, especially since Lex would be there.

In early 1953 Metro offered me a choice of two pictures the studio would be filming abroad. One was *Mogambo*, with Clark Gable as costar, and the other, *Flame and the Flesh*, would be shot in Italy. The *Mogambo* script didn't appeal to me, and I elected

147

Flame and the Flesh. A big mistake! Ava Gardner took the *Mogambo* role and played it beautifully but with a script very different from the one I read. There was another reason that I turned it down, too. My doctor had counseled me not to bury myself in darkest Africa because my blood type increased my risk of contracting some rare infection. Later, though, Clark told me that during the shooting they'd had all the comforts of home.

After *Flame and the Flesh*, I would move on to Holland to make *Betrayed*, with Gable and Victor Mature as costars. For both films the interiors would be shot in an English studio. This meant virtually a whole year's work for me in Europe. Lex would be working on two pictures in Rome, one of them a jungle epic called *Tiger of Malaya* and the other a costume spectacle, *The Temple of Kali*. In that one he wore a turban and balloonlike pantaloons. Well, at least he was breaking out of his Tarzan mold.

Paris would be my headquarters, I decided. I arrived there in April 1953 and found a lovely penthouse to rent in the elegant Sixteenth Arrondisement. I actually took two apartments and had a wall between them knocked out. The year's lease was frightfully expensive, and with the added cost of shipping over furniture, my business manager saw my supposed tax advantages going out the window. But I wanted my family with me, and as soon as Cheryl's spring term was over I had my mother bring her to Paris.

Location shots for *Flame and the Flesh* were done mainly in Naples and Positano. A week in chilly London for wardrobe tests gave me a cold that threatened to become pneumonia. From London to the blazing sun of Positano was a drastic and tiring change for me. I wasn't always in the best mood. Lex frequently joined me in Positano between his stints in Rome, and his strong, cheerful nature comforted me immensely. He was persistently talking marriage but I wouldn't give him a final answer. Three marriages were bad enough. But *four*? Besides, could this one work? Both of us had career problems at the time. And he had his two children, who stayed mostly with his first wife, and I had Cheryl to consider. There was a lot of room for mistakes. What would guarantee the success of this marriage? Luckily, I had some breathing space—his divorce from Arlene Dahl wasn't final yet.

MGM set the European premiere of *The Bad and the Beautiful* at the Cannes Film Festival and asked me and Kirk Douglas to attend. Lex escorted me, and we attracted a considerable amount of attention. Once more I was caught between my reluctance to marry again and the pressure of the moralists. I doubt that in today's moral climate I would have married Lex. We could have traveled together and lived together, and very few eyebrows would have been raised. But it wasn't that way then. In those days, when you fell in love, you married.

Lex had to return to Rome, and I went back to Paris and from there to London to shoot the interiors. Away from Lex for several weeks I found myself missing him badly. I hadn't realized how much I relied on him, on his strong support. So when he proposed again, I agreed to a wedding in Italy. There were a lot of premarital requirements there, posting banns and waiting for a specified period, but somehow Lex got them waived.

He rented a villa near Turin for all of us. And I do mean *all*. I had Cheryl and her governess with me, and Lex had his children, Lynne and Zan. We plotted carefully to keep the marriage a secret from the paparazzi, who kept their lenses trained on the villa. The civil ceremony would be held in the Turin town hall on September 8, 1953.

To fool the press Lex sent the children off to the movies with the governess. Surely if we were to be married we would have our children with us. Then, to further confuse the photographers, he would hide me in the car and drive through the gates of the villa, supposedly alone. He had me lie on the floor of the backseat, then spread a rug over me. But the paparazzi weren't all that easy to fool. They followed the car anyway.

I felt the car careening and the tires squealing beneath me. Lex had speeded up. He was a good driver but a little reckless. I was being tossed back and forth on the floor, and my pretty wedding outfit was becoming a mess. 'Must you drive so fast?' I called to him.

'Hang on!' he called back. 'I'm losing them.'

But he was wrong. It was like outrunning a swarm of bees only to find a much larger swarm in front of you. There were hundreds more paparazzi, it seemed, crowded in front of the town hall. Getting up the steps was like fighting your way upstream in a raging torrent. But somehow we got inside, and the doors were barred. We got through the ceremony in relative peace. But the moment we said our 'I do's' the door was thrown open and the photographers streamed in. Thank God it wasn't Artie Shaw I was marrying, or somebody might have been killed.

We spent our wedding night at the villa, but there was little time

149

for a honeymoon. We had to get the children ready for their trip back to Paris, where I was also soon due for wardrobe fittings for *Betrayed*. Lex and I managed to get away to Sorrento and Capri for a week, giving the staff strict instructions not to divulge our whereabouts. But there was a mixup about the date when I was supposed to report for my fittings, and our secrecy made for a lot of anxious cables and telephone calls.

Later I heard that the production people got so worried that they began considering Ava Gardner or Jennifer Jones to replace me. They were afraid that maybe I had decided not to come back at all, and Clark Gable had been waiting impatiently in London. After the fuss had died down and I was off to Balmain's for my wardrobe fittings, there was another problem. From all the publicity about it, you would have thought it was a major setback. My hair had been dyed dark for *Flame and the Flesh*, and now in *Betrayed* I played a schoolteacher in the Dutch Resistance, who was supposed to be blond. Finally, they decided to keep me dark-haired for *Betrayed*, and I rather liked the change.

Betrayed turned out to be Clark's last picture at MGM. He was in his early fifties and his girth showed his age a bit; the studio decided not to renew his contract. He spent his last days at the studio where he had reigned as King dubbing some scenes of *Betrayed*. And when he left, I'm told, there was no one to say good-bye except the guard at the gate. Many of us were shocked at that. What a disgraceful lack of appreciation for his years of service! But there would be no ceremonial farewells for any of us as, one by one, we left MGM's famous star stable. The heads of the studio were intent on reducing the overhead their stars' contracts represented. MGM was on the decline and we all knew it.

It was a time when the moralists were demanding wholesome, American movies, but audiences were rejecting the 'escapist' glamour vehicles of the past in favor of more realistic, even depressing films. And then there was the competition of television. The studios were losing money, and it seemed impossible to fight back.

But still MGM held on to me, mainly because my box-office standing remained high. I had begun to explore the idea of going free-lance, as so many of my colleagues had, but there was a hitch. My business managers, intent on fulfilling my tax debt to the government, had put me in debt to the studio. Now MGM held the advantage when contract negotiations came up.

My picture after *Betrayed, The Prodigal*, would be shot at the California studio, so I gave up the Paris apartment and returned to the States. Lex followed when he finished his work in Rome. Once he got back we had another wedding, in case anyone challenged the legality of our Italian one, and we decided to live in the house on Mapleton Drive.

Now it was back to work. Lex accepted a contract offer from Universal, and I started fittings for *The Prodigal*. Dore Schary told the press he hoped to make the picture one of 'the really significant spectacles of all time.' But when I read the script I wondered what Schary had been drinking. I was to play a creature called Samarra, the high priestess of Astarte, goddess of the flesh, who was the very temptress who incited the prodigal son of the Bible to leave his home. It was strong stuff! The prodigal son they named Micah and, to play him, chose Edmund Purdom, a young man with a remarkably high opinion of himself. His pomposity was hard enough to bear; worse yet was the garlic breath he brought back from lunch. My lines were so stupid I hated to go to work in the morning.

Even the costumes were atrocious. They were ornate concoctions dripping with heavy beads, and the material was so stiff that I felt I was wearing armor. 'Well,' I thought, 'I may be trapped in this picture, but I'm going to make myself as sensuous, sexy, and gorgeous as possible.'

If Dore Schary was going to mold me into his idea of a sex object, I was going to give him a sex object. I wanted to show flesh. Afraid of losing her job, the wardrobe mistress refused to tamper with the costumes. 'Then give me those scissors,' I said, and I proceeded to cut huge pieces out of the costumes.

Executives came running. 'Lana,' they protested, 'you can't do that to the costumes.'

'Am I in this picture?'

They agreed that certainly I was.

'Then,' I said, 'what you see is what you get.'

Actually I was quite pleased with my alterations, daring though they were for those days. I revealed more than the Production Code allowed, and they had to airbrush my publicity stills before their release.

Lex's first wife was planning to marry again, and she asked him to take the two children off her hands for a year. To make room for

151

the expanded family I added a two-room wing to the house on Mapleton Drive. Lex and I were happy there, living peacefully, but less so with the children around. Although Cheryl liked Lynne and Zan, they were precocious children who had been brought up leniently. They didn't accept discipline well and, when criticized, never hesitated to answer back. I had a hard time handling them while I was working. One of Cheryl's governesses couldn't stand their uppity ways. One day, without notice, she simply threw up her hands and declared, 'I've had enough!' Eventually Lynne and Zan turned out fine, as so many children do after going through a difficult period. I suppose it wasn't easy for them either, being shifted around as they were.

Once I finished *The Prodigal*, the studio immediately loaned me to Warner Brothers for *The Sea Chase*, with John Wayne. And I mean immediately—I finished my work at six one evening and at six the next morning I was on a plane along with Del Armstrong and Moss Mabry, the costume designer. Moss had time to make only one costume for me, a champagne-colored dress. The studio had told me that Warner's was holding up production until I arrived. But I suspect the real reason for the haste was that MGM wanted to make as much money off me as they could, by loaning me out as often as possible, before my contract expired.

We flew first to San Francisco, then to Honolulu, and from there to Kona, where the cast and crew were quartered. I was exhausted by the time our entourage pulled up to the Kona Inn. I had wanted Del to stay in a nearby room so he could do my makeup for early calls, but he was lodged at the opposite end of the long building. My room was small and furnished with twin studio couches, which would be made up as beds at night.

As I waited for my bags to be brought in, I noticed a sliding door. When I opened it my room became a two-room suite. Puzzled, I asked the production manager why Del was so far away and who would be sleeping in the other half of the suite.

'John Farrow has the room next to you,' he told me. Farrow was the director, a man I knew only by reputation. And he had a reputation as a womanizer.

'And where's Mr. Wayne?'

'Oh, he's taken a house on the end of the island. He's sharing it with his fiancée, Pilar.'

'Couldn't I have been granted a house?'

'That's not the way it's been set up.'

The setup, I realized, was that Warner's was paying MGM more than $300,000 for my services, and they were probably cutting a few corners. Or was it that Farrow had something extracurricular in mind? One has such thoughts when one is far away and rather out of touch with familiar territory.

I asked Del to come into my room. I showed him the sliding door and explained that Farrow would sleep on the other side.

'I won't have him next to me,' I protested. Del offered to talk to the production manager to see what could be done. He reported that the production manager was reluctant to talk to Farrow about it. So Del warned him that I might well get on the next plane to the mainland if something wasn't done. Del knew me well and he hadn't exaggerated.

I was sitting amid my luggage when the production manager came to see me. Farrow was off hunting locations somewhere and couldn't be found. 'You haven't unpacked,' the production manager noted gloomily.

'No.'

'How can I explain this to John?'

'There's no explanation.'

He chuckled and said he understood. He went off to search for Farrow while Del and I wandered down to the beach. About an hour later the production manager found us. Farrow, he said, had not take my attitude lightly. He couldn't understand what in the world was in my mind. He hadn't dreamed, etc., etc., he had just thought it would be a good idea to be close so that we could discuss the script.

'By the way, where *is* the script?' I inquired.

'Oh, they didn't tell you? It's still being written.'

'Then what was all this hurry about my finishing at Metro and getting here?'

At that he looked surprised. There had been no reason to rush. John Farrow and Wayne were working on the script along with two writers. That didn't bode too well. The production looked troubled already.

There was no wardrobe other than the dress Moss had made for me, so I used my own clothes. When I finally did read the script ten days later I found that the supposed Nazi spy I played was sailing back to Germany, bringing all her worldly goods along with her. Among her possessions was a jewel case. Now, when I wore jewels in a picture, I wanted them to be genuine. So I used my own, the ones I'd brought along.

Most of the story took place on a German freighter, called the *Ergenstrasse* in the film. It was actually a steel-hulled tramp steamer anchored in the harbor, forty-five minutes away by speedboat. We had to wake up at the break of dawn to take advantage of the light. Around two every afternoon clouds would roll over, and we'd all be drenched in rain. And when the sun shone we couldn't touch anything—all that hot steel. They set up fans to cool the metal but they didn't help much.

John Wayne had come before production started. He had gone snorkeling and had developed an ear infection. The ear festered and swelled up, and the pain was so severe he had to take codeine for it. The medicine didn't help his memory for his lines. Often his eyes were glazed from the pain and the codeine. His ear was so swollen that for a number of days they could shoot only one side of his face. Between takes he'd go to his bunk and lie down, suffering quietly. I'd go to him and try to help by putting icepacks on his forehead and ear.

Meanwhile Farrow, perhaps understandably, was rather abrupt with me. We had no script discussions. In fact he gave me almost no direction at all. God forbid I should miss a cue! Then he would snarl, 'You know your lines, don't you?' I resolved not to fight with him. It would only have made things worse. And he was not very pleasant with the other actors, either. Certainly he did not make my list of favorite directors.

Farrow was an Anglophile though he was born in Australia. It so happened that Captain Cook was buried on an island near Kona. Each year a British ship would visit that island and fire off a salute in his honor. Tradition! When Farrow heard that the ship had arrived, it roused his pride in his British citizenship. He contacted the captain, who invited Wayne, Farrow, and me aboard for lunch. I tried to beg off but Wayne told me, 'Honey, these are command orders.'

The tender took us out to the destroyer, where they piped us aboard as though we were visiting admirals. Then we reviewed the officers smartly lined up in their dress whites. When they asked us to go below to meet the sailors we could hardly refuse. So we made our way down to the three lower decks. On each deck the sailors greeted us, and they insisted on toasting us from their rations of rum. Of course we had to return the compliment.

154

Well, by the third deck I was reeling—all that rum on an empty stomach. Somehow I got through lunch and back into the tender to return to the *Ergenstrasse*. I was so woozy my speech was slurred. 'I'm loaded!' I said. 'How can I work?'

'Ah, the hell with it,' Wayne said, and the afternoon's filming was called off. Farrow had paid his full respects to the Commonwealth.

Riding in the speedboat to Kona, I found myself singing at the top of my lungs. Everyone joined in my hilarity. I'd never been so drunk—and never felt so good in my life.

'It's a wonderful world,' I shouted into the spray, 'and I love everybody, all of you, the whole lot of you!'

But when we got back to the hotel the headache started. I got desperately sick to my stomach, and all night long I paid and paid for paying my respects to Captain Cook and the British.

When my ten weeks on the picture were over Lex and I headed off for a month's vacation to Acapulco, which had become my favorite resting place. I loved that town, but it was very different then. No high-rise hotels—it was hardly more than a sleepy fishing village. High cliffs framed the gorgeous white beaches, so wonderful for swimming and fishing, under the dark blue sky. I usually stayed at the Villa Vera, a secluded and unusual place run by Teddy Stauffer, a former band leader and a former husband of Hedy Lamarr, among others. Lex and I liked Acapulco so much that we talked about buying property and building a house there. Eventually I did take an option on a beautiful piece of land with a fantastic view of the bay and paid for it with Bob Topping's engagement ring. Who knows? Maybe that fabulous diamond has shown up since in someone else's martini.

During that trip Lex bought a German Shepherd puppy, which he named Pulco. I didn't really want a dog in the house, but at eight weeks old Pulco was small and cute. Then he grew to all of 175 pounds. He guarded us fiercely and was forever lunging at the postman, the telephone repairman, and the delivery boy. Lex kept threatening to get another dog so he could call him Aca, but desisted when Pulco bit the postman's leg and he sued. To keep Pulco under control we confined him to a dogrun surrounded with chain-link fencing or to the carport, which was enclosed by iron gates and a high stone wall.

Sid Luft and Judy Garland and her little daughter Liza (Minnelli) lived on the other side of the wall. One day Liza, who was younger

155

than Cheryl, climbed over the top. She was halfway down to our driveway when Pulco got her. He seized her right leg in his jaws and yanked her right off the wall. Liza's screams filled the air, and I rushed outside to rescue her. The child was shaking and sobbing, terrified. Cradling her in my arms, I carried her home, where her governess was already at the door.

'Oh,' she exclaimed, 'don't let Mrs. Luft know. She's not well.'

But Judy had gotten out of bed and come downstairs. When she saw the blood on Liza's leg, she went stark white. I kept apologizing, practically crying myself, screaming, 'For God's sake, call a doctor.' Poor Liza got twenty-one stitches in her leg, and her face was badly scraped from hitting the cement. The messy situation got worse when Sid Luft came home. He wanted to sue me, but Judy well knew that Liza had been sternly warned about the wall and the dog.

As for Lex, he was so attached to Pulco that he refused to give him up, and in all fairness, he did have good reasons for wanting Pulco at the house. I'd been receiving some strange threatening letters, some of them worrisome enough to report to the police. And there had been that kidnap threat against Cheryl some years back. I no longer went out publicly as much as I had before, and when I did it would be to someone's home. Seclusion became important to me and Lex, and Acapulco appealed to us more and more. When we weren't working we'd often fly down and stay for a month at a time.

Later, when we parted, Lex took Pulco with him. That was a part of the divorce settlement I was delighted to grant him.

13

THE MOTION-picture industry was changing rapidly, trying to adjust to the new age of television. But MGM was adapting poorly, relying on supposedly proven formulas for success. They kept producing musicals when musicals were falling from fashion with audiences. Noting the success of a rival studio's CinemaScope production, *The Robe*, they tried spectacles. *The Prodigal* was one such misguided effort. Only with a marvelous production of *Ben-Hur* did the studio exhibit some of its former glory, but by then Dore Schary was gone, with a handsome settlement. One new president after another took his place.

My last few years at Metro were like working amid the ruins. Familiar faces disappeared. The wardrobe and the prop departments began to thin out, and publicity people I'd known for so long were dismissed. In the past when you walked down a studio street there would always be waves and greetings. You stopped to gossip, to catch up on what your colleagues were doing. But now those streets were deserted. It was all doom and gloom.

I was deeply saddened by losing my comrades—so many skilled and talented people I'd worked with over the years. They had treated me like a princess. Now strangers filled their places, and I had to adjust to a different and less comforting environment. I no longer had support from the top, the kind of protection I'd enjoyed under Mayer, Thau, and Mannix. I had little reason to feel loyal to the studio that had bred me. I didn't owe the new, distant executive branch a thing. My contract would expire after two more films, and I wanted out.

Another costume picture, *Diane*, was the last film I made for MGM. I owed them still one more but for that one they loaned me to Fox. When I finished *Diane* I remember leaving the studio literally without looking back. How strange it was to see those empty streets! They had been my second home—perhaps my most stable home—for seventeen years. I remembered how it had thrilled me at first when I saw those famous faces, in the golden era of MGM, and how awesome it was to find myself among them. For a

157

minute I thought of visiting my old sound stages for one last nostalgic glimpse. But I resisted the impulse. It was empty sentiment. Now the glory was gone.

There was a new day dawning in the industry. Not that movies as I knew them would disappear from the screen. But for me it was time to shift direction. The studios could no longer guide stars' careers. Now I'd have to become independent. I'd left William Morris long before, after some new contract disputes, and had signed on with Paul Kohner. He had new plans, big plans, in mind for me. My new work would be very different.

'Finished?' someone asked as I walked to my car on that last day at Metro. I couldn't speak. I could only signal *Cut!* by drawing a finger quickly across my throat.

My loan-out was for *The Rains of Ranchipur*, a remake of *The Rains Came*. Before filming began Lex and I returned to Acapulco. I nearly didn't come back. One day while we were out swimming, a huge wave just seemed to sweep me up. I was sucked underwater, spinning around and around. Short of air, I thrashed wildly, trying to break the riptide's hold. Then suddenly a powerful grip seized my ankle, and I was yanked up out of the water by a great force.

I managed to crawl out of the water and flopped down on the sand, trying to get my breath back. 'What happened to me?' I asked Lex, who was now beside me.

'While you were swimming,' he said, 'I dived under for a bit and when I came up you weren't there. I never swam so fast in my life.'

Then back at Villa Vera, when I was getting out of the shower, my foot slipped out from under me. I fell backward, cracked my head on the inside of the tub, and passed out. I suffered a concussion that caused me headaches and dizziness for most of the next year.

I warned Frank Ross, the producer, that the headaches might affect my work on *The Rains of Ranchipur*. He insisted that he would work it out so I could stay in the picture. That August of 1955, when shooting started, Los Angeles had one of its most severe hot spells. Fighting the headaches and dizziness I persisted through the hot weather, and everyone—the director, Jean Negulesco, and the whole crew—encouraged me and accommodated me and nursed me through shooting.

Everyone, that is, except Richard Burton.

One of the hardest chores for me as an actress is to have to simulate real feeling in love scenes when there is no chemistry between me and the leading man. Burton and I were supposed to be madly in love. He played a dedicated Indian doctor. I was the selfish wife of a titled man who had married me for my money. I would fall in love with the doctor, and he with me. Well, the plot was a little more complicated than that, but anyway, we were really supposed to swoon over each other.

Burton, who had come from *The Robe*, the first CinemaScope production, had a bloated self-image. The rest of us joked about his ego, and someone even advised wardrobe to make him bigger turbans. He strongly resisted Jean Negulesco's efforts to help him deliver a good performance.

'You're supposed to be an Indian,' Negulesco would tell him.

'I'm *not* an Indian,' Burton would reply loftily.

Yet he spent a good deal of time in his dressing room entertaining our dusky little extras, for whom he seemed to have developed a great fondness. For someone who didn't want to play an Indian, he did seem to enjoy playing *with* them.

I became pregnant again the following year. I took the same rigorous precautions I had in the past, hoping to carry the child to full term, but after seven months the child, a girl, was stillborn. My severe disappointment deepened the physical and mental pain. This time I had been more hopeful, for I had been told that Lex's blood type would lessen the risk of a miscarriage.

The loss of a third child depressed me, and new indications that Lex was unfaithful made me feel even worse. One day a 'friend' phoned to report that Lex was having a fling with one of the ladies in his low-budget film at Universal. Such 'friends,' I suppose, you can do without. But it did seem to me that Lex had been getting home later and later in the evenings, and I had tried to ignore what that might mean.

The marriage was already rocky. We were bickering a lot. Often we quarreled about the fact that my income was much larger than his, so I was again paying most of the bills. I think my star status threatened his ego. Universal wasn't giving him important pictures to do, and he felt his career was going nowhere. He kept talking about leaving Hollywood and going back to Italy, where he thought he'd find better opportunities.

I didn't see how our marriage could work with Lex in Rome and me in Hollywood. I had signed with Universal and was already committed to my first film, *The Lady Takes a Flyer*. We were fighting about that, but what is it really that breaks up a marriage? There are those accusing discussions: *You're cold to me lately. Why? Are you frigid?* And in return: *No, you're the one who's cold. I'm here, and you're home late . . . And when we went to that party I saw you flirting with . . .* In return: *I wasn't flirting. I was only being polite.* And so on and so on.

Finally I faced Lex with what I'd been told. He denied it, of course, but his defences seemed weak, and I saw my marriage tottering and about to fall. There came a point when I asked him to leave, early in 1957. He wanted a reconciliation, but by then I'd heard about more infidelities. I could not accept that kind of betrayal or his dishonesty about it. I remained firm and made arrangements for a divorce.

Painful as divorce always is, this one had some comic, even silly aspects. Lex insisted on taking a new Ford station wagon I'd bought mostly for driving around Cheryl and her friends. I didn't see why Lex needed the car, since he was already planning to go to Europe to appear in more Italian epics. So I refused to give it up. He persisted, saying, 'Then we should sell it and split the money for it.'

Why on earth did that station wagon mean so much to him? I decided to take the station wagon to a body shop and have it sawed in half. I'd give the driver's side to Lex. When I mentioned my almost-serious plan to Jess Morgan, my business manager, he laughed at first but prevented me from carrying it out.

Another irritation was the disappearance of a diamond ring Lex had given me. I loved that ring, beautifully set with round and baguette diamonds. When I called Lex to ask him if he'd taken it, his denial didn't convince me. Once he left for Europe, Lex's sister telephoned Jess Morgan to confess that Lex had given her the ring and that she felt guilty about it. I had stayed on good terms with Lex's family, and his mother had done her best to reconcile us. Anyway, the ring was returned to Jess and then to me.

Such stupid things! But once love evaporates, people become smaller and meaner. What a feeling of emptiness they gave me, those petty wars. Worse yet was thinking of the years I'd wasted. But I was grateful that I'd continued to work. I had my career if nothing else. Cheryl was now an adolescent. I was in my mid-thirties. When and how would I ever find the normal marriage I'd wanted? Why was I always attracted to the wrong man? Why did I always end up the patsy?

160

So there I was, alone once more, rattling around in a fifteen-room house with all the bills to meet for its upkeep. That house with its memories of two failed marriages depressed me. I had gone through two pregnancies there and had miscarried both times. It wasn't a lucky house. So I told Jess Morgan to put it on the market while I looked around for an apartment. By now Cheryl was attending the Academy of the Sacred Heart, a fine boarding school at Flint Ridge, despite her wish to live at home and attend Beverly Hills High School. She thought the students at the public school would be more sophisticated.

About two months after Lex moved out, I arranged for Cheryl to join me for a weekend in Palm Springs. We stayed with my friend Virginia Field, whose daughter Maggie also attended Sacred Heart. When it was time to return on Sunday, a young actor friend, Michael Dante, offered to drive the girls back to school. Virginia suggested that he drop them off at Union Station instead, where they could get a cab to Flint Ridge.

I rode with them as far as Union Station and put them in a taxi, then Michael circled back to take me home. The Sunday traffic had swelled by then so it took us fully an hour to reach the house. By that time the police were there too.

A call had come over the police radio. Cheryl was missing! Maggie had gotten back to school in a panic and told the mother superior that Cheryl had stopped the cab a block or so away from the station. She said to Maggie that she was never coming back, and then simply got out and walked away. The cab had dropped her off in one of the sleazier sections of Los Angeles. When the mother superior called but didn't find me home she had telephoned the police and then Stephan. It wasn't long before he arrived at the house, too.

We were both frantic with worry. Where had Cheryl gone? Who would find her? And there was the agony of self-examination. What had happened over the weekend? She hadn't seemed unhappy. Did I do anything? Did I say something wrong? What could have made her run off like that on her own?

Minutes of anguish. They seemed to stretch into weeks until the police finally called. Cheryl was safe at the station-house downtown. Stephan and I rushed down, and when I saw Cheryl both of us burst into tears. Stephan and I held her in our arms, all three of us rocking gently as the story slowly came out.

Cheryl had walked around for a while and gotten lonely. Men

161

kept eyeing her suggestively, and she began to grow frightened. So she approached a young man who looked kindly and asked him to help her find a cheap hotel. She told him that she hated school, that her parents were splitting up, and that she wanted to live on her own. At thirteen! Fortunately the young man called the police.

The incident was my first real sign that my marital problems were hurting Cheryl. How I had tried to hide them and protect her! But what I had thought were the normal trials of adolescence were responses to our unstable homelife. I hoped and prayed that I could set things right for her.

She desperately wanted to leave her Catholic school and go to Beverly Hills High. Stephan and I discussed it and agreed to concede if that would make her life somewhat easier. We persuaded her to finish out the term and then she could switch schools in the fall.

Maybe that would have made the difference. But none of us could know what was coming. Soon we would be swept into a whirlpool so strong that we would all be beyond rescue. It would leave us spinning for the next decades of our lives.

14

THE NIGHTMARE began innocently enough, with a series of telephone calls. In April 1957 I was filming *The Lady Takes a Flyer* at Universal, when a Mr. John Steele called me. I didn't take the call myself, and I had no idea who he was, so of course I refused to talk to him. As a matter of fact, after he'd phoned several more times, I left word that I wouldn't accept his calls. But even though they were headed off at the switchboard, the calls kept coming.

One day Mr. Steele phoned the studio while Del Armstrong was doing my makeup. By now I was fed up, and I asked Del to call him back and find out just exactly who he was and what was on his mind.

'All he wants,' Del told me after he'd talked to him, 'is to send you some flowers. I told him there wouldn't be anything wrong with that.'

The next day flowers arrived. And arrived and arrived, and kept arriving. There were so many of them that they wouldn't fit into my dressing room. And what magnificent flowers. A vast variety of them, as luxuriant as they were profuse. There was a card, of course, with just the name *John Steele* and a telephone number. No other message. Now I was intrigued, and certainly I was flattered. After Lex's behavior this floral compliment was gratifying and ego-boosting.

A few days later I phoned the number on the card. The voice that answered was pleasantly masculine. After hellos I said, 'The flowers are overwhelming. But do I know you, Mr. Steele? Have we met?'

No, he admitted that we'd never met, adding that he'd admired me for a long time. 'I know your good friend Ava Gardner,' he said.

Ava had been living in England for some years, and we had all but lost touch. But I still cared about her, and if this man had been her friend, that would certainly be a recommendation. Still, I was not really interested in taking up with strangers, so when he asked me to have dinner with him, I told him truthfully that I almost never went out when I was working.

163

'But on weekends?' her persisted.

'Weekends I spend with my family, my mother and my daughter.'

He offered lunch, or even just a drink, but I continued to refuse, adding that I had his telephone number; I might phone him again if I found myself with free time.

But John Steele did not give up easily. More flowers came the following day, followed by record albums of exactly the kind of sweet, melodious music I liked. How did he know what kind of music to send me? It seemed that he had managed somehow to reach the young woman in charge of playing my music on the sets. He knew how to get things done. He had mysterious ways of obtaining information and access, as I was to learn to my bitter cost.

And more flowers, followed by more, followed by phone calls I didn't accept. At last I telephoned him to inform him that he'd made his point.

Once more he pressed me to have lunch or dinner with him, or to meet him for a drink. My curiosity was piqued by now.

'I'll tell you what. I'll be working late here, but if you'd like to stop by for a drink after I get home, I might be able to see you for a little while. But call first.' And I gave him my home number.

And that's how the blackest period of my life began, a period that I've tried to block out of my mind for almost twenty-five years. It started with flowers and an innocent invitation for a drink, and it was to end in screaming headlines, in tragedy and death. It would make me and my precious Cheryl notorious, the butt of sick jokes, vile rumors, and malicious speculations. Hundreds of thousands of loaded words would be written about what I can still think of only as 'the happening.' Gossip writers had a field day with our tragedy, but nobody ever knew or told the true story—because I could never bring myself to tell it all, until now. Even now, as I look back reluctantly, as I attempt to analyze the events that are burned into my memory, I shake my head, defeated. *What* happened I can never forget, but *why* it happened I'll never really understand. I was weak, I'll admit it. Weak, lonely, persuadable. But I never meant anybody any harm—God is my witness to the truth of that.

I believed the lies a man told me, and by the time I learned they were lies it was too late. I was trapped, helpless because of my fear for my own life, for Cheryl's and my mother's.

But I'm running ahead of my story. I suppose I want to get it over with, finish with the nightmare forever. Maybe now that I'm dealing with it head-on, talking about it frankly, with nothing held back, it will finally go away.

It was an evening in mid-May. In those days I drove a big grey Cadillac I called the Baby Whale. After I pulled it into my usual spot outside the apartment house and went to get my script from the backseat, I happened to glance across the street, where a street-light shone onto a parked car. It was a black Lincoln Continental, with a man sitting inside. As I walked toward the building I saw him get out and begin walking in my direction. That seemed a bit strange, and I shivered as I hurried to the elavator and pressed the button.

My Mexican maid, Arminda, told me no one had called. But as I headed for my bedroom, there was a knock on the door. Arminda answered, and a moment later she came to tell me it was Mr. Steele.

'But he was supposed to telephone,' I said, and asked her what he looked like.

'A nice-looking man.'

'Well, show him into the living room,' I said.

The man I found there was tall, husky, and dark-haired, and he appeared to be around my own age. I strongly expressed my annoyance that he hadn't phoned beforehand, and I asked if he drove a black Lincoln Continental. He looked a little flustered and admitted that he did. 'I didn't mean to start off on the wrong foot,' he said apologetically.

'Well, you really have.'

'Would you like me to leave?' he asked, so abject that I began to feel a little sorry for him. 'Oh, well, you're here now,' I said. 'Just don't do it again.' And I offered him a drink. He didn't stay long because Arminda was making signs that my dinner was ready. Mostly we talked about Ava. He said they had dated but that there had never been a romance. When he asked if he might see me again, I said it was possible, but only if he called in advance.

More flowers arrived at the studio, and when he phoned, I suggested a light lunch at my apartment. I didn't want to be seen in public with a man I didn't know or to see my name in the columns linked with a stranger. He said he didn't want to trouble me and offered to bring lunch. He showed up with vermicelli in white clam sauce, prepared by a restaurant called Mario's. A favorite dish of mine! How had he known? His cunning in finding things out about me should have made me cautious. Instead I'm afraid I was foolish enough to be flattered.

Before he arrived that day a little package was delivered. It contained a bracelet fashioned of little gold leaves inset with diamonds, which held a fine gold watch with my initials engraved on the back. Over lunch I told John Steele I couldn't accept it. He said that he couldn't return it because it had been engraved, so he insisted that I take it.

By now I was thoroughly curious about what John Steele did for a living. But he had his own way of dealing with my questions—not so much by ducking them as by leaving me with an assumption that he was involved in producing records. But whatever his profession was, he clearly knew how to court a woman. He had the kind of dark good looks that had always attracted me, and his attentiveness soothed the hurt of those last grim months with Lex. The gifts continued—a brooch, another bracelet, and then a ring, all in the same leaf design. When I asked him, 'Do you happen to have a money tree?' he replied, 'No, just the leaves.'

I became cautious about mentioning anything I liked for fear that he would give it to me. After that first breach of courtesy he was utterly considerate, and I began to warm toward him physically. His wooing was gentle, persistent, and finally persuasive. By the time I found out his real name we were already having an affair.

He had commissioned a full-length portrait of me by an artist I had never met. It portrayed an astonishing likeness of me reclining under a filmy cloth. I found it embarrassing, but John was so pleased with it that it wound up on a wall of my apartment.

After John met Cheryl he told me that he had bought himself a horse and wondered whether Cheryl would like to ride it. I asked if the horse was well broken.

'Oh yes,' he said. 'She has an excellent bloodline. Her name is Rowena.'

I could only gasp. Rowena was the horse I'd learned to ride sidesaddle while I was making *Diane* at Metro. When I asked John how he had obtained her he only shrugged and smiled. To this day I don't know where he got the horse or how he knew her name. There are many more questions for which I still have no answers. What was the motive behind the gifts and the courtship? Was he ever truly in love with me, or was it all some mad campaign of a warped and calculating ego? Perhaps my own fascination with him was eventually fed by just that kind of uncertainty. But at the beginning I had no sense of danger. Not yet.

While I was working at the studio John began picking up Cheryl after school and taking her to the riding academy, where he would wait for her while she took Rowena along the trails for an hour or so. Then he would drive her back to my mother's apartment. Cheryl apparently liked John well enough, but she had really fallen in love with the horse. And one day she told me John had said she could have Rowena for her very own. I didn't want John to *give* Rowena to Cheryl, so I offered to buy her from him. But there was no way he would sell me the horse. Now Cheryl was caught in the middle. I finally agreed to let Cheryl accept Rowena as a gift from John.

I had hoped to spend the summer with Cheryl, but before my work at Universal was completed, Jerry Wald at Fox phoned me. He planned a production of the huge best-seller *Peyton Place* for Fox and offered me the role of Constance. To play the mother of an eighteen-year-old girl was a radical departure for me, but the script was too tempting to turn down. During the filming of *Peyton Place* I wore the jewelry John Steele had given me—it still chills me to see his gifts if I happen to catch the film on television.

One day a friend of mine—I won't tell you his name—came to see me, with something on his mind. He just blurted it out, 'Lana, you can tell me to go to hell, but for your own good there is something you should know. It's about your friend.'

I bristled. 'Well, what is it?' I demanded

'You're seeing a man whose real name is Johnny Stompanato.'

'But that's impossible! He wouldn't lie to me. We care for each other.'

'Lana, I assure you his name is Johnny Stompanato. He has a record. And not only that, he is associated with Mickey Cohen. You've heard of *him*?'

Yes, I was familiar with Mickey Cohen's name—at least to the extent of associating it with the mob, gambling, and violence. But the more my friend talked about the man I knew as John Steele, the more things began to make sense.

'Those flowers he's been sending you,' he said. 'Do you know where they come from?'

I mentioned the name of the shop.

167

'That shop,' my friend told me, 'is owned by Mickey Cohen. I doubt very much that your friend Johnny had to pay for the flowers.'

Del Armstrong was once again with me on the set of *Peyton Place*. In utter turmoil, I took him aside and confided what my friend had told me.

'My God, Lana, Stompanato! I've heard that name.' Del had watched what was going on, but had said nothing.

'I can break it off,' I told Del.

But even as I said it I felt a shiver of fear.

As a lover, the John Steele I knew was considerate and gentle. He didn't speak like anyone associated with a mobster. He had told me that he had been married and had a son. Although he looked younger, he said he was thirty-nine. I was growing to love him, and I couldn't believe he would just lie about his name. Maybe there was a plausible explanation.

'I've always told the truth,' John said the next time we were together.

'Then why are you using the name John Steele?'

'It is my name,' he said. 'I've been using it for years.'

When I said that I had learned that his real name was John Stompanato, a dark red color came into his dark cheeks. I held my breath, still hoping—for what I don't know. Then I said, 'John, just give me the truth. Why did you lie to me?'

'All right,' he said. 'I'll be honest with you. I felt that if I used my name you might have read something about me in the papers and made the connection with Mickey Cohen. So my name is Johnny Stompanato. So what?'

'So I think we'd better cool this whole thing. I think we'd better not see each other anymore.'

'Lana darling,' he said, 'just try and get away from me!' And he laughed in my face.

The sound of his laugh chilled me and, in bad moments, I can hear it now. Yet I didn't see him for what he was—but then who can say exactly what he was? I knew a few things about him but most of the story came out later.

Now I know he was born on October 19, 1925, in Woodstock Illinois, the son of a barbershop owner. His mother died soon after his birth. When his father remarried John was sent to Kemper

168

Military Academy in Bonneville, Missouri. He graduated from Kemper in 1943, and here the records vary. One report has him attending Notre Dame University for a year. Another (and probably more valid) has him enlisting in the Marine Corps immediately after graduation. His service took him to China, and he got his discharge there in 1946. In Tientsin he opened a nightclub, met a Turkish girl by the name of Sarah Utish, and when the nightclub failed he took her back with him to Woodstock, with a baby son, John III. There they separated. His wife and child remained in Illinois, while John went to southern California. Some reports have him arriving there in 1947; others fix the date as late as 1949.

According to police records, he was quoted as saying he met Mickey Cohen just before his discharge from the service. 'I got to know him because I went into his store to buy some clothes.' Cohen at the time was described by *Time* as a 'runty gambler,' tied up with mob interests. He hired Stompanato as a bodyguard. But John also had interests of his own. He worked as an auto salesman; at one time ran a pet shop; another time, a furniture store. He had married an actress by the name of Helen Gilbert who divorced him three months later. Then he married another actress, Helene Stanley, and they stayed married for three years.

In 1949, known to be associated with several Los Angeles gangsters, he was arrested on a vagrancy charge. He was found guilty, appealed the conviction, and the charges were dismissed.

In 1951 Lee Mortimer and Jack Lait, two yellow journalists, wrote in their book, *USA Confidential*: 'One of the minor tough boys is handsome Johnny Stompanato, who was general stooge for Mickey Cohen, introducer of gals for visiting mobsters, and dancing escort to the stars and would-be's.' In 1952 he was arrested on suspicion of armed robbery, but the charge didn't stick. At the time I met him his only visible means of support was a gift shop he ran in Westwood.

I began going out with others, making a point of being seen in the company of other men. But John's calls never stopped coming. After a while I would simply hang up but he'd call back immediately, and I'd let the phone go on ringing. I had a strange premonition that he might somehow manage to get into my apartment at night. So I locked not only the front door but also the door of my bedroom. And amazingly my fear came true.

One night I forgot to lock my bedroom door. That night John climbed a fire escape and managed to get into the apartment through the locked back door. I awoke to the sound of my bedroom door being opened. By the glow of a small nightlight I saw a shadow coming toward me. With a jump he was on the bed, shoving a pillow over my face. At just the moment when I was beginning to black out, he took away the pillow. Holding my arms pinned to my sides, he straddled me and held my legs tight with his feet. I shrieked at him while he tried to kiss me, using every foul word I could think of. I ended up with, 'Get the hell out of here, or I'm calling the police.'

But almost the last thing I would consider was calling the police, and John knew it. He knew I was paranoid about what people used to say or write about me. After this night-time appearance, he kept after me. I wasn't strong enough to resist. And there was another reason I didn't get help, though for a while I couldn't even admit it to myself: His consuming passion was strangely exciting. Call it forbidden fruit or whatever, but this attraction was very deep—maybe something sick within me—and my dangerous captivation went far beyond lovemaking. In fact the sex was nothing special. People have analyzed my attraction to John by pointing out that my father was an occasional gambler and that he was murdered—the connection seems obvious enough, but I can't say for sure that it's valid. Most of what I felt at this time was fear. I felt trapped, and John took pains to remind me that he had the power to harm me and my family. His threats were vague in the beginning—that rather than let me go, he would see me dead first.

Then an escape hatch seemed to open. It would soon be time to head off to Europe for several months of filming *Another Time, Another Place*. The title of the movie seemed to provide an answer. In England, I thought, I could finally break with him. As his threats continued I considered notifying the police—but once again I couldn't face the prospect of screaming headlines. Better to make a truce between us when I was an ocean away. During the three weeks before I left I saw him several times. He was gentle, more like the person I'd known at first. He said I must not judge him by his past—he was a changed man, even his threats meant nothing. I would see—the old Johnny Stompanato was long gone. I began to believe him.

But when I told him good-bye and left for England, in my own mind it was good-bye for good. Another time, another place.

170

He was there to see me off, along with my mother and Cheryl. Until the last moment John had pleaded to come with me, but I absolutely refused. Not only was I starring in the movie but I would also be coproducer. I insisted that my responsibilities would leave no time for him. 'But I'll write,' I said, thinking that a long, gentle separation might be the safest way to handle it. Deep down I feared some act of violence if I was too abrupt.

As always, I wanted Del Armstrong to come with me, but because of the British union rules he couldn't go as my makeup man. So I turned him into my assistant producer for Lanturn Productions. I took a suite at the Dorchester Hotel in London and Del found himself an apartment. But the long ride from London was taxing, so I moved to a rented house in Hampstead Heath, not far from the Elstree studios. The house bordered on a golf course, and on Sundays I played a round or two to relax.

I had never liked England. The damp, bitter climate depressed me and I could never seem to shake the malaise. In Cornwall, where we shot on location, the food and lodgings were grim. There was no central heating and all the coal fires on earth could never make me feel warm.

Then there were problems with the script. I quickly realized that the picture was a poor vehicle for me. The actors were inexperienced—as I remember, it was one of Sean Connery's first films, and he often missed his marks or forgot his key lights, to the annoyance of the director. Because I was coproducer I had to work to smooth things out to ensure that the schedule went ahead as planned.

I had Del, of course, but there was no one else around who I could consider a friend. I was lonely and felt sorry for myself and missed the liveliness of Los Angeles, the company of my mother, Cheryl, and my friends.

John called regularly from California. I suppose I shouldn't have talked to him, but he seemed the only one who could understand my problems. He was interested and sympathetic. He kept telling me how terribly he missed me, and in my loneliness, I began to feel that I missed him, too. He wrote me long, loving letters, begging me to write in return. And I did, with appreciation and caring. Those letters would live to haunt me.

And it doesn't seem reasonable even to me as I recount it now, but I got myself right back into trouble. The cold, the loneliness, the problems on the set, my weakness and vulnerability—they all

171

contributed, and before I thought through my problems I called my travel agent in Los Angeles and charged a one-way ticket to my account. Then I asked John to come.

He travelled under the name of John Steele. How he got a passport under that name I can't imagine, but then he had peculiar talents. Still, considering the nosiness of the British press, using the alias was probably a good idea. I had my chauffeur pick him up at the airport and drive him straight out to Hampstead. The truth was that I didn't want to be seen with him in London. That much sense I did have.

Our reunion was a joyful one and for a while John showed only his loving, docile side. The arrangement seemed pleasant enough for a while. John pursued his stated interests in becoming a producer by trying to acquire a book to develop into a screenplay. He hoped to act in the film himself. Eventually the negotiations fell through. With nothing to occupy him John grew bored with Hampstead, although I let him use my chauffeur to drive into town for shopping or lunch or whatever, so he wouldn't feel so isolated. But he still complained constantly and began to resent my long hours on the set.

There wasn't much I could do to entertain John, as my schedule might as well have been engraved in stone. The chauffeur would pick up Del in town very early in the morning and bring him to my house, where he would make me up and put on the artificial hair-laced eyebrows that I never learned to handle myself. When he'd finished we'd head for the studio, leaving John alone until my return late in the evening.

One unusual feature of English studios is the pubs that are available right on the lot or just outside it. Those working on a film dropped by the pub at lunchtime and usually at the end of the day before going home. Frequently I would join them for a drink after work. But if I got home a little later than John expected me, it would spark his jealousy, and we'd argue bitterly about it.

John also insisted that I bring him to the studio and this repeated demand provoked impossible quarrels, since only the director and Del, the people I could trust, knew of John's presence at my house. I was afraid the others would talk, and we believed the publicity would hurt the picture. John almost seemed to crave that publicity, to want to be seen as my lover. But despite his constant attempts to coerce me, I stood firm.

One Friday after an especially trying week on the set I came

172

home and went straight to bed. I was fighting a bad cold and I needed some rest so I could work the following Monday. We had the full weekend off. John came up to my bedroom to nag me about his boredom and my reluctance to be seen with him in public. He began slinging preposterous accusations about why I wouldn't allow him on the set. Finally, provoked beyond toleration, I screamed at him, 'Get the hell out of this room. I want you to pack your bags and go home!'

He left the room and I lay there on my bed, sick at heart and in body, watching television distractedly, knowing that John was off fuming in another part of the house. Suddenly he kicked open the door. 'I've had it with your orders,' he shouted. 'You get this straight—I'm not leaving here and you can't force me out.'

'The hell I can't,' I snapped. 'I'm calling the police!'

I reached for the phone, but he knocked it away and lunged for my throat. As his grip closed around my larynx, I managed to let out a loud scream, though I could feel the strain on my vocal cords. I didn't know I had that much lung power.

My maid, Annie, in her room upstairs, heard me scream and came running. I didn't know she had the strength, but she grabbed John by the shoulders and spun him away from me. His face purple with rage, John started toward me again, but Annie stepped between us, protecting me with her body. 'Don't come near me,' she warned in a deadly voice. 'I'm not afraid of you. Miss Turner is, but I'm not. So help me God, you come any closer and I'll kill you.'

At that, John turned and slammed out of the room. Annie and I tried to comfort each other, both of us trembling convulsively. 'Don't leave me,' I pleaded, unable to speak above a whisper. 'No, no, I won't,' she promised, and she stayed in my room all night.

On Monday I had Annie call the studio to explain that I had a terrible case of laryngitis. The doctor came out right away, and he told me my cold had become influenza. To treat my laryngitis, he placed metal prongs on either side of my throat and used some sort of ultrasonic device to release the pressure on the vocal cords. Only Del knew that I was suffering from something worse than laryngitis. The crew had to shut down production, and I was guilt-ridden over the costly delay. I literally could not speak, but I could never let anyone know why.

After a few days John cooled down and came by to see if I was better. All I could do was point to the door to show him I wanted

173

him out. If he ignored that signal I would wave him back to keep him from coming near me.

Standing a few feet away from the bed, he kept repeating that he refused to leave. 'I'm not kidding around,' he warned me. 'I can take care of your mother, and Cheryl, too. Don't think I won't do it. I can have it done; no one will ever know where it came from.'

Finally I was well enough to return to the set, but it was still another week, almost three weeks in all, before I was able to speak in my normal voice. I did as much as I could, mostly walking shots and scenes without dialogue. Even so, valuable time was lost.

Del and I began to consider how to get John out of England. First he talked to John to try to convince him to leave on his own, to face the fact that we were through. Then Del suggested that I could have him deported.

'That wouldn't be possible, would it?' I asked.

'I've already checked—I went to Scotland Yard.'

'You did! You told them about me?'

'I didn't mention any names,' Del said. 'But they would have to have cause to do it. Not only is it possible, Lana, it's the only way.'

I had cause enough, but I also didn't want anyone to know about it. Still, Del had a point. It was the right move. So I called Scotland Yard myself, explained the situation, and requested John's deportation, as Del stood beside me. I made the call during lunch break at the studio, and something really bizarre happened. I put Del on the phone to arrange the details, and while he was talking, the studio operator took a call from John and put him on hold, but left the key open. So John *heard* the conversation with Scotland Yard and learned exactly what we were planning!

Less than an hour later he came racing to the studio by taxi to tell me he knew my plans and to make more threats. It was his first and only time on the set. Fortunately he couldn't carry out his threats in public. When Del and I appeared at the house with two detectives, we found John seated on a couch in a little sitting room next to my bedroom, calmly reading a newspaper. The detectives watched him pack, making sure he took only his own possessions. Then they escorted him out of the house and, I heard later, right up to the steps of the plane that would take him back to the United States.

Relieved that he was gone, I still worried about those threats he had made against Cheryl and my mother. I didn't entirely believe them—not at that point. It was Cheryl I feared for most because I knew she trusted him, so I asked my mother to send her over to

174

spend the holidays with me. Meanwhile, there was more location work at Elstree and then the postproduction looping, the process of synchronizing the actor's voice with the image seen on little loops of the film projected on a screen.

If I thought I was finished with John, I soon learned otherwise. The minute he landed in California he phoned me. I had instructed the studio operator not to take his calls, so he left long messages and followed them with cables. John seemed so obsessed that I was afraid his dark, violent streak might reappear. I wrote him two more letters, as gentle and regretful as I could make them, emphasizing that our relationship was over. During our conciliatory periods in England he had given me a little black poodle called Gypsy; in one of those letters I drew a little pawprint, so that Gypsy could say good-bye, too. I wanted to placate him, but I soon realized that the letters were too sentimental and probably encouraged him to persist.

15

IN MY last letter to John I told him that the picture was finished and that I was going to Acapulco for a long vacation, but I never mentioned my itinerary. I didn't even tell the studio where I was going because I was afraid they'd leak it to the press. All I wanted was to get into the sunshine where I could rest my weary body and soul. At home I had no pending obligations so I planned a three-month stay.

At that time the most direct way from London to Acapulco was via Copenhagen. I landed in Denmark late on a bleak January day. As usual, I waited quietly in the plane until the other passengers left. I always like to be the last one off, to avoid the crush.

As I sat there waiting, a young man in a trench coat came on board and handed me a single yellow rose. I looked up, surprised.

'Who is this from?'

'A gentleman,' he answered and then said, 'Would you please step this way?'

So I followed him to the exit, and he stepped aside to let me go first.

It was pitch black outside and raining, and I had to grope my way down the steps. I clutched my purse and jewel case and the rose in one hand, and fumbled for the handrail with the other. I could barely see the stairs. Then out of the darkness a hand reached out to me.

I took it and descended a couple of steps, and then I saw the face. It was John's white face, looming out of the darkness. He was smiling that now-I've-got-you smile of his, a real smirk.

Well, I just froze. I wanted to turn around and get back on the plane but I couldn't move off that step. John gripped my hand firmly and led me down those steps one at a time, and all the while his smirk got bigger and bigger. When we reached the tarmac he took the jewel case from my hand without a word. There was no breath in my lungs; I became a robot. It's not that everything went

176

blank—no, I remember it all quite well—it's just that I was unable to speak one word.

He guided me to the terminal building and there, in the waiting room, sat a half dozen reporters around a large oval table; photographers began snapping pictures, and someone handed me flowers—I was so bewildered I couldn't think. There wasn't even a studio representative there. John must have set it up! But how? And why?

To this day I can't tell you exactly how John Stompanato knew when I was leaving England or that I was flying to Mexico via Copenhagen. He proved over and over that he had the power to do anything he wanted; but never so forcibly as that rainy evening when he caught me totally by surprise.

I knew I had to keep my composure in front of the press. I was trapped. I sat down at one of the table mikes, accepted a cup of coffee, and began to answer the questions mechanically. Meanwhile my mind raced ahead. John was sitting at a smaller table nearby; he never took his eyes off me. I felt them burning into my body.

Finally the 'conference' was over, and the reporters and photographers stood up to go. John came over and helped me into my coat, then took my arm and led me out to a waiting limousine.

We hadn't spoken a single word to each other, not a syllable from the moment he'd held out his hand. But as the limousine pulled away from the airport, I finally burst out, 'What the *hell* are you doing here?'

'I wanted to surprise you.' That smirk again.

'Well, you certainly did!' I conceded.

'We've been apart too long, and I'm going to Acapulco with you.'

'The hell you are!'

'I'm already booked on the same flight. Lana, you know in your blood that I'm never going to let you go. That was some stunt you pulled in England—'

'It was the only way I could convince you we were finished,' I interrupted.

'But we're not finished.'

And by God if he didn't pull out a ticket and it *was* for the same flight. I don't know how he managed it, or where the money came from, but he was booked on the same plane. His seat was next to mine!

I suppose at that point I could have changed my plans and returned to Los Angeles, but what good would that have done? John would still have remained attached to me like a leech. Somehow I had to get rid of him without attracting the press or challenging his mean streak. I needed time to develop a plan, and right now I needed some rest. To me that meant getting to Acalpulco.

As usual I had arranged to stay at Villa Vera. Teddy Stauffer had reserved me a one-bedroom suite overlooking the bay, with a private pool.

'And you're not staying here,' I told John sharply. 'Get yourself a hotel.'

'You know I can't find anyplace now,' he said. 'It's January, the big season. If you want me to stay in a hotel, call Teddy Stauffer and tell him I need a room.'

I reached Teddy at La Perla, his restaurant-nightclub.

'Oh, Lana,' he greeted me, recognizing my voice. 'You're at the Villa? You have the flowers? Everything is fine?'

'Yes,' I said, 'but I need another room.'

'Oh, this one is not . . . or you brought someone?'

'Not exactly,' I said, 'but there's someone else here with me and it's important that I get another room.'

'Ah, a big romance!'

Teddy was not only Mr. Acapulco, but Mr. Romance as well.

'No, Teddy, but I can't explain anything over the phone.'

'Lana,' Teddy pleaded, 'I'm booked, completely. I can't throw someone out.'

'That's too bad,' I said. 'Then can you think of another place for me? Another hotel?'

'You're trying to tell me something?'

'Yes,' I said. '*Yes*, dear!'

Throughout this conversation John kept his eyes focused on me; he was alert to every inflection in my voice. I was keeping my voice light and happy, trying to get the message to Teddy that I needed more than a room. I needed help. I glanced at John and saw that slow flush rising to his cheeks, with a purplish tinge. It always scared me. 'Well, call me back,' I said to Teddy.

'What the hell are you telling me, Lana?' Teddy was asking.

178

'Okay, Teddy,' I said, brightly, 'you call me back and let me know. Thank you, dear.' I hung up.

John looked at me suspiciously. 'Did you signal him that you were trying to get rid of me?'

'You heard every word I said.'

He gave me a measured look, then lit a cigarette and walked into the kitchen of the suite. 'Would you like a drink?' he called to me.

I told him yes and he fixed me a vodka and tonic and carried it out to the garden. I followed him, explaining, 'Teddy's going to call me back. He's trying to find another hotel.'

'Oh, I see,' John said.

The evening sky had turned a deep, dark blue, and from the garden we could see the glittering lights of the town and the small boats on the bay. The sight must have turned John mellow, for he said, 'Look at that beautiful sight. I've heard about Acapulco, but I didn't think it was like this.'

'Just like a tourist,' I thought, at the same time wondering how I could get out of this mess.

'Let's go into town and have dinner,' John said.

'No, I'm tired. The cook is fixing dinner in.'

'My first night in Acapulco,' John sulked, 'and I don't get to go out.'

I went into my room, and for a while I heard him shuffling around in the garden. I didn't realize that he'd gone out until I heard the door open and he was back.

'It's all arranged,' he said, with a satisfied expression.

'What is?'

'I spoke to Teddy. He found me a room here.'

But Teddy had said they were all full. What had John said to him? I was sure Teddy had guessed that I didn't want John here. But if he hadn't understood . . . Suddenly my heart began to sink, and I felt my one hope for rescue was gone.

In a little while one of the maids arrived to show John his room. In minutes he came storming back. 'That's not a room,' he fumed. 'It's a utility closet with a cot set up! And there's just a sink, but no toilet!'

'You're lucky they found you that.'

'This has gone far enough,' he shouted. 'I'm sleeping with you!'

Just then dinner arrived but John continued to rave.

179

'Go to your damn room!' I finally yelled at him. 'And I hope I don't see you here in the morning.'

'Oh, you'll see me.'

He left, and I ate quickly and got into bed. I lay awake all night, exhausted though I was, tossing and turning. I finally fell asleep at dawn, but around seven in the morning there came a sharp knock at my bedroom door.

'It's John,' he said.

'Look, I'm exhausted,' I told him. 'Just let me sleep.'

'Open this door.'

'Just go away,' I screamed.

There was a crash as his shoulder struck the door, and there he stood. The wooden louvers had given way. 'Goddamn you, you know better than to lock doors on me.'

Seeing the look on his face, I tried to placate him. 'I wasn't trying to keep you out. I'm just tired . . .'

He sat down and began telling me that the night before he'd taken a cab and gone into town, where he'd walked around, thinking about his resolve to make it work between us, and I must give him another chance and time . . . I hardly listened.

'Don't worry,' he said. 'I'll take care of everything. This is going to work. It'll be okay . . .'

A few days later Teddy moved the person in the room next to my suite and gave the room to John. More of John's finagling? I suppose by now he had finally convinced Teddy that we were really together.

The days drifted by, and we developed a sort of armed truce, marred by a few violent arguments. They arose because, in spite of his pleading, I absolutely refused to have any intimacies with him.

Then we found the iguana.

I'd seen baby ones before when they came down from the mountains looking for water and drank out of the pool. We had been sitting out in the sun, and when I walked back into the living room, I saw a long green monster stretched out on the red pillows of the sofa. I immediately began screaming for the maid, the gardener, anyone.

John came running in, and stopped short. He was as frightened of the iguana as I was.

'Get it out of here,' I kept screaming.

'I can't do anything,' he blustered and went to get help.

Soon the maids and the gardener arrived. All three of them stood there laughing hysterically at us. None of them was in the least afraid. Instead they all seemed absolutely delighted. They grabbed the monster and carried it out triumphantly. It turned out they loved to eat iguana meat, and the bigger the beast the juicier. Uggh!

John and I had drinks to calm ourselves. The fact was I drank plenty to blot out John.

'Those things scare the hell out of me,' John said. 'Do you think there are more around?'

'Well, the mountains are full of them.'

'I'm going to talk to Teddy,' John said.

'What about?'

'I'm going to ask him for a gun.'

Sure enough, John told Teddy that I was terrified and Teddy gave him the gun. My big lover was going to protect me!

With the gun in his possession, John grew bolder—especially toward me. Now he was carrying it around with him all the time, supposedly to deal with the iguanas that might invade my quarters. And he was becoming more insistent about sharing my bed—or else . . . I dealt with his threats in the wrong way, escaping him by drinking. If he made another threat, I took another drink.

Friends wanted to see me but I pleaded exhaustion. I'm sure they assumed that I was there with a lover; even Teddy had become convinced of that. And I was so intent on keeping my problem private that I made no effort to get help.

One evening I was in bed half-reading, half-dozing, believing John was in his room, when suddenly he appeared at the foot of the bed, pointing the ugly snub-nosed automatic at my head. He had that purplish color in his face. Holding the gun on me, he got into my bed.

'If you're not going to be with me, you aren't going to be with anyone else,' he said. 'I'm not kidding with this gun. Take your choice.'

I endured his lovemaking with no feeling whatsoever—the vodka I'd drunk took care of that. He tried everything, even kindness, to win me over. And I kept thinking, 'I have to wait this out . . .'

*   *   *

Finally I decided that my only choice was to return to Los Angeles. But when I told John, he insisted that we stay. 'I haven't been to a nightclub yet. Why won't you go?'

'Because,' I said, 'I don't want to be seen with you.'

It was the wrong thing to say. His hand whacked me across the face. I slapped him back, smartly. His fist smacked into my stomach, and I doubled up.

'Get out of my life,' I sobbed. 'I hate you! Can't you understand? I *hate* you.'

All he did was smile.

After that John was forever holding that gun on me—when I was out by the pool, in my bedroom, or even sitting on the toilet. He gave me no privacy, and there was never any letup. 'Put that crazy thing away, for God's sake!' I'd scream. 'Do you really want to shoot me?'

And he'd taunt me, 'When I decide, then you'll know,' flaunting the gun and showing his power over me.

Sometimes I'd wish he'd get it over with. And I kept drinking, which he hated, because when I had a few drinks in me I could tune him out and that would lessen his control.

I knew how important it was for him to go out with me, to be seen with me in public, to show himself off with a movie star. He kept insisting on it, demanding it. I never wanted to go, but I eventually went—anything to stop the fighting. And people would look at us, of course, and whisper about us when they saw us in restaurants. I felt deeply ashamed for ever getting caught up with a man like him, for being too weak to get away.

At that point he never let me go into Acapulco by myself. If I tried to resist his dictates he'd slap me around. I had to believe that once I got home to my friends and family in Los Angeles, things would be different. There, on my turf, he'd have to behave, I reasoned. But how could I convince him to leave? Hour by hour I lay in the sun and tried to plan my escape.

Finally salvation came in the form of a phone call from Los Angeles. It was my agent, Paul Kohner.

'Lana, Lana,' he said, his voice high with excitement, 'you've been nominated for best actress for *Peyton Place!*'

'What? Nominated?'

'By the *Academy.*'

'But I didn't do all that much in *Peyton Place.*'

'Well, others think it was a wonderful performance,' Paul said, almost bubbling over. 'Aren't you happy about it?'

'Yes, I guess so . . . Yes!'

And suddenly I felt myself lifted up out of my gloom straight onto cloud nine.

16

JOHN WAS so impressed by my Academy Award nomination that for a while he behaved. Naturally I was so elated that I felt like celebrating in some way. The next evening John asked me to go out to dinner with him, and I surprised him by agreeing. Afterward we went to a nightclub and danced. As long as John remained in this mood, I could ride it out and eventually get out from under.

John misread my high spirits as a sign that I was at last accepting our relationship. He would slip into town and buy me thoughtful gifts, like the lover he had once been. Later I learned that I had bought them for myself, as they were charged to my account.

I could hardly imagine that the nomination was real because whatever fantasies I had about winning, the reality was that I remained John's captive.

When I finally decided to leave Acapulco a month early, John's mood became threatening again. One day I was reading in the sunny living room, and I looked up to see him sitting across from me, holding the gun in his hand. I had become even more frightened of his stealthy movements than I was of the gun.

'Just to remind you I have it,' he said, 'and that it's still aimed at you.'

'And if you killed me, what would that get you?'

'I'd throw myself on top of you and shoot myself.'

'You'd kill yourself?'

'If I don't have you, I have nothing to live for.'

That astonished me and filled me with dread. Now I thought he might even be insane. I was relieved that John returned the gun to Teddy just before we left Acapulco.

The Oscar nomination gave me a new resolve, so I simply went ahead and made the plane reservations and phoned my mother to tell her when I'd be home. She and Cheryl were waiting when John and I arrived at the Los Angeles airport. Somehow the newspapers anticipated my arrival, too, and sure enough, the photographers were there. They snapped me with Cheryl and John, who seemed to be basking in the limelight. He made it appear as though we were a happy couple who had just returned from a marvelous vacation.

I had reserved a suite at the Bel-Air while I looked for a house to rent. John stayed in his apartment on Wilshire Boulevard, but he did his best to remain glued to me. He insinuated his presence into my every act, even to the point of criticizing every house we saw. Finally I found the house I was looking for, with a tennis court in back, on Bedford Drive in Beverly Hills. It was a beautiful neighborhood then, as now, filled with stately manors and Moorish castles flanked by palms but also with the finest creations of the brilliant young architects of the day. I arranged to rent the house fully furnished, beginning April 1.

John assumed he would be escorting me to the Academy Awards ceremony. Not only had I been nominated but I had also been tapped to present the award for best supporting actor. But I certainly wasn't going to appear among the leading lights of the industry with John on my arm. I screwed up my courage and told him I would not allow him to come. I wanted only my mother and Cheryl there to celebrate with me. Despite his threats and pleadings, I wouldn't budge an inch.

What a thrill to be nominated in the company of such wonderful actresses as Joanne Woodward and Anna Magnani! I didn't expect to win. I was happy enough to know the Academy had finally decided to look beyond the glamorous shell. I was only disappointed that it wasn't for *Postman* or for one of my better roles.

As I dressed for the evening, John stuck close by me. I was nervous and his heavy presence made it worse. He couldn't say much while the hairdresser and dressmaker were around, but once they left he tried all his old tricks.

From coaxing he turned to bullying. 'But you're not going to the ball afterward,' he said, with that familiar deadly look.

'If I win, which is unlikely, I have to go.'

Before we could go another dismal round the limousine arrived. I warned John not to badger my mother and Cheryl because I didn't want our fight to spoil their evening. Cheryl was ecstatic when she saw me, saying that I had never looked so beautiful. My dress evoked the image of a mermaid, and I almost felt like one. I wore a strapless gown of exquisite white lace that was form-fitting down to my knees, where it flared out into three glorious tiers of lace

185

stiffened with tulle. Underneath it I wore a deep tan slip, to match my own tan, and I'd had my short curly hair bleached to set it off. With sparkling diamond earrings, diamond necklace, diamond bracelet, and diamond rings—glowing with health, at least outwardly—I really wanted to knock them out of their seats as I walked down the ramp of the Pantages Theater.

As we swept up to the theater I looked out at the corner of Hollywood and Vine, that magical intersection, symbol to millions of the glory that was Hollywood. In the fifties it looked just like any other corner in any downtown in America, with a department store, a drugstore, and a restaurant. Next to the luggage shop the marquee of the Pantages, its thin spire with fanciful lettering, glowed brightly in the neon of the street. As unprepossessing as that corner seemed, the dream it stood for had come true for me.

I had on the most dainty high-heeled slippers imaginable, and as I rushed inside the theater, one fell off and got lost in the crowd. I almost panicked. The usher was already steering us down the aisle. I had to limp along to my seat while my publicist and friend Glenn Rose was sweet enough to recover my shoe.

A few minutes later an usher came by to escort me backstage, where I would wait for my cue to go on. It was a small reunion back there—five or six familiar faces, alive with gaiety. What a charge—I was thoroughly delighted. And there was no John Stompanato to spoil my evening. When I came down that ramp to the stage, what a thrill! The audience responded with gasps followed by a torrent of applause for the blond, tanned vision I created as I walked onstage. I felt I was floating on a sea of warmth and love. As I read the names off the teleprompter in front of me—Sessue Hayakawa for *Bridge on the River Kwai*, Red Buttons for *Sayonara*, and three others, I was almost delirious with excitement.

Slowly I opened the envelope—I had been secretly rooting for Red Buttons—and when I saw his name I gasped, then broke into a wide smile. What a pleasure it was to announce his name. He ran up the ramp, and we hugged each other. When I handed him the statuette, he kissed me impetuously as the audience roared.

The suspense mounted as they rolled the clips for the best actress award. As I saw myself in *Peyton Place* I suddenly felt calm. Before they even announced it, I knew Joanne Woodward had won, and God knows she deserved the honor for her multiple roles in *The Three Faces of Eve*.

186

After it was all over we went on to the ball, but not without a moment of anxiety. The limousine never showed up. We just stood on the pavement, looking dumb, as star after star rolled away. For a minute I wondered if John had fouled things up, but as I found out later our driver had simply fallen asleep. The resourceful Glenn Rose managed to commandeer a cab, and off we dove to the Beverly Hilton Hotel.

After the Mexican ordeal this was the tonic I needed. The ballroom sparkled with color and life, and there were all those important people paying me compliments and condolences. The orchestra was in full swing, and both Cheryl and I were invited to dance. Oh how we danced! I adore music, and dancing has always been my special form of therapy. That night all my tensions just seemed to float away on the waves of sound.

All too soon the lights dimmed and it was time to leave. Glenn hired another limo to take us all home, and we dropped my mother off first. Cheryl came back to spend the night at the bungalow at the Bel-Air Hotel. I had a living room and two bedrooms, and I had left the living room light on as I always do.

I knew something was wrong because I heard music, and I didn't remember leaving the radio on. Well, maybe I had, I figured, in the rush and the excitement. Then I didn't give it a second thought. I went directly into Cheryl's room to help her out of her dress, and we chatted a while, giggling about the party. We were both very tired but we still felt the evening's happy glow. I'd been so pleased to have her there beside me, and I was thrilled to hear that she'd been proud of me—that she loved me as her mother and as Lana Turner, too.

Finally, I smoothed her coverlet and kissed her good night.

'Well, I'd better go to my room and get out of this dress.'

'Oh, you shouldn't,' Cheryl mumbled sleepily. 'It's so beautiful.'

'But I do have to sleep. So, good night, dear. I'll see you in the morning. Do you want me to close your door?'

She said no. So I picked up my wrap and purse, and turned off her lights.

My bedroom was dark, but the music was playing. When I flicked on the lights there was John lying propped on my chaise longue, smiling at me. That damned smile of his. A triumphant smirk that said, you didn't expect me, but here I am. You've had your evening of fun, but now I'm here. You can't get rid of me that easily.

187

For a minute I stood there looking at him, not saying anything, trying to guess what he had in mind. I prayed that there wouldn't be a noisy argument for Cheryl to overhear. I put down my things and went over to the little bar to make a vodka and tonic. If I ever needed a bracer, it was now. Then I began in a reasonable tone, calmer than I felt, 'John, I don't know why you're here. But you can't stay. Cheryl is sleeping in the next room and her door is open.'

'So close it,' he demanded.

'Look, I don't want to fight with Cheryl here. I'm asking you to leave.'

'I'm not leaving.'

I finished my drink quickly and poured myself another, all the while considering what to do. I had to break the impasse, but I didn't want to provoke him.

'Don't have another drink,' growled John. 'You're always boozing. Sit down. I want to hear about the evening.'

'John, I'm very tired. Please go home.'

'You spent enough time yakking about it with Cheryl,' he said accusingly. 'But now you have no time for me, is that it?'

So you could hear from bedroom to bedroom, I thought. Keeping my voice very low, I tried to head off the ugly scene that was brewing. 'Look, John, it was a lovely evening, and you say that you just heard all about it. Don't make me repeat it now. Please, just go. Just go, and I'll call you sometime tomorrow.'

Now he sat up on the chaise and glared at me, with his hands on his knees. My skintight dress was getting unbearable. I had been hooked into it all evening. Partly from the discomfort and partly to escape his gaze, I grabbed up my robe and went into my bathroom. Although I tried to appear calm I was shaking and tormented by indecision. Should I close Cheryl's door so she wouldn't hear us? Would I have to let him stay to avoid an argument? Cheryl still had no inkling of the irrational, violent monster lurking underneath the charming suitor. And I didn't want her to find out, especially not tonight.

I was without a plan as I came out of the bathroom, pulling the sash of my robe tightly around me. I was still wearing my elegant diamond earrings, as well as my necklace, wide bracelets, and several rings, all of diamonds. I hung up my dress carefully, then I turned to John with as much coolness as I could muster. 'John, I'm going to bed. Now will you go?'

With one pantherlike spring, he leaped from the chaise and

188

grabbed me tightly by the shoulders. 'You no-good bitch! How dare you tell me to leave!'

I was afraid to raise my voice, and I spoke in an urgent, sobbing whisper.

'John, please don't start anything, for God's sake. Cheryl is here. Her bedroom door is open so she can hear everything.'

He swung his hand toward me, and before I could raise my free hand to protect myself, I felt the searing sting of his palm across the left side of my face. Two thoughts hammered in my brain at once: *Don't hurt me* and *don't let Cheryl hear*.

My face burned, especially my ear and jaw. His hard slap had caught one of my earrings and driven it painfully into my cheek.

'Don't you dare touch me again,' I hissed at him.

But he was advancing on me, his face that purplish color it always took on when he was violent. 'I'll not only touch you, I'll give you the beating of your life,' he snarled back, then he spun on his heel and went to close Cheryl's door.

The act of closing the door filled my heart with fear. He was deadly serious. Automatically, my hands went up to my face and I tried to unfasten my earrings. Instinctively, I knew he'd go for my face, and the heavy, sharp diamonds could cut my cheeks. But my fingers wouldn't respond. Before I could remove the earrings he was back in the room grabbing me, spinning me around.

He cracked me a second time, this time knocking me down. I staggered back against the chaise and slid to the floor. He yanked me up and began hitting me with his fists. I went flying across the room into the bar, sending glasses shattering on the floor.

John had slapped me around before but this was a full-scale beating, and I was in fear for my life. He punched and slapped me again and again. He finally slammed me against the closet door, and the back of my head hit the door good and hard. And through the enveloping mist of grogginess and fear cut the knife of a deeper dread, that Cheryl would be hearing all of this, that she might even come through that door and see her own mother's agony and humiliation.

When my head hit the closet door, my knees began to sag, and John grabbed me by the shoulders and socked me again. As I crumpled to the floor, he grabbed me and hurled me onto the bed.

I was gasping for breath, and I couldn't have screamed, even if Cheryl hadn't been there. He leaped on top of me on the bed,

189

crouching over me like an animal. He began cursing me; a string of vile names spewed from his lips, every foul word he could think of.

All I could do was shake my head from side to side and mumble, 'No, no, no, please. Don't. Don't hit me anymore. Please don't hit me anymore. Stop it, please, please stop it.'

But he wouldn't let go of my shoulders. I could feel the heat of his breath as he threw his words directly into my face.

'Now do you understand? Do you? You will never, never pull anything like that on me again. You will never leave me out of anything. If you go anywhere, I'll always go there, too. I let you get away with it this time, but never again as long as you live.'

I nodded in defeat, and my head throbbed in agony as I moved it. 'Anything. Anything you say. But get off me. Leave me alone.'

John laughed at me harshly and shook his head no, but he did let go of my shoulders. I staggered off the bed and headed for the bathroom. I had to see my face, to see if it was bleeding.

There were welts all over my face and neck, and the beginnings of what would be terrible bruises, but my eyes were all right. The insides of my cheeks were cut and sore, where my teeth had cut into them with every hard slap. My chin was swollen and red, and where the heavy earrings had hit my face it was scraped but not bleeding. My breasts ached, and every part of my body throbbed. But I wasn't going to take off my robe to look beneath, because John stood in the doorway watching me. So all I did was rinse my mouth out with cold water, spitting out the blood. I could see him in the bathroom mirror and I glared at him. Anger was coursing through all my veins, replacing the fear. How dared he do this to me, especially with Cheryl in the next room!

After I dried my face, I went toward the chaise to sit down, but John grabbed my arm and said, 'Go to bed.'

'I don't go to bed until you leave.'

But he gave me a push in the direction of the bed, so I climbed on. I didn't get under the covers or lie down, but pulled my robe around me and huddled up against the pillows, on top of the spread. I was shivering, and I felt numb and sick inside. What the hell was I going to do about my face? And what could I possibly tell Cheryl?

I was still wearing my jewelry, and the bitter irony of a battered woman in diamonds struck me like another blow from John's fist. And the incredible contrast of the evening—the exhilaration of the Awards ceremony and the love I'd felt from everybody, their

190

encouragement and approval. To go from that to this . . . this degradation, this vicious beating at the hands of a madman. Shame washed over me, deep scalding shame, as though it were my own fault.

John was sitting on the chaise, staring, not taking his eyes off me. Finally, I said, 'You've done your worst. Will you please go now? I'm getting awfully sick and I need some sleep.'

He got up and came toward me. I flinched as he climbed onto the bed next to me and stretched out full length on top of the covers, with his clothes and shoes on. 'Go to sleep,' he commanded.

I closed my eyes but sleep wouldn't come. I was conscious every second of this man lying next to me. I knew that his eyes were open, watching me. I pulled a bit of the bedspread over me, but I couldn't get warm.

And he lay there and I lay there, and neither one of us got a wink of sleep. At last the gray light of dawn broke outside the window and I heard John get up. He walked around to my side of the bed, and I felt his eyes on me, then he bent over and gave me a gentle kiss on the cheek. I kept my eyes closed tightly as he walked out of the room and closed the door behind him.

For a few minutes I lay there, waiting to hear the front door close. But all I heard was silence, and it frightened me. Was he still in the bungalow? Still waiting for me? I stood up painfully and walked out into the living room. The lights were still on, but John was nowhere to be seen.

Sighing with relief, I turned out the lights and stopped at Cheryl's door. It was closed, and everything inside was quiet. I opened it a little and looked in. Cheryl was either asleep or pretending to be; to this day, I don't know which. I was too distraught to go near her, too much of a mess—emotionally, mentally, physically. So I closed her door very quietly and went back into my own room.

I was cold, very cold. Without bothering to take off my robe or change into a nightgown, I pulled back the covers and slipped underneath. There was no question of sleeping; I just huddled under the covers for a few hours, trying to keep warm.

Then Cheryl came tapping at my door.

'Mama? Are you awake?'

Christ, I thought, I can't let her see me like this. 'I'll be right with you, darling,' I called to her. 'Don't come in. Just go back to your room, and I'll see you in a minute.'

'Okay.' And she left.

191

I got out of bed and walked stiffly to the bathroom. I examined my face in the mirror. The swelling on my jaw and chin had increased, and you could see finger marks on my cheeks. My entire face was lopsided and swollen; later my jaw would turn an angry blue. I had worn very little makeup the night before, but my mascara had run from the smarting tears when John had beaten me. I looked terrible.

Very gingerly I brushed my aching teeth and washed my painful face. Then I applied as much powder as I could to hide the marks and the redness, put on a little lipstick, and ran a comb through my hair. And now, at last, I took off the jewels.

I was apprehensive about Cheryl seeing me, but I knew I couldn't put it off, and I was determined to keep my composure. Maybe she'd give me some kind of signal as to whether or not she had heard last night's beating. When I walked into her room she was still in her pajamas, and I took her into my arms.

'Good morning, Mama. How are you?'

'A little tired, darling, I didn't sleep too well. How about you? Did you sleep well?'

'Oh yes, just fine.'

And I wanted to believe her.

Over and over again, in later years, people would ask me the same questions. Why didn't you try to get away from John Stompanato? Why didn't you call for help? Weren't you seeing friends and business associates all the time, talking to your business manager or your agent or lawyer? Why didn't you confide in them, ask them for help? Why didn't you go to the police? These are hard questions to answer.

There were a number of reasons I kept my troubles to myself. The first is that John had made repeated threats, not only against me but against my mother and my daughter. He would have Cheryl kidnapped, he said, or have them both killed. And he did have underworld connections. He could have had anything done and been miles away when it happened, probably with an airtight alibi.

He threatened me, too, constantly. He'd kill me or cripple me. He'd disfigure my face, carve it up with a knife, so that no man would ever want me again. I'd never act again or be able to earn any living. And of course these were private threats, made only to me. In public he never uttered a word against me or my family. There he was all smiles. A hood to some, but a charming hood.

And then, too, there was the publicity. I was terrified that the

192

ABOVE: Cheryl, my
mother, and I at the
invitational press
preview of *Madame X* in
1965. Three years later
I married hypnotist
Robert Dante (RIGHT),
the last of my husbands.

Three debuts (ABOVE): My
first television work,
teamed with George Hamilton
in the short-lived
series *The Survivors,* 1969;
my first live
theater work, touring with
Forty Carats, 1971; and being
honored as a 'Legendary
Lady of the Screen'
at New York's Town Hall,
1975. LEFT: Cheryl
and I at a recent
Hollywood party. She
has grown into a
beautiful and successful
businesswoman.

Today

newspapers would get hold of the story, get wind of what was happening, and have a field day with it. They'd crucify me, and along with me my family would suffer. Of course my career would never survive. My God, if Fox and Metro wanted to separate Tyrone and me because 'living in sin' might be bad for the box office, just think what this would mean. Disaster. Things were very different then, even in the late 1950s, from the let-it-all-hang-out philosophy of today.

Remember that in the late 1950s a man and woman who weren't married to each other had trouble getting a hotel room together. And most of us in Hollywood were recognizable throughout the world. Sure, we could get married and divorced, but I don't need to remind most of you what *they* said about Ingrid Bergman—and that was a grand passion, artistically and otherwise.

The studios were already running a bit scared, and it was obvious to me that I couldn't use much more bad publicity. A little scandal was tolerated and was even good publicity—but Lana Turner mixed up with a gangster who held her a virtual captive *right here* in Beverly Hills? Not a chance.

And what about Cheryl? What would the screaming headlines say to her? Besides, for much of that year with John I had vacillated. Much of the time I really didn't know how I felt about him. Sadly for me, drink was the convenient way out. I wasn't an alcoholic, but I was weak and confused and used vodka to blur the edges, even the center of my life.

I had only myself to blame for getting involved, too deeply involved, with John Stompanato. By the time I'd gotten in over my head I didn't have a clue about how I was going to get rid of the man. I just hoped he'd go away—and peacefully.

But underlying everything was my shame. I was so ashamed. I didn't want anybody to know my predicament, how foolish I'd been, how I'd taken him at face value and been completely duped.

I couldn't see into the future, and I was afraid even to look. If I ever tried to picture how it would end, I'd have a vision of myself dead or mutilated, and I could see no other way out. I knew what the man was capable of. Not only had he beaten me viciously but from time to time he bragged to me about jobs he'd pulled, how he'd blackjacked people and beaten them half to death, and how he'd go away feeling good about it. I didn't know whether to believe him or not, but in my heart I feared he wasn't lying.

I felt as though I was slowly being smothered, and I lived in a state of continual terror. His love for me was so bizarre, so twisted, you really couldn't describe it as love at all. He was like a puppet-master, pulling all my strings, demanding total control, complete possession. He wanted to break my will entirely, to have me come and go at his command. It was sick, demented.

But what finally broke his hold was something we only refer to as 'the happening,' Cheryl and I, because we could never bear to give it its rightful name.

17

T HE WEEK after the Academy Awards I prepared to move into the house I'd rented on Bedford Drive. Before I packed up my things I went through the house to determine what else I needed. John was with me, and I mean *with me*. No matter what I did, no matter where I went, he was a hovering presence. It was as though he thought I'd escape somewhere if he freed me for more than an hour.

Although the house was completely furnished, even to glassware and some awful china, I discovered there were no pots and pans or cutlery. So the day before I moved, on March 31, I stopped by to pick up those supplies at Pioneer Hardware. John helped me pick out the inexpensive silverware, an extra set of simple china because mine was still in storage, and a set of kitchen knives, all to be delivered the next day. I didn't bother to look at the carving set John selected—after all, knives were knives to me, and he was the expert in that department.

Cheryl was on her Easter vacation from school, and she planned to spend a long weekend helping me fix up the new house. John came with me to pick her up at my mother's apartment. Once we got over to the new house another argument broke out. It was the latest in the series about whether he would stay, or whether I could be alone with Cheryl for the weekend.

Cheryl was up in her room putting some things away, and I knew she could hear us quarreling. I kept telling John to keep quiet in case she was listening. But he got angrier and angrier, and began to threaten me. Now I didn't doubt that Cheryl could hear him. Finally I managed to get him out of the house, and Cheryl came down to see me. Her little face was pinched and tight. I thought she might have been crying.

'Why does he say those things to you?' she asked. 'Can't you just tell him you don't want to see him anymore?'

'I've tried, Cheryl. Believe me, I've tried for some time.'

'Then you're afraid of him. Does he hurt you, Mother?'

195

'Well, I never wanted you to know about it.'

Then she said, 'What happened that time when you were in London?'

I told her of his violent behavior, the constant threats he made, including threats to harm her if I should leave him. Cheryl was reserved, a family trait, but her shock and fear registered on her face. And I believe she was less frightened for herself than she was for me.

'But why, Mother?' she kept asking. 'Why can't you stop seeing him?'

'I wish it were so easy, Cherry,' I said. 'But he almost never leaves me alone. It won't go on, but I must do it in a way that will be safe.'

I talked with my mother about it, too. She insisted that I call the police, but I knew that press people hovered around the Beverly Hills precinct hoping for just such news. I thought that John might be more reasonable if Cheryl moved in for a while. At least then if I wanted to keep him out I would have a plausible excuse.

Then came Friday, April 4, 1958. Earlier in the day I had gone shopping again—of course, John went with me—and we returned to the house about four-thirty in the afternoon. I was expecting Del Armstrong to come by for a drink, and when we got home he was already there, with a friend we had met while making *Sea Chase* in Hawaii. The man's name was Bill Brooks, and I knew little about him, only that he was a businessman who traveled frequently around the islands.

As John took the bags to the kitchen, I sat down to chat. Bill Brooks turned to me with a thoughtful look. 'Who did you say that fellow was?' he asked.

'John Stompanato.'

'I believe I used to know him,' Bill said.

'Really? Where?' I asked, as I made us drinks.

'If it's the same one, we were at military academy together. Kemper, in Missouri, class of Forty-three.'

Class of Forty-three? But John was older than that! Before I could press Bill about it, John returned.

'Remember me?' Bill asked, as they shook hands.

'Yes,' John said. 'Sure I do.'

196

His response struck me as cool for someone meeting an old schoolmate after such a long time. And John did seem uncomfortable around Bill. After a short time he excused himself, saying he'd call me later. He'd mentioned something to Cheryl about seeing a movie.

'What's he like now?' Bill asked me after John had left the house.

Del and I exchanged glances, and Bill went on, 'When we were at school together, he was bad news.'

'What do you mean?'

'He caused a lot of trouble there. He was a thief. I'd be careful of him,' Bill said.

I was not surprised by what Bill was saying. But I couldn't imagine why John had lied about his age. It was one more strand in that web of deception he'd been spinning and weaving around me. We chatted a while longer, and then the two got up to leave. Del suggested that I join them for dinner.

But the afternoon was fading, and I still had a lot to do. I'd hardly begun to unpack my clothes. My luggage from Acapulco was piled in the closet. I hadn't even looked at it yet. Once they were gone I spent a few hours sorting through boxes until John called around eight. I told him I was tired and wanted to skip the movie, adding that I'd turned down dinner with Del and Bill.

'But I might see them for dinner tomorrow,' I mentioned conversationally.

'Without me?'

'Surely I have the right to see old friends,' I said.

'I'm coming over and we're seeing a movie,' John said, and hung up.

He arrived within half an hour, in a black mood. How long had they stayed, he wanted to know. Why had they stayed that long? I didn't want to argue so I went upstairs, where Cheryl was watching television. I hoped that John would cool off soon. But he followed right behind, still haranguing me about making plans without including him.

'Now look,' I said, from the doorway of Cheryl's room, 'I've told you time and again not to argue in front of Cheryl.'

'Let her listen,' he snarled. 'I want her to hear the truth about you.'

I could see it was going to be a serious fight. I don't know why,

197

but I remember telling Cheryl explicitly what I was going to do. 'I am going downstairs now. Then I'm coming right back up.'

'Okay, Mother,' she answered.

John followed me down to the bar, where I fixed myself a drink. 'You break promises,' he was screaming at me. 'You said you would go to the movie but then you changed your mind. And now you're going to get drunk. You drink too damn much—'

'Just leave me alone,' I interrupted.

But he wouldn't leave me alone. As I climbed the stairs his shouting echoed in the hall. He was right behind me when I went into my room, and he angrily slammed the door. '. . . And you'll do as I say,' he was screaming.

'I don't want any more of this,' I said. 'Please get out of here.' By then I was in tears, and seeing me cry enraged him even more. Suddenly I heard a tinkling sound in the hallway outside the door. I recognized the sound—it was the charms on a bracelet I'd recently given Cheryl.

'Cheryl,' I called out, 'is that you?' No answer came. 'Cheryl, I can hear you. You *are* there. Please go to your room.'

The tinkling faded away. Next to the bathroom there was a dressing room with a built-in vanity of pink marble. I lifted myself up onto it cross-legged and lit a cigarette to calm myself. But the cigarette didn't help. I was shaking, with anger, with fear, afraid to lash out at him but too unsure that I could keep my self-control. I needed a drink. I stubbed out the cigarette and started for the bedroom door.

'Where are you going?' John bellowed. 'To the bar?'

'I'm not. But I *will* if I want to.'

'Like hell,' he fumed.

Before I could get the door open enough, he grabbed me and spun me around, then shoved the door shut with his foot. I thought he was going to hit me, but instead he shook me hard by the shoulders. I broke away from him, screaming, 'Don't you touch me! I have had it! Now get the hell out of my life!'

I was close to the door, and again I heard the tinkle of the charm bracelet. 'Cheryl! Get away from that door! I'm not going to tell you again.'

John was screaming back at me. 'This time you'll get it. No one will ever look at that pretty face of yours again—'

I remember telling him to get out, something to the effect that 'this is a new house and you're not going to be around in it.'

198

There was urgent knocking on the door, and outside it, Cheryl was begging, 'Mother, don't keep arguing. Let me talk to you.'

Because we had originally planned to go out, John had brought over a shirt and jacket earlier in the day. They were on his own hangers, heavy wooden ones. Now, yelling abusively at me all the while, he went to the closet and took out his clothing, hangers and all. I felt a stab of relief. This meant he was going!

'Please,' Cheryl persisted, outside the door. 'Let me talk to both of you.'

'Oh, all right,' I called to her. 'But the argument is over. John is leaving.'

Cheryl opened the door.

What she saw was me sitting on the pink marble counter, and John coming toward me, his arm upraised, with something in his hand. She didn't grasp the fact that he was carrying clothing on hangers over his shoulder. Just that upraised, threatening hand, and what appeared to be some kind of weapon. And he was right in front of the door, his body unprotected.

Out of the corner of my eye I saw Cheryl make a sudden movement. Her right arm had shot out and caught John in the stomach. I thought she'd punched him. There was a strange little moment, locked in time, as each stood looking at the other.

'Oh, my God, Cheryl,' John gasped out. 'What have you done?'

I darted forward off the counter, afraid that John was going to punch Cheryl back. Cheryl was backing up slowly, staring at John. John took three little circling steps away from her, in slow motion. He didn't clutch his belly; he didn't cry out. Just those three little steps, and then he fell backward, like a board, straight to the floor. His eyes were closed. Weird gasping was coming from his throat, as though he couldn't breathe. At that moment I realized suddenly what Cheryl grasped in her hand. It was a carving knife, one from the set John had selected a few days before.

At that instant of consciousness, a wave of shock hit me. I stared at Cheryl as she dropped the knife and suddenly began to cry. Numbly I turned to look at John lying prone and motionless on the floor, then took Cheryl by the shoulder and sent her to her room. John was make dreadful, soft, choking sounds. I went to him and leaned over, but I didn't see a wound, not until I lifted his sweater. It was a small wound, only a little slice. Strangely there was very little blood. I don't remember going to the bathroom to get a towel to cover the wound, but since there was a towel there I must have. John's eyes were closed as though he were in a sound sleep. I moved in a dream. None of this could be real. What made me do it, I don't know, but I picked up the knife and dropped it into the sink.

Do something, my mind commanded. Call a doctor. Call my mother. But I couldn't remember the numbers for a while. Finally my mother's surfaced and I dialed it almost automatically. When she answered I had to struggle to ask for the doctor's number.

'Are you sick?'

'Don't ask me, Mother. Just give me the number.'

'Lana, you sound dreadful. Is Cheryl all right? Tell me what's the matter.'

I looked at John and saw no movement. After a long minute all I could say was, 'Mother, John is dead.'

I cut off her questions with another demand for the number, then hung up and dialed the doctor. I got Dr. McDonald's service, and he called me right back. Somehow I managed to choke out the message.

'Don't do anything,' he ordered. 'I'll be right there.'

I tried calling my mother back then, but got no answer. Then I remembered poor Cheryl. I found her sitting on her bed, trembling violently. Sitting close to her, I held her, rocking her back and forth, trying to quiet her shaking. She began to sob again, but I didn't ask her questions. 'Shhh, darling, don't cry, don't cry.' I didn't know then that she had already phoned her father to tell him something terrible had happened. While I sat with her, soothing her, the doorbell sounded. I ran downstairs, and my mother rushed inside.

'What were you talking about?' she asked me, agitatedly. 'Where is he? Where is Cheryl?'

She brushed me aside without waiting for answers and went straight up the stairs to Cheryl's bedroom. She gathered Cheryl, who by now was crying convulsively, into her arms. After a moment or two she turned to me and asked, 'Where is he?'

I led her to the master bedroom. She started when she saw him, then looked at me. Then she dropped to her knees and listened to John's chest. I watched her as if in a trance. She went to the bed and got a pillow, then knelt down again and placed it under his head.

'Mother, don't touch him!' I cried.

She glared at me. 'I'm doing the right thing.'

Then she bent down and began to give him mouth-to-mouth resuscitation. I didn't want her mouth on his.

The doorbell rang. I raced down the stairs and let in Dr. McDonald, with a cry of relief.

'Where?'

'Upstairs. Mother's up there.'

He went up with his bag, calling, 'Mildred, Mildred.'

'In here,' she answered.

I realized later that he hadn't asked about Cheryl. He supposed I was the one who had done it.

In the pink bedroom he shrugged out of his jacket and threw it on the bed, and while opening his bag looked at John. He put his stethoscope to John's chest and felt for a pulse. Then he looked up at me. He didn't say a word. He just shook his head *no*.

Then reality broke in, like an explosion in my head. The haze gave way to a real horror. Now I watched Dr. McDonald take out a syringe and lock an ampoule of adrenalin into it. He plunged the needle into John's heart and pumped in the liquid. When he pulled out the needle he listened again for a beat through the stethoscope. As he waited for the sound he waved me toward the phone. 'Call Jerry Geisler,' he said.

I had to ask information for Geisler's number; after he answered I told him who I was and what had happened. I knew him only slightly from a few social occasions. He was the most famous lawyer in Hollywood, who had defended Errol Flynn and Charlie Chaplin, among others.

'John Stompanato is dead,' I told him. 'He's—he's here.'

'I'll be right there,' he answered. 'Give me your address.'

'Get me Geisler.' That was one of the jokes at the time. If you were in trouble, you knew whom to call. Only now it wasn't a joke. It was something unspeakable, all too real.

Time was playing strange tricks on me. It seemed to stretch out long and then recede. Things were happening all the while that I didn't know about until afterward. For one thing, Stephan reached the house moments after Dr. McDonald. My mother must have let him in. The police arrived, and then the ambulance was there. And then Geisler. I didn't even notice them.

Meanwhile my mother sent Dr. McDonald in to see Cheryl, and Geisler came in to find me. I told him that Cheryl, thinking to

201

protect me, had stabbed John with the knife. I took him into the bathroom and showed the knife still lying there in the sink. Then he and Stephan went to meet the police, and Dr. McDonald came in to check on me. And while he was doing that, Chief Anderson of the Beverly Hills police appeared at the door of the pink bedroom.

'Please,' I said to him, 'Let me say I did it . . .'

'Lana, don't,' he said. 'We already know it was Cheryl.'

I learned the police had found Cheryl's charm bracelet on the landing outside my bedroom. She had taken it off so that I wouldn't hear the sound as she listened outside the door. And when Stephan came she had told him, 'I did it, Daddy, but I didn't mean to. He was going to hurt Mommy.'

The police poured in. So many police! I was stunned at the number of blue uniforms all over the place. Kneeling over John's body, circling it, standing over it, running upstairs and downstairs and into Cheryl's room. You'd have thought they were making a raid. Were they all there out of curiosity? Surely three or four would have been enough. Then the reporters came, clamoring outside, yelling to the police to let them in. I heard them shouting directions: 'Bring a light.' 'Go around the back.' The police photographers must have given pictures to the press, for later the newspapers printed shots of John's body lying on the floor. How cooperative with the press, the Beverly Hills police!

Cheryl had to dress because she was still in her robe, and we all had to go down to the police station. My mother was badly shaken, so one of the officers escorted her home. Geisler took Cheryl and me in his chauffeured car, while Stephan rode with the policemen. When we arrived at the stationhouse Police Chief Anderson ushered us into his office. He told Cheryl that he needed a formal statement and asked for her version of what happened.

'Don't ask her,' I blurted out, 'ask me.'

'Lana,' he said, 'please be quiet. I want to hear it from her.'

She told him but I hardly remember her words. Now in the glaring light of the police chief's office, I began to grasp the enormity of what Cheryl had done and began to understand why. She had heard John say he was going to destroy my face, and she had brought the knife to protect me. A young girl, a child, against a big man. The thrust of the knife piercing the aorta was fatal by chance. She had been trying to protect me. She was now in terrible trouble. Nothing seemed to matter except protecting her.

202

The matron stood there waiting, and Chief Anderson was explaining, 'Cheryl, go with her. You'll be spending the night here.'

'No!' I screamed, and I heard Stephan asking why.

'Because that's how we have to do it,' Anderson said.

The events seemed to snowball, growing larger and larger, with no end in sight. 'Let me go with her,' I begged him.

'For a while you can,' he said. 'I'd like to talk to Steve.'

I rushed after Cheryl and the matron. Down a corridor I saw the matron waiting, and when I reached her I saw Cheryl—behind bars. That vision is one that will never go away. My child's face, behind bars.

'Will you open that door, please,' I ordered the matron.

She stared at me blankly.

'Open that door!'

Without saying a word she did it. Inside, I clutched Cheryl and she clung to me, then both of us sank to the cot and cried. 'You'll be all right,' I tried to reassure her. 'You're the most important one in the world now, to all of us. Don't be afraid. You *will* be all right, and in the morning we'll come and get you. Chief Anderson said we could.'

An officer arrived to lead me away. The matron stood at the door, holding it open. 'You must leave,' she said, and the officer took my arm as I stared back at my child. Cheryl stood there woodenly, impassive and silent.

When Stephan, Geisler, and I left the stationhouse, we saw why they were so anxious for us to leave. The press had gathered like vultures outside, cameras at the ready. And they got their damned pictures.

Geisler's limousine brought me home. What a horrible sight greeted me there! The ambulance attendants were removing John's body on a stretcher covered with a sheet. Still seated in the car, I watched the grisly procession on its way to the ambulance at the curb. I couldn't suppress a scream. Geisler held on to me, saying, 'Stop it, Lana, stop it,' and he shoved me down to the floor. He had seen the flashbulbs flaring as the body was carried away. When he got out of the car the reporters swarmed around him, as I hid, shaking, in the backseat. I heard him telling them that I had gone away for the night, and when the ambulance drove off the reporters followed it. Then Geisler came back to tell me the coast was clear.

I peeked out of the car. The street was empty. Quickly I ran into the house. There my friends had gathered, Del and the others, having heard the news on the radio. More questions, gentler this time. Yes, it was all true, but . . . All those kind faces, helpful, understanding, floated before me in a dream.

18

H ARDLY HAD my head touched the pillow, it seemed, before it was time to leave for the stationhouse. Stephan met me there in the chief's office, where we would be jolted by another agonizing piece of information. Cheryl could not go home with us today. Instead she would be held until arraignment at the juvenile center downtown.

We would have to wait another day to see her. By the time we arrived the next morning, of course, the press was already there. Flashbulbs popped like gunshots, and my ears rang from the barrage of questions. Propelled along by Geisler and another attorney, Louis Blau, we fought our way through the crowd to a waiting room.

Soon a matron came for me and led me to Cheryl's private room. They had allowed her a visit from Dr. McDonald, and mercifully, he had brought her a sedative the previous day. She looked pale and drawn, but she seemed relatively calm.

'Can you leave us alone?' I asked the matron.

Obligingly, she left. Looking back on it now, the talk I had with Cheryl seems mundane. *Are you all right, dear? Yes, Mother, I'm okay. And you?* And so on. Those empty words hid emotions too deep and complex to explain. Carefully we skirted the grim event itself, and we rarely discuss it to this day. It's always *before* and *after* that signpost in our lives. I didn't know that morning—I had no way of knowing—how 'the happening' would affect Cheryl's life. I wanted her out of custody, safely home with me. The attorneys fought for that but did not succeed. She would not be released until the coroner's inquest, which would be held in a week.

I spent that week under almost continuous sedation, with moments of dark despair. I sank into guilt as I was questioned again and again. But I answered as frankly as I could. Nobody let me see the headlines, but I got wind of what was turning up in print. My letters to John from England, for example. That sickened and

205

depressed me. The thought of a million strangers reading those letters, cackling over the affectionate lines . . .

On television recently I saw a woman journalist describing the triumphs of her career. Her big coup, she declared, was obtaining those letters from Mickey Cohen. How she gloated over them! How pathetic that it was the big moment of her life.

The inquest was held at nine in the morning, April 11, before a ten-man, two-woman coroner's jury. I testified for more than an hour, telling the whole sordid story. Radio microphones and television cameras recorded what became a spectacle. Although the curious public had been milling outside since the wee hours of the morning, they had little hope of seeing the proceedings. Of the 160 available seats, 120 had been reserved for the press.

It was a humiliating ordeal to explain on the witness stand what I barely understood myself, to confess before the cameras that strange helplessness that bound me to John for so long. I didn't think I could withstand it. More than once I nearly broke down on the witness stand from the mixture of agony and shame, of grief and relief that I felt about John's death. But all my emotions were secondary compared to Cheryl's release—that was what mattered now. The vision of her face framed by the bars was the only thing that got me through.

After the grueling questions relief came quickly. The jury took only twenty-five minutes to deliver the verdict of justifiable homicide. There would still be a hearing in a juvenile court, set for a date three weeks away, and my lawyers were sure Cheryl would be acquitted. But she would have to remain in the juvenile hall until the hearing date. I cried every night, thinking of Cheryl in prison. I hardly slept. Then one night Dr. McDonald came by to give me a sedative, and he suddenly realized I was still living in the room where the killing had occurred.

'My God,' he exclaimed, 'what have I done to you? You can't continue to stay here.'

He took me to my mother's. But I was paralyzed with despair and indecision, not knowing what to think or what to do about my future life and Cheryl's—waiting, simply waiting until she came home. Soon my mother found me another place, a small house on Roxbury Drive, and I immediately moved my things from the Bedford Drive house. I had lived there less than a month, and I've never wanted to see it again.

Cheryl's juvenile court hearing was held in the Santa Monica courthouse before Judge Allen T. Lynch, who mercifully closed it to the public and the press. We were in that courtroom from nine in the morning to almost noon. My lawyer, my mother, and I sat at a long table, listening to endless testimony by the police about who was the first to arrive on the scene, who was the second, and so on. It seemed interminable, and I was aching with anxiety for Cheryl, wanting the whole thing to be over.

Finally Geisler whispered to me, 'Come on, let's get out of here.'

'Don't we have to wait for the jury to go out? I thought we'd be here all day.'

But he shook his head and took my elbow, and I stood up.

'Mother, we can go now,' I told her softly.

'Oh, thank God!'

We made our way out of that courtroom, past the merciless battery of cameras and reporters, and went down to the curb. Geisler's driver was on the watch for us, but he was stuck in the parking lot, and it took him a few minutes to get the long green sedan to the curb where we were standing. Do I have to tell you that a large milling crowd of the curious public was on that sidewalk with us? Even behind my large dark glasses I felt vulnerable and unprotected. People were staring at us and muttering, but I kept my eyes down and forced myself not to hear anything.

The car pulled up at last. My mother and I got in, with Geisler between us. Just as the door closed, a woman detached herself from the crowd and came up to my open car window. She was truly a hag, with gray, stringy hair, a witch's nose, and very thick glasses, behind which I could see mean, angry eyes. I had been crying, and I was dabbing at my cheeks and eyes with my handkerchief. This hag thrust her face right up to mine and spat her words at me.

'Hah! Crocodile tears!'

Jerry reached over immediately and rolled up the window, but I'll never forget the hate on that woman's face and in her voice, the hatred of a stranger to whom I have never done any harm. It shook me profoundly.

While we were driving, the car radio was on. Suddenly words caught our attention: '. . . regarding the case of Cheryl Crane, Lana Turner's daughter . . . stabbing . . .' and I leaned forward to hear better. I was so tense that my long fingernails were digging

207

into the leather back of the driver's seat in front of me. 'The jury has just returned a verdict . . .'

We were all holding our breath. 'Justifiable homicide . . .'

'Oh, thank God!' I cried. My mother and Jerry Geisler also let out their breath in relief; there were smiles on their faces.

'Oh, thank God! Thank God!' I couldn't stop saying it. And all the while I was pummeling that poor driver with my fists—not too hard, I hope—but the joy and the excitement wouldn't let me sit still. Jerry, laughing, pulled me by the arm and I was suddenly aware of what I was doing.

The jury wasn't out more than twenty-five minutes before they brought in that true verdict, and we weren't even in the courtroom to hear it! Judge Lynch upheld the verdict, as the lawyers had predicted.

In his ruling the judge addressed the question of 'proper parental control and supervision.' He was unsure that Cheryl had suitable guidance at home, so he made her a ward of the court for an undetermined period. Meanwhile he entrusted her to my mother for sixty days, with visitation rights for me and Stephan. Geisler told me that it was the best arrangement I could expect, and I accepted it, knowing that I would have to order my own life before I would be able to help Cheryl.

The judge also ruled that Cheryl, Stephan, and I had to undergo psychiatric consultation. I went to a Dr. Fisher faithfully once a week, but after six weeks I'd gotten little out of it. He would just sit there and nod, or murmur 'hmmmm . . .' During one visit, I burst out, 'Why don't you ask me some questions?'

'This takes patience,' he replied.

But by then he had exceeded mine. When the court-established period was over I decided to end our sessions. I've never believed in psychoanalysis as a way to solve my problems.

I almost never allowed myself to think of John. My fascination with him in the early days of our relationship had turned to terror and then to hatred. Now I do not doubt that his efforts to bind me to him had to end in some violent way. If that freakishly accurate knife thrust hadn't hit a vital spot, I wonder if Cheryl or I would be alive today.

The coroner's report at the inquest was a shocker. It revealed, among other things, that John had a serious kidney ailment, and he probably wouldn't have lived much longer, no more than a matter of months. That caught me like a blow to the middle! He would have died anyway, and we would have been free! My mother, my daughter, and I—we would have been free of his threats and his menacing presence! And instead *this* had to happen.

Irony piled on top of irony, all as bitter as the bitterest gall. All the *ifs* came rushing back at once to engulf me, one by one.

If John had left a few minutes earlier. *If* he had carried his clothing in front of him instead of slung over his shoulder. *If* Cheryl had seen the hangers in his upraised hand. *If* it had been I who opened the door, and not Cheryl. *If* John's body had been turned an inch to the right or the left . . . Oh, there were so many ifs and now this! This monumental *if. If* we'd known that John Stompanato was terminally ill . . .

There were a lot of things I hadn't known that came out in the publicity about the case. One was that he kept a little brown book filled with dozens of telephone numbers of Hollywood women—Anita Ekberg, Zsa Zsa Gabor, and June Allyson, among them—and some prominent male personalities as well. That especially made me wonder what he had wanted from me. Money? Love? Marriage? What was the obsession that drove him?

One other discovery especially puzzled me. A week or two after the inquest one of my lawyers, Louis Blau, came by the house. He took a spool of exposed film out of a little box and explained how he happened to have it. My maid, Arminda, had come to him a few days before and handed him a package that John had asked her to keep for him just before he met me in England. He had told Arminda that the contents were extremely valuable to him, and that she should keep it safe until he returned to reclaim it. Arminda had put the package in the trunk of her car and, as time went on, forgot about it. Then, not knowing what else to do, she had passed it on to Blau, who was shocked by what it concealed.

'Now, you look at it,' he said.

I held up the strip of film to the light. Several of the frames showed me lying on my bed, completely nude. Another sequence showed a blond woman I didn't recognize performing fellatio on John.

'Do you remember him taking those pictures?' Blau asked.

I shook my head. I had never even seen John with a camera. There was only one explanation. I remembered making love with John on a weekend afternoon. He brought me a drink afterward, and almost at once I fell into a deep sleep. I didn't wake up for

209

several hours, and when I did, I felt groggy and dull. In retrospect, I suppose he drugged me.

But why had he wanted the pictures? All Blau could suggest was that he had planned to do some trick photography, using the other woman.

'Then he could hold them over you for blackmail,' Blau surmised.

'Or,' I said, 'to make sure I wouldn't leave him. He was always threatening to ruin my career.'

'Do you have any scissors?' Blau asked.

I got a pair and he cut the negatives into tiny pieces, then burned them in an ashtray before flushing the ashes down the toilet.

'Now,' he said, 'we'll both forget about this.'

But it wasn't easy for me to forget, and my confusion about John's twisted motives persisted.

Throughout the ordeal my mother and Del had kept the papers from me. But once the crisis passed I was determined to read every single word that had been printed. My mother pleaded with me. I had been tortured enough, she said. But I didn't know any other way to get through the nightmare my life had become. So I gathered up all the newspapers and locked myself in the bedroom of my house on Roxbury Drive. All I did for several days was read, quickly at first, then more slowly, column after column. Then came the editorials and the letters from readers. I finished them all—the slanderous ones, the moralistic ones, the sympathetic ones, the pathetic ones. I read everything, then reread it, attempting to analyze the whole awful happening. I wanted to understand and then to step outside of it. And after I had done that I felt totally drained. The press had done their worst, and now I knew exactly what the worst was. And I'd have to survive it.

I took stock of my situation. My overriding concern was Cheryl and the effects on her of those three weeks in detention at the juvenile hall. The aftermath of the happening had not yet subsided, as the newspapers and the columnists continued to milk the sordid story to death. There were threats of violence against me and also against Jerry Geisler; a damage suit against me brought on behalf of John's eleven-year-old son, which implied that I might have done the actual deed; and a mountainous stack of mail from all over the world, nearly all of which supported both me and Cheryl.

My financial prospects looked grim. I was again in debt, and I had my mother and Cheryl to look after. For a while I was convinced that my film career was finished, that the scandal would haunt me for years, probably forever. After some heated debate Paramount's management decided to rush *Another Time, Another Place* into release. Although the early returns were brisk the box office soon faltered, and my fears seemed to be confirmed.

It was time to start over. Could I do it? I knew that I had to somehow.

19

MY AGENT Paul Kohner never lost faith in me. He called me about six weeks later to persuade me to do a picture. It was a remake of *Imitation of Life*, the Fannie Hurst story, and Ross Hunter, the producer, wanted to meet me.

'See him, Lana,' Paul urged. 'This is just what you need to come back. It's a proven story.'

But I was scared. What if the picture flopped? And maybe it was too soon. Maybe I was still too notorious and people wouldn't come to see me. If the movie bombed I knew what could happen— I probably would never work again.

Paul kept trying to coax me into it.

'Ross has a great track record. And listen—it's only you they want. More than that, they need you. Ed Muhl insists on it. Otherwise he won't give the go-ahead.'

Ed Muhl was the head of production at Universal. The studio was having some lean years, and he was keeping budgets tight. Because Ross delivered glamour and opulence on the screen without spending large sums of money, he'd become Muhl's fair-haired boy.

I only half-listened to Paul at first, but eventually I consented to see Ross Hunter. One Sunday afternoon he came to my house bearing an early draft of the script. His mid-thirtyish rosy-cheeked face and his winning smile could have sold me on anything. And he played out the parts so enthusiastically—he was a frustrated actor—that at one point I laughed outright. I hadn't laughed in a long time.

The 1934 *Imitation of Life* had starred Claudette Colbert. In developing the update Ross had changed the main character from a successful businesswoman to a Broadway stage actress. That wrinkle certainly appealed to me, but one element of the story spooked me. It was the relationship of the actress and her teenage daughter, to whom she had given every advantage but love and attention, the only important ones. I knew that painful comparisons would inevitably be made.

212

'No, I can't do it,' I said. 'I'm frightened.'

Then Ross began to tell me what I already knew but maybe hadn't fully believed, that I hadn't reached my fullest capability as an actress because I had been a commercial commodity at MGM. Women lived vicariously through Lana Turner. The studio had emphasized my looks rather than my talent to maintain that glamorous ideal. What Ross wanted to do was combine the two, the actress and the image.

He did have me there. It was just the kind of offer that I wanted. Then he and Paul ganged up on me, insisting that the role was the perfect way to show people that I could rise above the tragedy. Sooner or later I would have to face the world, and now, they assured me, was the time to do it.

Finally I caved in, but not without great trepidation. 'Oh God,' I prayed. 'I've survived so far, but this is a giant step. Please help me to help myself.'

How Ross handled the budget I don't know, but I had never before encountered such lavish beauty on the set. The sound stage was filled with lush real flowers, yellow roses that were changed every day. The props were real, too, including some fabulous jewels supplied by Laykin et Cie, and Jean Louis designed a dazzling wardrobe for me. It seemed that Ross was trying single-handedly to restore glamour to the screen. And Douglas Sirk, Universal's most polished director, put his own special gloss on the production too.

We knew the press would be dogging us for news on my comeback, so we decided to throw open the first day of shooting. I would meet with individual reporters, who could ask me anything but questions about John or his death. And all the reporters respected that restriction, except one, a woman. When she asked the one question I didn't want to hear, I felt as though she'd belted me one. But I managed to smile and say that I didn't care to discuss it. Still, in a way I was thankful she asked. I'd been able to stand up to the worst, and I knew I could take it from then on.

My big scene in the film was the funeral of Annie, the longtime black companion of the actress star. In the original version Annie had been the star's business partner, but Ross had made her a housekeeper-friend. I most dreaded the part when Annie's repentant daughter would throw herself on the casket, reminding the star of her troubled relationship with her own daughter.

The casket was covered with a huge blanket of gardenias.

213

Hundreds lined the streets of Harlem to see the cortege pass by, and Mahalia Jackson sang a heartbreaking spiritual. When I heard the first strains of that song in rehearsal, I simply broke down. Images of my own life, my own dark fears flooded my mind, and I dissolved in tears. I fled.

My hairdresser, Patti Westmore, saw me getting out of the pew and running out of the side door. Tears were beginning to spill from my eyes. Our dressing trailers were in the parking lot outside the church where we were filming, and by the time I got to mine I was close to hysteria, running in my high heels and weeping. When I reached the safety of the trailer, I slumped onto the chair in the front of my little dressing table, burying my face in my arms. By now I was shaking with sobs, unable to control myself. That casket, with its blanket of heavily perfumed gardenias, had wakened unexpectedly all the crushing thoughts of death I had been trying to suppress.

Patti rushed into the trailer, concern on her face.

'Lana, what is it?'

I couldn't even speak to answer her, and motioned to her to go away. But she came over to me and pulled me by the shoulders, making me sit up and face her.

'Stop it!' she ordered. 'You've got to come back and finish the scene.'

'I . . . can't . . .' I sobbed. 'I can't stop.' And I couldn't. The tears were gushing from my eyes like a waterfall of bitter regret. My emotions had me in a grip of iron.

With that, Patti slapped me, knocking the breath out of me, but it worked. It also knocked the hysteria out of me. Then she put her arms around me and hugged me. 'You're gonna be all right, Lana. Come on back now, honey.'

And I did go back to finish the scene. And I cried, but I had myself under control now, and the tears rolled silently down my face, as I sat there in the pew with John Gavin and Sandra Dee, and Mahalia singing so beautifully, and that casket, all covered with flowers.

'Cut and print,' called the director.

'Brilliant!' he said to me. 'You gave it just what it needed.'

Later Ross told me a theater owner had wired him about the scene: 'Good God, even strong men are crying!'

Imitation of Life grossed more than any Universal film ever had. And, thanks to Ross, it was my financial salvation as well. I had

214

accepted a fairly modest fee because Ross had a limited budget, so he suggested that I gamble and work for half the profits. This was a new trend in Hollywood, and I was taking a big chance—at the time (and today) few pictures ever broke even. But for me the gamble paid off. I don't know exactly how much I made—my managers took care of that—but it was more than the highly publicized million dollars that Elizabeth Taylor got for *Cleopatra* some years later.

I'll never forget Ross for saving my career, and for more than that—for saving my sanity. Without his support and his respect on the set, I probably wouldn't have had the courage to come back. He came along in my darkest hour.

Throughout the shooting my confidence grew, although I rarely left the house except to work, and if I did I would see only my closest friends, among them Del Armstrong. Sometimes I met with Stephan to discuss Cheryl's welfare. But to all other invitations and intrusions I gave a firm no.

An actor friend, Kim Dibbs, kept calling me despite my refusals. Finally one summer Saturday he persuaded me to come to a beach party in Malibu. An executive, Bob Whittaker, was our host, but I didn't know him well. And I didn't recognize any of the other guests. Kim hovered protectively near me as Bob introduced me around, but I felt too shy to mingle freely or take part in the horseplay on the beach.

As I sat there watching the crowd, a man coming down the beachhouse steps happened to catch my eye. He was dressed all in brown, everything about him seemed brown—his tanned face, his sandy hair, even the dark glasses that he wore. Something about him grabbed me. Maybe it was his resemblance to Tyrone. I had been so blocked off emotionally, so dead for so many weeks, trying to keep down the terrifying conflicts inside. But something about this man awakened my interest and I hoped that I would meet him.

But not right away. I wanted to watch him circulate for a while, move around in the crowd—partly because I wanted to figure out why he attracted me and partly because I was afraid. Now I wasn't the *famous* Lana Turner but the *notorious* one. Surely he would know about my troubles, and how would he respond to them? What had he thought of me when he saw those lurid stories in the papers?

And other inner voices were crying, *No, no! Don't get involved again. Emotional entanglements bring nothing but sorrow and pain.*

215

You're back on your feet, so stay there! Don't let your heart trip you up again.

But there was another woman inside of me who wanted to be with a man, who was still looking for warmth and caring and love. Then he was standing in front of me, and someone was introducing him as Fred May. That was it. He had shaken my hand and just as quickly drawn away. I saw him talking to a lovely little actress. 'Well,' I said to myself, 'sometimes it goes that way.'

But later he came over to chat a bit. He told he'd met me years before when he worked as an extra on *Dancing Co-ed*. I remembered him! How strange—that picture had led to my marriage with Artie, and now it had some connection with Fred. Was it some kind of sign? He went on to describe his horse ranch, where he raised thoroughbreds for racing. Impulsively I remarked that I'd love to see the place sometime. As we parted he asked nervously for my phone number, and just as nervously I told him. He didn't write it down.

I was afraid he wouldn't remember it but two days later he called. Because I still shunned public places we barbecued steaks at his apartment. That night he told me that, when he'd first met me, my name had hardly registered. He'd felt the same kind of magic as I had, but he was gun-shy, too. He was going through some unpleasant divorce proceedings that made him wary. So I wasn't the only one. So much for my foolish fears.

But a few weeks later those fears were temporarily confirmed. I had opened his closet to hang up a coat when I spotted a pile of newspapers. The huge headlines smacked me like a bucketful of cold water. He had collected all the stories on the Stompanato case! For a time I didn't mention it to Fred but I scrutinized him carefully. Why was he so fascinated by my humiliation? Was he some obsessed publicity seeker, too? Later he explained that as he began to care deeply for me, he thought he should find out everything about me—even the worst. And amazingly, he found it didn't matter.

His ranch was near the little town of Chino, about an hour's drive from Los Angeles. The life we led there was new to me and revitalizing. We'd wake at six o'clock and spend the morning working, feeding Fred's beautiful horses, cleaning manure from the stalls, and loading the bales of hay onto the truck. I wore sweat shirts and blue jeans, and kissed my long fingernails good-bye.

Working with Fred's thoroughbreds rekindled my interest in racing. We often went to the track to see his horses running. Under

Fred's guidance I bought two horses of my own, and my big winner, Grey Host, came from one of my mares.

With Fred's strong, reliable help I was coming to life again, and it was an idyllic, peaceful life, too. After the horror of the time with John, Fred provided the stable, loving support I needed. We were living together at the ranch, though never in town, where I still had my house and he had his apartment. So it was some time before the gossips caught on to us. By then it seemed that decision time was fast approaching.

20

D URING THE time I was seeing Fred my career was exploding. I needed a secretary to manage the volume of letters and the endlessly ringing telephone. Paul Kohner recommended Lorry Sherwood, a bright, humorous woman who had once worked for the director John Huston, and we took to each other right away. She was adept at driving off prying reporters, but now I wanted them around—I was doing publicity for *Imitation of Life*.

Ross Hunter had asked me to accompany him on a promotion tour for the picture. Of course I tried to refuse, still leery about the way I would be received. But eventually he convinced me, and I was amazed that audiences greeted me warmly. The outpouring of sympathy I encountered more than convinced me that my career wasn't over. I found my confidence slowly returning.

Film offers flooded in. Jerry Wald approached me for *Return to Peyton Place*, and Otto Preminger wanted me to star with Jimmy Stewart in *Anatomy of a Murder*. On Paul Kohner's advice, I accepted Preminger's offer. Preparations moved along nicely until costuming time, when Hope Bryce, Preminger's assistant, wanted to dress me in a simple little suit right off the racks. I have never favored ready-to-wear clothing onscreen. So I suggested that my dressmaker run up the kind of suit she had in mind.

The next evening I happened to answer the phone myself, and I heard a male voice shouting at me, 'You bitch!'

'What?' I gulped. 'Who is this?'

'Otto Preminger,' he yelled, in his thick Viennese accent. 'And you are to understand this is *my* production. You think you are the great star? *You* vill make the decisions? *No!*' Then after more expletives he screamed at me, '*I* vill choose your clothes, you—!!?!'

I banged down the receiver, then immediately telephoned Paul Kohner. 'Paul, get me out of *Anatomy* . . .'

'But you're signed for it.'

'I can't possibly work with that man,' I insisted, and told him about the hysterical phone call.

Throughout the years Preminger has repeated his own version—that he gave me the choice of accepting his wardrobe or withdrawing from the picture. But for me the decision was whether or not I could put up with his arrogance. I am by no means a prude, but Preminger's language was intolerable, not to mention the tyrannical behavior that went with it.

With *Anatomy* out of the way, I was signed with Ross Hunter again for *Portrait in Black*. It was a murder mystery based on a stage play. Ross saw it as another chance to develop the glamorous look that had enhanced *Imitation of Life*. Again Jean Louis designed my fabulous gowns, David Webb supplied my elegant jewels, and once more we reveled in the splendor that Ross considered 'psychologically important' on the set. The critics blasted the picture, but Ross had delivered what the public wanted. He racked up another success—and so did I.

After *Portrait in Black* I starred in *By Love Possessed*, another glamour vehicle. But though I was busier than every professionally, my major concern was still Cheryl. Although technically she remained a ward of the court assigned to my mother's custody, I tried to make her feel that she was again leading a normal life. For her fifteenth birthday I had arranged the traditional party but had to cancel it when she developed a severe case of mononucleosis. I planned to reenroll her in her old school, but the headmistress rejected her as a potential 'bad influence' on the other girls. So Cheryl got her wish. She entered Beverly Hills High School in the fall of 1958.

I feared she would attract a lot of morbid attention from her fellow students, but she seemed to be making a good adjustment. She was tall, slender, and strikingly beautiful. She was beginning to attract attention from boys, so when she turned sixteen I allowed her to date.

Six months later, in January 1960, I got an anxious phone call from my mother. 'Lana, get over here right away. Cheryl has a boy here, and she says they're getting married.'

As I drove over, my mother called Stephan and also Jim Bruce, Cheryl's court-appointed caseworker, who administered the terms of her probation. My mother explained that Cheryl had been sneaking out at night to visit her boyfriend, who worked at a drive-in. They had decided to elope that night but Cheryl had confided the plan to my mother.

It was Jim Bruce who suggested that we call her bluff. My mother went to get the 'lovers' from Cheryl's room. We offered them a big wedding in a church, with lots of flowers, and a reception for all their friends. We discussed how they would support themselves and the children they surely hoped to have . . . and on and on, until Cheryl interrupted, 'Excuse me.'

She took her boyfriend firmly by the hand and led him to her room. Soon they emerged red-faced. 'We've changed our minds,' Cheryl announced.

But the episode, silly as it was, had serious repercussions for Cheryl. By leaving the house at night she had violated her probation. The judge took a harsh view of her actions and recommended stricter supervision. So he ruled that she be sent to a special school, El Retiro, in the San Fernando Valley, for girls with emotional problems.

El Retiro was hidden by a twelve-foot wall with barbed wire strung along the top. It was really a reform school, and from the outside at least it resembled a prison. The gates in the wall were sheathed in steel.

The girls lived in cottages, and Cheryl shared a room with another girl. Her schoolmates were a mixture of caucasian, black, and Mexican, from the poorer neighborhoods of Los Angeles. She had assigned times for chores and psychiatric consultations.

We could visit her on certain days, and she could come home every other weekend. Despite the depressing atmosphere, we thought she was adjusting reasonably well. But less than six weeks after she arrived Cheryl ran away with two other girls. It made the headlines of course. After three horrendously anxious days they found her and returned her to the school. A month later she escaped again, but this time she was picked up in a matter of hours. Eventually, after nine long months at El Retiro, the judge allowed her to return home. Fred and I were married and living in Malibu, and Cheryl moved in with us. Fred took a genuine fatherly interest in Cheryl, and in time she grew close to him.

In the meantime Fred and I were discussing whether to make our relationship official. One day when we were driving to the Del Mar racetrack we impulsively decided to stop at Santa Ana and take out a marriage licence. It would be good for three months so we would have time to reconsider. Sure enough, the press discovered it and there were the usual headlines: LANA TURNER TO MARRY AGAIN. The publicity disturbed Fred, who was a very private man. In that respect he was utterly different from the other men in my life.

So we put away the license and we didn't discuss marriage again. But then one Sunday afternoon we both suddenly realized that the license would be good for only one more day. As if he were reading my mind, Fred said, 'Lana, do you to want to get married today?'

I didn't answer immediately. After four previous washouts I wasn't sure I was ready to take the plunge. But Fred was different in so many ways, so kind, so thoughtful, so stable. He had a life and a career of his own, things he believed in and wanted to share. He wasn't a spoiled playboy or a swell-headed star. He didn't want to possess me or control me . . . And I loved him, and he loved me.

We rushed to arrange the details. There was no time to waste. I invited Lorry Sherwood and called my close friend, Virginia Grey, to ask her to be my bridesmaid. Cheryl and my mother completed the wedding party. Meanwhile Fred looked for a minister and a place for the wedding. Several ministers he called refused to marry us because we'd both been divorced. Finally Fred's friend who managed the Miramar Hotel in Santa Monica found a Baptist minister to perform the ceremony. He also provided champagne and hors d'oeuvres for our little reception in a suite in the hotel. As his best man Fred chose George Mann, a well-known comedian, who had become my good friend, too. We went to choose rings from a jeweler friend of Fred's who agreed to open his shop for us on Sunday.

Not that I was anticipating the women's rights movement, but I changed the traditional 'love, honor, and obey' to 'love, honor, and respect.' It seemed a far more fitting way to describe the life I had with Fred. And throughout our marriage I never lost that feeling, the respect I had for Fred.

He brought out a whole new side of me, a more natural side. Not only did I get my hands dirty mucking out stalls at the ranch, but we'd go marlin fishing in La Paz Bay off Baja, California. Or we'd go stream fishing, and Fred made me bait my own hooks. I'd take off my boots and roll up my jeans and wade right in, slippery rocks and all. And we cooked whatever we caught, trout mostly. But Fred couldn't make me clean them. Sometimes we'd go to a trout farm in Pomona, a town in the beautiful mountains, and in those days we'd pay $1.25 for half a day's easy fishing. It was strictly for beginners, but marvelous fun. They'd rent us rods and reels and we'd buy our bait, little worms or cheese. Did you know that trout love cheese?

Once in a while I'd catch sight of myself and do a double-take. I'd be wearing jeans and a big parka, with a knitted cap if it was really cold. And my face would be shiny clean, with no makeup at all, maybe just a dab of lipstick. And I'd think, 'Is this Lana Turner, glamorous star of the screen?' But it was me, another Lana Turner, and Fred had introduced me to her.

Back at the ranch, I'd paint furniture and plant trees—I'd always had a handyman or gardener for that. I even mowed the sheep meadow, although I made them get rid of the snakes first. Fred was good for me. He was my husband but also my best friend.

So why didn't I stay with Fred? Well, I suppose we each had quirks that the other simply couldn't tolerate. For example, Fred was perfectly punctual and well organized and demanded these qualities in others. Virginia Grey once called him 'the cruise director.' When it came to my work I believed in punctuality, too, but at other times . . . if I didn't *really* want to do something or *really* want to go somewhere, some perverse streak of rebelliousness sometimes made me stall. Maybe it was a hangover from my childhood, when I resisted the chores that were forced on me. Whenever Fred and I went out casually with people we really liked, and I could wear a comfortable pair of slacks, I was ready in no time. It was only when I was faced with some public function, where the spotlight would hold me in its remorseless glare and I would be stared at by the curious, that my shyness took over and I'd spend hours doing over my makeup, arranging and rearranging my hair, changing my outfits. The excuse was that I had to be perfect, but the real reason was that I was scared.

When I was shooting I had to be meticulously groomed, with every hair in place, every inch of clothing free of tucks and wrinkles. The most important tool of my trade was a mirror. I always had a three-way, full-length mirror placed outside my trailer door so that I could check my appearance before I went on the set. Once I was sure that I looked my best, I would forget all about it and buckle down to work. Then it would be up to the others—the makeup and hair people who stood by on the set, always ready to remedy any fault they spotted. It was their job now, and I let them handle it.

222

In public I knew that eyes would always be on me, and sometimes less than friendly eyes. Photographers would be ready to pounce on any spontaneous gesture, and the gossips would document what I was wearing. I took great care to maintain my appearance even offscreen, to make sure it conformed to the image that had built up over the years. Often I preferred to stay home rather than face the chore of getting ready to be on display.

Sometimes, if we were going to sit-down dinner, Fred would say to me, 'Honey, lay out all your clothes for tonight at ten in the morning, get everything out—clothes, shoes, jewelry; take your shower at noon, so that all you'll have to do is get dressed. We'll leave at six.' Still, I must confess we'd be lucky to be able to leave by eight.

I can understand why Fred found my fastidiousness one of the penalties of being married to me. But that constant problem of time, of being on time for Fred, caused me hellish anxiety. When I was working at a studio I couldn't always insist that I be finished by six. Even if we completed shooting, my co-workers sometimes pressed me into that obligatory one for the road. I couldn't always estimate what time I'd get home.

While Fred and I were married, I made a picture at Paramount called *Who's Got the Action?* Dean Martin was my costar, and he believed in the value of time a lot less than I did. In his happy-go-lucky way, he paid little attention to the shooting schedule. Instead of the ordinary one-hour lunch break, he would stretch his into two or three.

Dean kept urging me to join his group for lunch, which he usually took in the bungalow reserved for him on the lot. I went there once, to find the place filled with his cronies. There was much mixing of martinis and a lot of heavy Italian food. 'Drink up,' Dean kept saying, 'drink up.' I accepted one martini, then seeing there was more drinking going on than eating, I filled some plates with food and brought them back to Lorry and Helen Young in my dressing room. It was some hours before Dean strolled onto the set as though he had just decided to drop in on us. All the director could do to make up for lost time was to keep us working well into the evening. Late again!

After one of these late sessions I was riding home with Lorry Sherwood when I suddenly began shaking. She was alarmed until I told her I wasn't sick. It was just that I knew I was late, and I so much dreaded having to face Fred.

223

Fred hadn't been himself for weeks; he was morose, uncom-municative, withdrawn. I was really worried. Was it something I had done? Was he seeing another woman? I pleaded with him to tell me what was wrong. It took me a long time and a lot of hard work to pry it out of him, but at last he admitted, with his head in his hands, that he was in serious need of $5,000. Everything he had was tied up for the moment, and he wasn't, as they say in business, liquid.

'Oh, if that's all,' I breathed in relief. 'Well, honey, I'll lend it to you.'

He wouldn't hear of it; he didn't want it; he wouldn't take it. It wasn't an act. Fred's masculinity cringed at accepting even a short-term loan from his wife. But I insisted and finally he agreed. He even drew up a businesslike document setting the duration of the loan at three weeks.

Now we come to one of the great puzzlements of my life.

It was only a few days later that Fred, George Mann, and I went out to dinner together. Fred insisted on stopping at a Cadillac dealership, claiming he needed some parts for his Caddy. At that time we were a two-Caddy family; each of us owned a black Cadillac. I didn't even want to get out of the car, but Fred insisted and, taking me by the hand, led me through a maze of offices and out onto the lot where all the new cars were parked. A bright spot-light was shining up ahead, and I remember remarking caustically, 'Is this another supermarket opening?' But when we came closer, I saw that an actual klieg light was shining straight on a brand-new white Caddy, decked out with a huge blue bow on its hood.

'Somebody's going to be getting a present,' I said, innocently.

Fred beamed at me. 'It's yours, darling.'

Mine? What was he saying? I didn't understand. I looked from the car to Fred, who was nodding at me, then to George, who was grinning, then back to the car again, then to Fred, and all of a sudden anger exploded inside me.

'How *dare* you do that to me!' I raged, and Fred realized that I was really, really mad.

To this day, I can't tell you what actually happened. Did Fred borrow $5,000 from me and immediately put a car on order for me? Were his business problems solved much sooner than he'd expected? Was the car a repayment of the loan, made in a cute kind of way, or was Fred paying *interest* on the loan in advance with the gift of the car? Did he really *have* business problems? I'll never

224

know, because I didn't give Fred a chance to tell me any of the answers to any of these questions.

Instead I went into a fury. I wouldn't look at the car, let alone get into it. I wouldn't touch my dinner. I didn't want Fred to bring that car back to the house. I never wanted to see that car again. I already *had* a Cadillac! All the way back to Malibu I yelled at Fred, and by the time we reached home we were in the middle of a battle royal that broke up our marriage.

I was wrong. I admit it. Whatever my first reaction was—and it was confusion more than anything else—I should have given Fred a chance to tell his side of the story. But I was too angry to listen. I felt used. I felt cheated. I felt stupid. Here I'd been worrying my head off about my husband, happy and relieved when he finally told me that it was money trouble, which was something we could deal with. And now to be faced with a car I didn't want and didn't need! Well, it threw me, and I overreacted. Overreacted, hell! I exploded. I wasn't thinking clearly, and I was wrong.

I flew off to Juarez and got a divorce. But when I came back, Fred and I began seeing each other as friends, and we've been friends ever since, dear friends. But who knows? Maybe if I hadn't been so hot-headed, maybe if I hadn't been so ready to jump to conclusions, Fred and I might still be married today.

Maybe.

I moved into a Malibu hotel complex while trying to decide where to live. Then Fred came across a house in the Malibu Colony, a private enclave along the shore. The colony was a colorful grouping of beach-style homes with walls of glass, sundecks, and glazed tile chimneys—one of the most exclusive sections because of the splendid, sweeping surf front. Fred advised me to buy there, so I took the house, with its ninety-five feet of private beach. Today its sands are literally worth their weight in gold. I redid the house and put in a swimming pool. I lived there for the next seven years.

But before the divorce deeper problems had surfaced with Cheryl. Her defiance had a tough edge that made her impossible to control. For her seventeenth birthday I had presented her with a Ford Thunderbird. Late at night she would sneak out of the house to meet her friends, and they would roll her car out of the garage and onto the road. We were still living in the five-bedroom Spanish-style house we'd rented, and Cheryl's bedroom was on the far side, over the garage. There was a back staircase. Fred and I never knew she was gone until one night the police brought her home. They had picked her up wandering alone in a rather notorious place called Tuna Canyon.

Technically she was still a ward of the court until she turned eighteen, and I told her I would stand for rebelliousness no longer. Fred and I talked to her parole officer, and at his suggestion we sent her to a psychiatrist. As I talked with him I began to realize that Cheryl still had deep-rooted emotional difficulties, and I wanted her to have the best help possible. He advised us to send her to the respected Institute for Living in Hartford, Connecticut. Cheryl, Fred, and I flew out to see it and Cheryl was impressed enough to stay.

It proved to be a wise decision. After eight months there, Cheryl began to appreciate her own intelligence and to use her innate abilities. With that, her behavior changed. She developed an interest in Stephan's restaurant business, which by then had become enormously successfully. So she entered the Cornell University hotel and restaurant management school and graduated with straight *A*'s. She became one of Stephan's partners; later she moved to Honolulu, where she lives today, a highly successful businesswoman in real estate. I now spend more and more time in Hawaii, and whenever I'm with Cheryl I'm impressed at how effectively she's taken charge of her life. It's been a long, hard journey for her, but she's made it—made me proud, too, to be her mother. Late in 1981 I bought an apartment in Honolulu, and can now look forward to sharing some of my grown daughter's life as a mother and a friend.

21

O NE DAY late in 1962 Bob Hope called me up to offer me a trip to the Far East. He had invited me along before on his annual holiday visits to troops overseas, but I'd always been busy filming. Now I was free and delighted to accept. I'd always wanted to see Japan, and the two-week tour would also take us to Okinawa, the Philippines, Guam, and Korea. But as it turned out we were so busy that I seldom managed more than three hours of sleep at night, and I caught my few glimpses of Japan from the windows of cars and helicopters.

I created a minor international incident at Panmunjom on the border between North and South Korea. As I stepped off our helicopter I saw some North Korean soldiers standing impassively on their side of the fence. I gave them a friendly wave and a smile. They stayed expressionless, except for one soldier whose lips twitched in a suppressed grin.

'Miss Turner!' a shocked American officer said, 'we don't do that!'

Bob then explained to me that protocol required us not to acknowledge their presence in any way.

'You'd think they'd at least smile a little,' I said.

Bob cracked, 'They probably saw my last picture.'

The trip was a continual grind of shows for the troops, receptions for officers, and dinners with local officials. By the time we reached Taipei my voice had given out. I had to carry my own microphone and croak my lines into it. But one night my throat was so raw that I couldn't speak at all. An Army doctor offered to fix me up, and he sprayed my throat just before the show. When I got onstage, not a sound came out. The doctor had sprayed it with novocaine! But I had no regrets about the tour except for missing Japan. When it was over I took some R and R of my own in Hawaii. My mother flew there with me, but we missed Cheryl. So we called her and persuaded her to join us. After she got there, we all missed Fred! He was harder to persuade than Cheryl, but the 'cruise director' finally gave in and joined us, organizing our days and escorting us out

227

at night. Yes, Fred. Mother, Cheryl and I—we all still cared for Fred.

Once I returned to the house in Malibu, life continued, in essence, as a long vacation while I waited for the right script to come along. It was a quiet time, made somewhat livelier by the life of the beach colony—swimming, sunning, entertaining. I made friends with one man, a casual sort who made no romantic demands on me but who always seemed to be around during cocktail hours. After a while he brought his friends to the house, and soon he was running my social life. He even tended bar.

He wanted to invest in a business, and he asked me for a loan in return for an interest. I sent his proposal on to Jess Morgan, who thought the idea was sound. So I loaned him roughly $6,000 and he went off to New York to work out the details.

While he was gone a young man, Robert Eaton, who was part of my crowd during that period, stopped in to see me. He was friendly with my new business partner, whom I'll call Larry, and also with Clint and Maggie Eastwood.

As I made him a drink he fidgeted. I didn't know him very well, so I tried to make small talk to put him at ease. But he still seemed uncomfortable. Finally I asked him what was wrong.

'Well,' he said, 'I have to tell you. You're quite a person, and I don't like what's being done to you.'

'What do you mean?'

'It's Larry,' he said. 'I know about that business deal. You should know that he's not in New York.'

He went on to report that Larry was in Palm Springs. And what had he done with my money? He'd bought himself a Cadillac, and he was driving around telling people I'd bought it for him.

'And people now think you're keeping him,' Bob concluded.

His story utterly appalled me. I simply couldn't believe it was true. But Bob's sincerity convinced me, and I was touched that he'd compromised his friend to protect me. I wasn't all that surprised that once again I'd take someone at face value and had ended up the loser. When, oh when would I ever learn?

Finally Larry resurfaced in Malibu as though nothing had happened, and his stories about New York didn't seem to ring true. So I confronted him with Bob's story, not mentioning who'd told me of course, and told him he'd better steer clear of me or I'd report him to the police. Larry disappeared from my life, but I gained a new friend in Bob.

228

His full name was Robert P. Eaton, and he came from a solid Virginia family. His father was a retired Navy captain. Ten years younger than I, he was handsome and athletic. Like so many good-looking young men, he'd come to California to act but had little success. I'd heard that he had squired certain actresses around town, among them Ginger Rogers. At the time I met him he wanted to become a film producer. He was close friends with Clint Eastwood, who hadn't yet really broken onto the screen successfully. He and Clint planned several films that sounded both commercially solid and interesting to me.

Maybe if I had been working then I wouldn't have spent so much time with Bob. But the scripts coming in to my agent seemed too shoddy to consider. I decided to wait until Ross Hunter put together a project that Paul Kohner and I had found, a remake of *Madame X*. So while I was waiting I had a kind of never-ending social season. Bob was always attentive, full of humor and gossip, and he just couldn't seem to do enough for me. It was a combination of qualities that had ensnared me before. And it worked again. I fell for him.

Not only his charm impressed me. Speaking frankly, Bob introduced me at long last to the real, fulfilling pleasure in sex. Sex, as I've said, had never been a compelling need for me, and I often pleaded that familiar headache. What I always looked for was romance, the excitement of it, rather than sex. At forty-three, after five husbands and a few lovers, I finally experienced passion for the first time. The way he made love was new to me—nothing crude or unusual, it was sensual, gentle, and sensitive. I felt adored, womanly, and beautiful. There was something a little innocent about it—sometimes we'd break off, laughing—but Bob always knew how to rekindle the passion.

In time Bob and I became inseparable, despite the difference in our ages. It troubled me a little—maybe that's old-fashioned—but he insisted that to him it wasn't important. He wanted to be with me always, he said, and the feeling was mutual. I wasn't surprised when he asked me to marry him, but I postponed making a decision.

After almost two years, Ross Hunter finally completed his work on the remake of *Madame X*, and production was under way. I liked the character Holly Anderson, the neglected young wife driven to infidelity then prostitution and alcoholism, but she aged twenty years in the course of the story. That meant five different hair colors and many makeup changes, all squeezed into a tight production schedule. Worse yet, the changes weren't progressive because the film wasn't shot in sequence. Sometimes I had to age decades in a single day.

In my most critical scene I lay on my deathbed in prison, having been convicted of killing a blackmailer. I had been defended in court by my own son, but never suggested that I was his mother until my dying moment. It was a real five-handkerchief scene. When we shot it the crew was in tears, and even the director's eyes were red. I cry when I see it on television now, as though someone else were playing Madame X.

To prepare for the role of the broken old woman, the first thing Del did was to turn my chair away from the mirror. When he finished with my makeup I was afraid to look. 'You've got to,' Del insisted, and when he turned the chair around and I saw my reflection I started to scream. What a horrifying sight, that strange, aged face! I didn't want to leave the trailer. Finally they were calling and I couldn't delay any longer. But when I left for the set I hid my face in a scarf.

One day I finished a scene at two and had to shoot another one at four. My character gained or lost—I can't remember which anymore—twenty years in those two hours. That meant a major makeup change, and they had to redye my hair. There was no way I'd make that four o'clock call.

Del told the assistant director, who agreed that shooting should be postponed. But when Ross heard about the delay he hit the ceiling. He stormed into the dressing room, raging that the schedule had to be maintained, we were on a tight budget, we had to work faster, and so on. Everyone tried to explain the problem but Ross was too angry to listen. He was driving me to exasperation and tears.

I'd been wiping off my makeup with a tissue. In frustration I tossed it at the mirror and said, 'Oh, fuck it.'

That was all Ross needed to hear. 'Did you say "fuck you"?' he exploded. 'Do you realize you just said "fuck you" to the producer of this picture?'

'Ross,' I said, 'I didn't say "fuck you," I said "fuck it."'

'I heard you,' he shouted. 'You said "fuck you."'

He was raving with anger, and he kept repeating over and over, 'She said "fuck you."' No one could persuade him that he had misheard it. Finally he spun on his heel and marched out the door of the trailer—and right into my three-way mirror. Confronted by three images of himself, he didn't know which way to turn. 'How do I get out of here?' he screamed. Red-faced with laughter, the assistant director grabbed him and led him back to the set, where the rest of the cast, who had caught sight of the floundering, outraged Ross, were doubled over with laughter.

Humiliated, Ross jumped into my waiting limousine and sped away—I guessed where—to the executive offices. Even though the situation was hilarious, I realized Ross's anger might have serious repercussions. So I called Ed Muhl and told him my side of the story.

That's all there was to the incident, but somehow the press reported that I was the temperamental star who had driven Ross to distraction. Actually he'd been driven home, probably in my limousine. I heard later he went straight to bed. He may have been coming down with something, anyway. During the final eight weeks of shooting, he never appeared on the set again.

At the close of production I sent Ross an arrangement of lemons in an elegant epergne. Ross loved lemons during that time, and his house was filled with real and artificial ones of every kind. When we met again, the quarrel was forgotten, and we were friends once more.

By 1965, I conquered my misgivings and married Bob Eaton at his family's home in Arlington, Virginia. I knew I would have to support him for a while, but I expected his production plans to come through eventually. Besides, he'd given me happiness, so money didn't matter. I was the perfect picture of a silly grown woman in love.

I bought him a car and dressed him well, I must say. I rented him a handsome office suite on Sunset Boulevard, as his production headquarters, and furnished it beautifully. When I got tired of digging into my pocketbook, I put him on an allowance of $2,500 per month out of which he would pay the office rent, the secretary, and his own bills for clothing, gasoline, whatever. I am sure it made him feel more independent. As for me—well, I just looked the other way.

22

IN JUNE 1967 I made a three-week USO 'handshake' tour to Vietnam. At that time the popular sentiment against that war was just beginning, but my work consumed my life so completely that I never got involved in politics. I didn't go over to take a stand for or against anything. I simply went to bring cheer to American men and women who were stationed far away from home.

Before I left I filled a huge trunk with $5,000 worth of presents. That trunk traveled with me wherever I went, by jeep, by truck, or by helicopter, so I could distribute gifts to the nurses and the wounded. I felt a bit like Santa Claus squeezed into his tightly packed sleigh. When I gave the men Polaroid cameras they immediately snapped my picture, and I loved seeing the nurses' faces when they received cosmetics and other feminine frills.

Shortly after I arrived I sprained my ankle badly, and for a while I was wheeled around in a chair. Even so, I got a good glimpse of the strange jungle war when I was flown over enemy terrain in a helicopter. A Captain Paul saw to my security and arranged for me to visit the Montagnards, a remarkable mountain people whose primitive culture intrigued me. It was an unforgettable experience to visit their simple houses, built on piles, and to observe their village rituals, including fertility rites and ancestor worship. I even went through one of their rituals myself (no, not the fertility rite!) and I have the bracelet to prove it. I'd better not describe it or I might be breaking tribal taboos, but I *can* tell you that it was a test of courage, strength, and endurance, and it involved drinking a nameless, indescribably acrid substance out of a vat, not once but three times! How I got through it I'll never know; but at least they didn't cut a chicken's throat over my head, as they did with others who undertook it. That I don't think I could have survived!

When I returned Bob spent the night with me at the San Francisco military base. I was so keyed up by what I'd seen that I wanted to talk all night. I was surprised that Bob didn't take much interest in my adventures. He fell asleep, while I lay awake in the dark.

Back home in the Malibu Colony house I spent a few days resting. I have never before appreciated home so much and the comforts of American life. I kept rattling on about the trip to anyone who would listen, describing the lush greenery and the tiny hamlets I'd seen. My mother listened patiently for a day or so until I finally realized she had something important on her mind.

When I asked her what was wrong, tears came to her eyes. 'Lana, this place was a madhouse while you were gone,' she said. 'The parties didn't stop from the moment you stepped on the plane.'

But that wasn't all. The maid had been so appalled by the debauch that she had saved my sheets as evidence. I was sickened by the lipstick smears and stains on the linens from my own bed. I went straight to the phone and dialed Bob at the office.

'Get home fast,' was all I said.

He raced home, and I was waiting there with the sheets in a pile at my feet. When he saw them he mumbled lame protests and confused explanations. Then he realized that I didn't believe him, and he began to plead earnestly, assuring me that he loved me, he needed me, and only me. By now I recognized lines like that— maybe I was beginning to wise up. Infidelity was bad enough. I've never been able to stand that. But in my own bed!

In a couple of hours he had packed and gone. I was too angry to cry. All I could do was literally beat my head against the wall and curse myself as a fool. I vowed that I'd never see Bob again, never trust any man ever again. But in the words of the song, I always pick myself up, dust myself off, and start all over again. It wasn't long before Bob was back, and I was giving it one more try.

How Bob met Harold Robbins I don't know even to this day. One afternoon at the country club I found myself shaking his hand. Although it was nearly ten years since the happening, his exploitation had kept it alive in a distorted version he had hardly had the grace to disguise. He had turned the worst tragedy of my life into a best-selling novel.

Surely Bob knew I hated the man, and we fought bitterly about the introduction. But then a short time later his name came up again. Bob was hired to do some minor job on a television project with Robbins. While I didn't approve, I was even more surprised when my agent Stan Kamen approached me about the most lavish

233

series ever concocted for television. And again, who was behind it? Harold Robbins.

I had considered seeking television work, and I had shifted my representation back to William Morris because so much was changing in the movie world that I had known. Stan was my agent now and he strongly urged me to consider the project. 'Let bygones be bygones, Lana. This could be the turning point of your career.'

It's said in Hollywood that you should always forgive your enemies, because you never know when you'll have to work with them. I wasn't about to forgive Harold Robbins yet. But Stan convinced me to look at the outline Robbins had prepared, and I could give him a definite answer then.

All Stan sent over was one triple-spaced page. For that Robbins supposedly made a million dollars! They wanted me to play Dolly, a troubled married woman with a habit of leaping into strange men's beds. I didn't mind playing a woman with marital problems, being something of an expert on the subject, but I didn't like all those affairs. My reputation was bad enough without that. Besides, I thought Dolly would be more sympathetic if her husband was unfaithful too. I called Stan back and told him that.

'Any other problems?' he asked.

'Well, I hate the name Dolly.'

'Make a suggestion.'

I pulled a name out of the blue. 'How about Tracy?' I said.

When he called me back later, he reported that Universal would make any changes I wanted. Then we began to talk wardrobes and figures and schedules . . . Before I knew it I was signed for twenty-six hour-long shows.

Many months went by but not a single script was written about the jet-set family of a banking tycoon. Writers were hired and fired every day, it seemed, and I spent long hours working with some of them. Before anyone ever developed a single show, we set off for the Riviera to shoot background scenes for the stories that would somehow evolve.

We hadn't been shooting there long before a nasty scene erupted between the producer, William Frye, and the costume designer, Luis Estevez. Frye had imbibed too heavily at a party, and suddenly he was dumping all his problems on poor Luis's head. As far as I knew Luis was blameless, so I stepped in to defend him. Then I became the brunt of Frye's ugly abuse. When he wouldn't let up, I slapped his face and he immediately slapped me back. Another

234

backhanded whack knocked me against the fender of my car. When I recovered from the shock of being clobbered, I told Frye to start packing. Luis stood frozen, and my chauffeur stood ready to take on Frye.

When we got back to the hotel I put ice on my face and called Grant Tinker, a Universal executive. Tinker had been sent to France by the studio to see what the hell was going on. 'I've had it,' I told him. 'Either Frye goes or I do. I've had enough.'

Tinker came over on the double to inspect my face; Frye was replaced, and we returned to California to shoot the interiors under a new producer and to see if the show was really going to continue. 'The Survivors' title was taking on an ironic ring. The sound grew more and more hollow when the scripts came in late, and more writers and directors were replaced. With the constant rewriting I'd get ten pages in the evening to memorize by the next morning, but when I arrived at the studio I'd get a brand-new version to use for the day's shooting.

Harold Robbin's million-dollar storyline all but disappeared. One director was hired just to glue scenes together and fill in the hour with action sequences from other films—that was at the end. We only shot fifteen episodes of the proposed twenty-six. Luis Estevez walked out in a huff because an interviewer reported that I'd called his costumes matronly—at least *she* said I told her that—and was replaced by the fine designer Nolan Miller. Nerves were frayed and tempers short as we all tried to pick our way through the shambles.

My marriage to Bob was not to survive. While we were on the Riviera his job on the production had left him time to whoop it up with some new female chums. His earlier infidelities had weakened our bond and now it finally snapped. We stayed in the same hotel for most of the location work, but we weren't speaking. By the time we got back to California, it was a foregone conclusion that we were through.

My divorce from Bob Eaton came through, and wouldn't you think I'd look carefully before leaping again? Not this impulsive character!

His name was Ronald Dante—and still is, I suppose. His real name was Ronald Peller, and he called himself a doctor, although of what I'm not exactly sure. He was a nightclub hypnotist, and I met him at one of the discothèques that were springing up all over

235

in Los Angeles. This one was called The Candy Store, and it was usually packed—discos then were either jammed or empty, depending on how 'in' they were. I was watching the dancers when I caught sight of Bob standing at the bar with a striking brunette. So when a tall man in white asked me to dance I didn't turn him down. I thought he was rather attractive, and as we chatted he described his nightclub act, which intrigued me. He asked if he could call me, and I gave him the number of my service. Sure enough, two days later he phoned.

I must admit that he had an original style of courtship. One day he appeared at my door on a motorcycle. I had never been on a motorcycle before, but I was game. He told me to climb on behind him and hold on tight. Then off we sped through the hills of Malibu. I loved it! Then there were times that we flew kites and took long walks on the beach. It was idyllic, thoroughly romantic. I hadn't learned my lesson yet, and, as you can guess, I was drifting.

He had a persuasive voice and strange, compelling eyes. My friends often wondered if he had hypnotized me somehow, but I don't think so. His personality was mesmerizing to a degree, but he was hardly a Svengali type. To me he was a welcome relief from the turmoil caused by my divorce and the disastrous television series.

Shortly after I met him he asked to marry me, but for once I knew I really didn't want to. After I declined he left for Arizona to do his nightclub act. Clever man, he didn't call me for a few lonely days. Sensing my mood, he again asked me to marry him. This time I agreed. Our wedding took place in Las Vegas. Why, oh why?

He claimed to have been brought up in Singapore and to have earned a doctorate in psychology there, but the press dug up something to debunk that. Shortly after our wedding he was shot at, or so he said, in an underground garage, by a gunman wearing an Australian bush hat. It got a lot of attention in the papers— maybe that was what he wanted. I asked him if he could help me stop smoking. But he said no, he would prefer not to hypnotize me. Some time later I was told one of his previous wives alleged that he (as Ronald Peller) had hypnotized her, married her, then bilked her out of her savings account. The judge, according to my source, annulled the marriage and gave her the money back.

Meanwhile, I sold the house where I'd lived with Bob Eaton and found another one to rent, with extensive grounds, high on Coldwater Canyon Drive. Life there would be completely different

236

from the easygoing, sun-worshiping party scene of the Malibu Colony. It was more isolated, more private, a handful of majestic modern and Spanish-style homes clinging to the mountainside, a stark, dramatic, setting. I was still struggling through 'The Survivors,' and I wanted peace.

Around this time I began looking for a new secretary. My trusted right hand, Lorry Sherwood, had left me a few years before, and I'd had a succession of replacements. None of them had been able to match Lorry's efficient organization and bright humor, and none had been quite as dependable. I felt rather lost without someone I could truly rely on at a time when major events in my life were changing. A new husband, a new house, and now I needed a new secretary—what would change next?

Some aspect of my life *had* to stabilize, so I looked hard for someone reliable. Finally I met Taylor Pero, who for the next ten years would help manage my life. I'm not sure what his qualifications were supposed to be, other than that he was personable and free at the moment. He'd never been a secretary of any kind before, but then I didn't need the usual kind of secretary, just someone to look after details. Taylor had toured for a few years with the Johnny Mathis troupe, and he had helped out on public relations work so he had some familiarity with show business. He wanted to become a singer on his own, and his voice was good though it lacked full professional training. Very likely the reason he applied for the job at all was that he would be working for a 'star,' and he'd meet the kind of people he hoped to cultivate.

He was in his late twenties, had been married and divorced, and had a small daughter who was then living with her mother. I'd heard that he was gay, and I mention this only because Taylor himself was frank about his private life. Whether someone is straight, gay, or neuter has little to do with employability in my business.

Dante sat in on our interview, his eyes as usual hidden behind the dark glasses he wore. I decided that Taylor gave off the right vibrations, and he even had the same astrological sign as mine. I offered him the job. He came to work for me in August 1969. One of his first tasks was to sort through those pink and blue and yellow and white pages, each color a different version of the same 'Survivors' script. But they wouldn't be rewriting much longer. The

237

series was clearly a disaster. I wasn't at all surprised when Stan Kamen called to say the studio had asked if I would settle my contract for fifty cents on the dollar.

Yet I still run into people who say, 'Miss Turner, I loved you in "The Survivors."' I did have some lovely costumes but I was told no one could make head or tail of the stories. Oddly, those fifteen episodes of the scheduled twenty-six are still shown in syndication now and then, and twelve years later, small residual checks flow in.

Taylor caught on very quickly to the kind of pressures I faced, and he became my guardian and protector. And he proved his value on one especially difficult occasion a week or two before the series folded. I had flown to San Francisco to be the guest of honor at a benefit for the Presbyterian Children's Hospital. A public relations man, Phil Sinclair, who had set up the affair, met us at the plane when we landed. We had arrived later than we'd arranged.

'Oh, thank God,' Sinclair said when he saw me, 'you've already changed for the evening, and we can go right to the dinner.'

But I was wearing a traveling costume, a black jersey jumpsuit, and over it a long red coat with a collar and border of black fox fur. 'No, I'm sorry,' I said, 'but I'm planning to change. And Doctor Dante is going to wear a dinner jacket.'

An escort sped us through the city and to our suite at the Mark Hopkins Hotel. By the time we changed and got to the Museum of Natural History, we'd missed dinner but the evening turned out well anyway. With the limousine still at our service, Dante, Taylor, Sinclair, and I went on a nightclub tour, and when we got back to the hotel I was hungry.

Sinclair offered to get some sandwiches and bring them to our suite. Dante said he'd go, too. I didn't see why it took two to get sandwiches, but I assumed Dante wanted to pay for them, and Taylor and I went upstairs alone. As I was getting undressed the phone rang, and Taylor went down to the lobby. He returned about fifteen minutes later. I could see by his face that something was wrong. Dante had disappeared, or so it seemed. As Taylor recounted his talk with the Sinclair, I grew heartsick with worry.

After the limousine dropped us off Dante had told the driver to stop and had simply gotten out and walked off. He didn't return that night, and Taylor and I sat up until morning waiting for word. The next day I called my house to see if he was there, but no one answered the phone. 'Why, why?' I kept asking. Taylor soothed my panic and offered to call the police. 'Not that,' I said. 'Not yet.'

The next day was Sunday, and I decided to wait it out in San Francisco, certain that Dante would contact me with some kind of explanation. I never suspected that I had been deserted by my husband of six months. Later, when it became clear, I was surprised by my ability to adjust to the knowledge and the situation. If that was his cowardly way of ending our marriage, all right. I felt more shock than sorrow. Deep down I knew I hadn't really wanted to marry him, but having been persuaded, I had tried my best to make it work.

It was a sparkling clear day, so Taylor and I decided to explore San Francisco. We wandered around that beautiful city between phone calls to the house and checking the hotel desk for messages. No word came, so at the end of the day all we could do was fly home.

The first thing I noticed when we got to the house was that Dante's motorcycle was gone. 'Maybe he's gone for a ride,' I said. I stood in the living room while Taylor searched the house for signs of Dante's presence. When he came back, he took me by the hand and said, 'Lana, you'd better come with me.'

The closets were empty, and so were the drawers. 'Now look at this,' Taylor said.

He led me into my bathroom. Taped to the mirror above the large marble sink was a note typed on my own blue stationery. It read, 'It's obvious that you have your thing to do, and I have mine, and I have to keep on doing it.' It was signed 'Muggs,' a name I'd never heard him use.

Taylor told me later that I gave a little gasp and slowly slid to the floor. He'd taken a cold washcloth and revived me. When I came to, he brought me to the living room and mixed me a drink. As we sat on the couch he turned to me and said, 'Lana, let me remind you of something. Friday at lunch you signed a check made out to him for thirty-five thousand dollars.'

Now I was really awake.

The check I'd written was a loan to set up Dante in business. He planned to invest in a 'stack sack,' a new kind of housing project. When he first brought up the idea, he claimed he didn't want to use my money. But then he babbled on about the project being such a good opportunity, and so on, and so on . . . Finally I just gave him the capital.

'All right,' he said, 'but only if we clearly specify that it's a loan.'

I had Jess Morgan draw up the necessary papers, and he wrote out the check to 'Tower Funding.' Of course, the coincidence of the loan and his disappearance aroused some justified suspicions.

Later I learned that Dante had stopped off at the Security Pacific National Bank on Friday afternoon and had drawn a number of cashier's checks on the $35,000. He made them out to several different people and drew one very large one for himself. Needless to say, none of the recipients was remotely connected to a housing project. On Monday the bank called to tell Jess Morgan about the withdrawals, and he informed them of Dante's misrepresentation, instructing them to stop payment immediately.

Charges were filed at once, but the case didn't come to trial until January 1972. Until then, the $30,000 or so that the bank had been able to recover had to remain in escrow. On the Monday following Dante's disappearance, I begged off work at the studio—with good cause, as I'd been up most of the previous night—and when the afternoon papers arrived I learned I'd been sued for divorce. I immediately filed a countersuit.

After 'The Survivors' folded, I was bored and depressed. I had no new films lined up, and the scripts I received were hardly worth reading. Taylor helped relieve the boredom by spending more time at the house, and eventually he moved into one of the guestrooms. After weeks of idleness—something unusual for me—I was delighted when, in February 1970, my interior decorator, Vince Pastere, invited me down for a week at his house in Palm Springs. Of course I brought Taylor along. We were all asleep in our respective beds when, around three in the morning, the telephone rang. It was Dante, of all people. Vince told him I was asleep, but Dante said it was urgent.

'I was thinking about you,' he said when I picked up the phone. 'I just had to hear your voice.'

'At three in the morning?'

He rambled on for a few minutes about how we should still be friends, how he missed me, and how sad it was that things hadn't worked out. 'This is crazy,' I thought to myself.

Then he wanted to know what I was wearing so he could 'visualize me,' and 'one other thing': How long would I be staying?

I told him three or four days.

'Have a good time,' he said.

In the morning I repeated the conversation to Taylor and Vince, saying it all sounded fishy to me. They didn't now what to think either. Dante's call had unnerved me so much that I suggested we cut our visit short and go home the next day. We pulled up to the house in my black Cadillac just as darkness fell. Taylor took the luggage out of the trunk; going into the house, he noticed that the doors to the pool were open. The wind was blowing the sheer draperies so that they billowed into the house.

I knew that Carmen, the maid who had replaced Arminda, would never have left the doors open. Now I was frightened. Taylor and I decided to call the police, and then we crept into the house cautiously, in case someone was hiding inside. Taylor led the way. Nothing was disturbed in the living room, but the bedroom we came in for a rude shock. My chest of drawers, which I always locked, had been pried open; and some of the contents were scattered all over the room.

But there was one special drawer that worried me. There I kept my most valuable jewelry when it wasn't in the vault. That secret drawer, too, had been roughly forced open. About $100,000 worth of jewelry was missing.

'Who knew about that particular little drawer?' Taylor asked.

I didn't answer. There was no need to; we both knew.

The jewelry was never recovered, and no one was ever charged with the theft.

When the divorce case finally came to trial, I had another surprise. My attorney presented a document stating that I would pay Dante $200,000 tax-free if we ever divorced. The paper was dated October 1, 1969, and although it bore my signature, I had certainly never seen it before. Fortunately the judge immediately suspected that something was amiss.

From the court records:

FINDINGS OF FACT

Dante carried out a pattern of acts maliciously designed by him to defraud, oppress, and victimize Turner and to take advantage of her trust in him. That pattern included . . .

(A) On or about October 1, 1969, Dante caused to be prepared a document purporting to obligate Turner to pay Dante the sum of $200,000 in cash or property should the parties ever get a divorce.

241

(B)   In addition, Dante caused to be prepared a document dated October 1, 1969, whereby Turner purported to grant to Dante the right to use Turner's name for various purposes and to sign her name to any document.

(C)   At some time during the period from October 1, 1969, to November 8, 1969, Dante surreptitiously, by false representation, obtained the signature, or a counterpart of the signature, of Turner on the documents described . . .

Need I go on? The final judgment charged Dante with malice, oppression, and fraud against me. He was assessed punitive damages—which were never collected, I might add. I would have had to track him down and sue him. It wasn't worth the bother or the cost.

So ended my marriages—and high time. Somebody asked me recently if I had ever sat down and added up what my husbands cost me in hard, cold cash. The question staggered me. Of course I hadn't! And I couldn't now, although I know that the figure must come to tens of thousands of dollars. With the exception of dear Fred May, who is still my good friend, all my husbands have taken, and I was always giving. Why? Well, I was always a giver, even as a little girl. If I had candy and you had none, I'd give you half of mine. If you admired a little ring on my finger, I'd pull it off and give it to you. I'm still that way; my friends have learned to be cautious about admiring one of my possessions, or they wind up carrying it home.

But that's an easy answer, one I've used all my life. Now I see that somewhere there was a pattern, something in me that made me choose takers, over and over again. Surely I should have learned that, when respect goes out the door, love flies out the window. So why did I lose respect again and again? I honestly don't know. Once would have been enough for some people.

Today things are very different, and I think they're healthier. People fall in love and move in together, and nobody bats an eye. They get to know each other first, to see if their romance can survive the mundane things like whether or not he picks up after himself, or she leaves hair in the sink. Or that all-important question of sharing expenses, each one pulling his or her weight. Honeymoon first, and if it lasts, then marriage. I like that.

242

With me the honeymoon never lasted. Something in me must have yelled 'patsy,' otherwise why would I have been taken advantage of again and again? Yes, I made mistakes, and when I did they were doozies. One thing I have to say about my husbands—all of them were able to make me laugh—at least at the beginning. I couldn't have married them otherwise. A keen sense of humor attracts me as strongly as good looks do. And thank God I could always laugh at myself. My disappointments haven't left me bitter. I've never lost a sense of youth and I've always loved a challenge. Certainly I'd had my share of those. And there were more to come.

23

B y spring 1971 I was unemployed again. And I'd turned fifty—the toughest age for an actress. I was a bit too mature to play a bubbling ingenue but certainly too young to be a frumpy dowager. Scripts still flooded in, but I read nothing even remotely suitable. I was waiting for a role with dignity, but with a little sparkle too.

Then one day Stan Kamen called with the perfect part. The script, *Forty Carats*, was clever and unusual, with moments of genuine comedy. I would play Anne Stanley, a glamorous forty-year-old divorcee (so, I was fifty—I looked ten years younger), who falls in love with a man of twenty-two. Talk about typecasting. The producers wanted me badly enough to be talking real money— $17,500 a week. Clearly the setup was ideal, but there was one hitch. It wasn't a movie or television script. It was a play.

A play! I'd never done live theatre, not even in school. I would have to perform in front of hundreds of people. After all my years in movies I still felt shy and nervous the first three days on the set. Only after those first nerve-racking days of profound anxiety did I begin to feel grounded enough to concentrate. How could I possibly do a play?

I called Stan back and told him to forget it. I'd be too terrified.

'Lana, this is hot,' he insisted. 'The producers are Lee Guber and Shelley Gross. And it's been running on Broadway for ages already, so it can't miss.'

The more Stan kept telling me what a great opportunity it would be, the more convinced I became that I couldn't do it. Finally he persuaded me to think it over one more day.

Taylor had become a fairly constant presence by then, and I used him as my sounding board. I told him I didn't know how to study for a play, didn't know if my memory for lines would hold up through a whole evening's performance. In films I'd start at the middle or even the end. If a line reading went wrong it could always be cut and redone. But Taylor assured me that my memory was good enough to swing it, and he liked the script, too.

'Oh, why don't you try it?' he said.

'Easy for you to say!'

There was also the matter of a director. For me the captain of the ship had always been my director. Never mind what the producer or anyone else would tell me, it was the director I obeyed. During filming everyone tried to put in his two-cents' worth, even the other actors. To listen to more than one person meant utter confusion. So I had learned to shut my mind to unsolicited advice. Whom could I trust to direct me on stage? I didn't know any directors of plays.

That day Dorothy Lamour, who was doing some stage work of her own, called to ask my advice on a makeup problem. Nervously I outlined the whole difficult decision to her. She laughed sympathetically at my anxiety, then delivered a brief answer: 'Get John Bowab.'

'Who?'

'He's a young director I've worked with. Don't accept anyone else,' she advised. 'Tell your agent that you want John Bowab because you know he's good, and you can say I said so.'

I phoned Stan and told him I would do the play on one condition, that it be directed by John Bowab. Stan hadn't heard of him, but he said he would talk to the producers. He called back a few days later. 'You've got John Bowab,' he said, 'and you're in the play.'

Now I couldn't back out, but I felt I had to meet Bowab. Stan set it up for a week later. Of course I was a bundle of raw nerves when the day finally came. I was sitting in my room agonizing when John arrived. I wanted to greet him with a semblance of professionalism and composure, but it took me a while to pull myself together. Quite a while, I'm sorry to say. I kept him waiting twenty minutes in my own home.

When I finally dragged myself out to greet him, I recognized the tall, handsome man. I had met him briefly when he had directed Ann Miller in *Mame* at the Huntington Hartford Theater in Los Angeles. He reminded me that when I complimented him on his directing he had offered to do a play with me sometime. I had told him, 'That'll be a cold day in hell!'

We both laughed at that, and I felt so reassured that I decided to confess my fears to him. I explained that I'd never done a play, that I didn't know how to study for a play . . .

245

'Well,' he interrupted, 'just start reading it with me. I'll take the young man's part.'

He listened carefully to my voice as we ran through the first page. He patiently corrected my reading and explained what to stress on the stage. How embarrassing, for a veteran like me, to have my voice criticized. But he laughed away my mistakes and tried to put me at ease. When we finished the page, I begged off for the day.

'Why?' he asked. 'It's early. Let's do another page. We're going to have to get started and now is as good a time as any.'

With another page finished, I put the book down again. 'I really can't handle any more today.'

'I understand,' he said. 'But, tell me, how do you think this woman thinks? Just explain her to me—how you feel she might react in certain situations.'

I hadn't yet analyzed the play to that degree, but John guided me, step by step. He stayed in Los Angeles for five weeks on his own initiative, and we worked every day for two or three hours. And because stage work requires endurance—it is tiring to stand up there in front of the audience, concentrating intensely, maintaining perfect control—he encouraged me to get myself physically in shape. I took long walks on the beach, saying my lines over the traffic noises and the sound of the waves, to give me more lung power and better voice projection. I took modern dance classes and exercise classes, to make my legs stronger and to give me more stamina. I began to be revitalized and, little by little, to feel better about the whole thing.

Meanwhile Nolan Miller designed fourteen extravagant costumes for me, plus two special gowns for taking my bows. Usually bow gowns were worn only for musicals, but John and I agreed they would provide an elegant touch. The fittings in Nolan's salon took endless hours, and I drove the poor fitters crazy with my usual perfectionism. But, if people were going to pay to see Lana Turner, by God, they were going to get Lana Turner.

The rehearsals were set for June. I arrived in New York a week early with the kind of entourage unknown to theater people. I brought Taylor, of course, and my own hairdresser and makeup man, and I'd asked Nolan to stand by to fly out on a moment's notice if I needed him. To me it was well worth the expense to have my familiar team with me. For security's sake I brought extra pairs of shoes and ten specially made wigs. If I was nervous—and surely I would be—my head would perspire, and I would have to change wigs often.

Everything was ready, I had my character and my lines fixed in my mind, but the night before rehearsals began I couldn't sleep a wink. I kept tossing around in bed, turning on the light to reread the play, tormented by fears of meeting the cast. Would I fall on my face? Would I miss my cues? Would they judge me as a rank amateur on the stage, unable to meet the demands of a live audience? I was still awake at six in the morning when I called John in a panic. 'Look,' I said, 'I haven't slept. I have a headache and a stomachache. You go ahead with the others and I'll start tomorrow.'

He simply roared with laughter. 'I'll be at the Plaza at ten to pick you up,' he said. 'And don't worry—everyone's as nervous as you are.'

When he came to get me, I was still fussing with my hair and trying on yet another outfit. I begged him to let me wait until lunch. But he took me firmly by the arm and marched me down to the lobby, encouraging me all the way. When we got downstairs I asked Taylor to call for the limousine. But John made me walk the five blocks down to the Broadway Arts Studios. He simply grasped my hand and started walking. He made me take long steps, and I went, protesting all the way, as the empty limousine followed us.

Finally we reached the rehearsal hall, where I met the rest of the cast. As John had said, they were as bashful as I was. Soon we were all chatting around the long Formica table, eating doughnuts and drinking coffee from paper cups. It was a far cry from Ross Hunter's lavish, flower-filled sets. I could hardly believe that all major plays were rehearsed in such ordinary surroundings. But by lunchtime I was concentrating so intensely that I didn't even want to break.

I found out the cast had accepted me a few days later, when John was rehearsing me with Honey Sanders. Honey had stopped in the middle of a line, her face frozen in a blank stare. John took her aside, and later he said to me, 'Do you know what Honey told me?' he said. 'I asked her what had happened and she said, "I just can't believe it. I just can't believe that I'm saying these lines to *Lana Turner!*" '

During the rehearsals in New York, every one of my lunch hours was taken up by interviews across the street in a little restaurant. When I should have been resting and taking some food, these press people were asking me all kinds of what to me seemed dumb

247

questions. I'd try to give honest and simple answers about this new phase of my career. I'd return to rehearsals in a daze, pick up a scene where we'd left off and find I hardly knew my own name, much less my lines. I had to apologize to the cast. So that first week of rehearsals was hellish for me, and I couldn't wait to get out of New York and start rehearsing in Shady Grove, Maryland, where our opening was to be. Naturally John was furious at the producers who were behind the interview sessions.

We completed rehearsals in the banquet room of a hotel in Shady Grove, which was not far outside Washington, and then opened at a huge theater in the round. My mother flew in for it. I had heard that all the Washington press was there. During the first five minutes I could hear the audience buzzing. It almost threw me. 'You have to do this,' I ordered myself and kept away from the footlights. I forced myself to look out at the audience but not see them there, as though it were only the darkened set that stretched away from the stage. And somehow I choked down my fear and got through it.

Finally the curtain fell. I raced backstage to put on my bow gown. Another moment of anxiety. Which one should I wear? They were magnificent, but they each weighed about thirty pounds. Finally I chose one, put it on, and ran up the ramp to greet the audience not as my character, but as myself.

How can I describe that exhilarating moment, that unbelievable, overwhelming outpouring of love? The roar of the applause, the whistles, as the audience, in a single mass, shot from their seats. I was dazed, deafened, and on the verge of grateful tears. *Time* magazine remarked in a review that, when I took my bows, it was as though the president had walked in and the Marine band had struck up 'Hail to the Chief.'

Ironically, live theater, the medium I had so dreaded, became the new backbone of my working life. I took *Forty Carats* to Westbury, Long Island; Philadelphia, Chicago, Valley Forge, and Baltimore. Later on I starred in *The Pleasure of His Company*, with Louis Jourdan, then went on the road for ten weeks in *Bell, Book, and Candle*.

As I continued with dinner theater work, Taylor asked to be listed on the programs as producer, but that was out of my hands. He was listed as my personal manager, to mollify him. Writing about Taylor Pero is not easy. Perhaps I shouldn't even include him in my story, but how can you exclude a decade of your life?'

Taylor was with me night and day for ten years. We worked together, played together, did everything, in fact, except sleep together. And we had some wonderful times. He was a bright, amusing companion and very protective of me. We went to Hawaii, where he took me to a gay bar in Waikiki—my first time in a gay bar and I had a ball. We'd dress up and go dancing. Once we even rented a helicopter to go to the Renaissance Fayre, and we 'buzzed' the fairgrounds in the 'copter, to the consternation of the management. Taylor was a good cook, and he'd whip up exotic and complicated dishes like ratatouille for my guests.

But here was a dark side to the relationship, and it began to grow larger and darker, until it all but eclipsed the sunny side. I've said Taylor was protective of me, but little by little he grew *too* protective. Perhaps he thought it was my wish to avoid people and pressures, but he began keeping people away from me, even people I wanted and needed to see. Sharing my life, he felt a need to control it. Part of that feeling arose out of his own ambition to be a singing star and his frustration when that ambition wasn't fulfilled. It's only my opinion, but I think he grew tired of standing in Lana Turner's shadow and wanted to push me aside and take my place.

The drinking was a large part of the control. I'm not pretending that I never took a drink before Taylor, but I'm a sipper, not a drinker. Even today, when I drink only fruit juice, I can sit in front of a filled glass for hours without the level of the liquid going down an inch. And that was also true when there was vodka in the glass. But Taylor would always take my drink away 'to freshen it,' as he said, and bring it back topped up with so much vodka it would make me choke. Taylor himself drank a great deal, and he wasn't a good drinker. When he got drunk he often became abusive, and once he even slapped me. There were clashes between us, and I sometimes wondered who was the employer and who the employee.

I continued to depend on him to get me to where I was going and on time, and I admit it wasn't always easy for him. My depression was growing, and so was my dependence on alcohol, and they fed upon each other.

Taylor look to deciding who I should and shouldn't see, who I should talk to on the telephone, what scripts I ought to be reading. He even turned down projects in my name without ever consulting me! At the end, I wasn't living my own life—Taylor Pero was.

249

Toward the close of 1979 I was appearing at a series of 'tributes' for the benefit of San Francisco's children. Two Chinese-American community groups were preparing a television show called *Bean Sprouts*, and these tributes, held in different cities, would help raise the production money for the series. Attorney Melvin Belli and his wife, Lia, were good friends of mine, were on the same committee for the tributes, and Phil Sinclair was the producer.

As usual Taylor handled my travel arrangements, hotel accommodations, and press interviews for the five-city tour. He was drinking, and while we were in Miami, he learned that his daughter had run away with a boy and couldn't be found. It made him so distraught he threw a telephone through the hotel window. By the time we got to Atlanta, he was drinking very heavily, and I asked him to stop. In reply, he attacked me physically, shoving me to the ground. Without thinking, I brought my knee up sharply and got him in the groin; only then was I able to push him away. I scrambled to my feet, ran to the bedroom, and looked the door. Then I called Eric Root, my hairdresser and trusted friend, on the phone, and he came running.

In the presence of Lia Belli, Eric Root, and Phil Sinclair, I asked Taylor for my keys back, the keys to my house and my car that I had entrusted to him so long before.

'Take them, bitch!' he raged, and threw them straight at my head. That big bunch of keys missed me by an inch.

'That's it!' I yelled back. 'You're fired! Now, get out!'

I never saw him again.

Last year, I was fortunate enough to have two great honours paid to me. In September 1981, I flew to Paris with Eric Root on my way to the Deauville Film Festival in the south of France. There, along with Joseph Mankiewiecz and Arthur Hiller, I was honoured with a retrospective of my films. Eric had never seen Paris and I longed to see it again, and after a glorious two and half days we made the beautiful drive down and along the coast to Deauville. After the gala, I made an appearance on the evening they showed *The Postman Always Rings Twice*. There were photographers there from all over the world, and were those flashbulbs popping! I had just come back from Honolulu, and I was wearing a deep summer tan and dressed entirely in red from head to toe—red silk pants suit, very dressy, with a deep V neck.

250

'You'll notice I'm all in red tonight,' I told the audience. 'You won't be seeing this in the film,'—this was a reference to the well-known fact that as Cora I appear entirely in white—'so I did it as a little surprise for you.' And how they applauded.

On October 25, 1981, the National Film Society selected me as one of the recipients of an Artistry in Cinema award. Because of a disaster that befell the dress I made for the occasion—it was unaccountably miles too big for me, cut entirely wrong—I had to have another dress made, at top speed, at the last minute. At nine o'clock on the night of the awards, I was standing there in my jewels, with my hair and makeup done, still being sewn into the dress! This was something I didn't want to be late for, but late I was. I was the last honoree to arrive, and when I came in the door I got a standing ovation!

It took me forever to get to my table, and when I finally did and sat down out of breath, I said to Eric, 'Were they applauding for me or the fact that I finally got here!' But I was deeply honoured and very touched by the wonderful things said to me and about me and the warm reception I was given.

Early this year, I did a revival of *Murder Among Friends*, a play rewritten especially for me, at the Fiesta Dinner Playhouse in San Antonio, Texas. Before that, I did an episode of *Falcon Crest* on CBS-TV. At this writing, I'm about to take *Murder Among Friends* to a number of cities, touring it for the first time and, also for the first time, performing it in proscenium instead of in-the-round and dinner theaters.

I've been blessed with a full, varied and satisfying career.

And a long one.

Afterword
The Past Ten Years

I N 1980 I was on a serious downhill slide, in terrible health. I was playing *Murder Among Friends* in New Orleans, and I was missing performances. My weight was down, way down to the point of emaciation. I wasn't eating, but I was drinking, even though vaguely I knew it was dangerous for me to continue. Eric was very worried about me and finally convinced me to go to a doctor he knew, a holistic specialist named Dr. Khalsa, a Sikh convert. Too weak to argue, I agreed.

When I got there, I was a total mess, ashamed of myself, wanting to crawl into a hole. I, who had always kept my commitments, had been letting my audiences down. But Dr. Khalsa looked straight into my eyes and said, 'Miss Turner, you are very ill. Are you willing to give up alcohol in order to get your health back?'

And a strange thing happened. A light came right straight down into my head, a light from God, and I said to the doctor, 'You've got a deal.' I stuck out my hand, and when we shook hands, it was a three-way partnership—God, the doctor, and me.

It wasn't a short or easy process, getting my health back. The day my weight was back up to a hundred pounds, I celebrated. I couldn't have done it alone. But when you accept God, you're never alone. With His help I entered a new phase of my life.

Not one of us lives in order to be an example to others. Not even the saints. You live because you live. You do the best you can, and if you're lucky it's good enough. Of course there are things I would do differently now that I know better. Who couldn't say the same thing? But if you ask me if I would trade my life for anybody else's, swap my sorrows for their security, my highs and lows for their peace of mind, well, I'd honestly have to say no. I've found a peace of mind of my own now. I've had a privileged, creative, exciting life, and I think that the parts that were less than joyous were preparing me, testing me, strengthening me.

The thing about happiness is that it doesn't help you to grow;

252

only unhappiness does that. So I'm grateful that my bed of roses was made up equally of blossoms and thorns.

For awhile there it looked as though I might hit bottom. What it took was a combination of miracles to bring me back into life. It took a good friend who was concerned enough to get me a doctor, it took a good doctor who knew instantly how to treat the illness, and it took the hand of God.

All my life God had held my hand, even in those darkest days. I always used to say that you can push me to the wall, but no son-of-a-bitch is going to push me *through* it. Many have tried, including a fair number of my husbands. But I've been pushed through the wall only once, that long-ago time when I tried to end my life.

God brought me back; He saved me; and I made the deepest vow that nothing would ever drive me to that again. I could be in the gutter, but I'd never try to kill myself again. Men I loved were unfaithful to me and broke my heart. They took everything I had to give and gave little back, but I never sank to the bottom. I've been vulnerable and heaven knows I've been gullible. I've been fooled by good looks and romantic ways, but in the last analysis the great loves of my life always were and always will be my mother and my daughter.

In mid-February 1982, I received word that my mother was dying. I flew to Honolulu to be with her when she died on February 22. Strange—she was born on Lincoln's birthday and she died on Washington's. Even though she was very ill and is now at peace, I'm still numb from the shock of losing her. Proud and powerful, she was always there for me when I needed her. I'm so glad to be able to say that I was there for her, too. All my life it was a source of gratification to me that I could look after my mother, give her everything she ever needed or wanted. And thank God I wasn't reticent! Thank God I was able to say to her, 'I love you, Mother.' I said it often, and she knew in her heart that I meant it. 'Perfect love,' they call a mother's love for her child. My mother was well aware of my faults and weaknesses, but she had perfect love and she forgave me everything.

Now I have only my beloved Cheryl, of whom I am so very proud.

Writing this book has been a difficult experience for me, because this is the first time I've ever dug down this deeply or revealed

253

myself to the public so entirely. In my time I've given hundreds and hundreds of interviews, and I've always hated them. My private memories I wasn't about to share with anyone. Even the people who were closest to me never got my innermost, agonizing thoughts. Now I've been forced to look down the years and evaluate my own life. I've had to ask myself *why*? Why did I do such-and-so? Didn't I know it would turn out badly? Hadn't I learned from my last mistake? Truthfully, even today, I don't know why. I'm still learning. For me, life is a wonder, a searching and a progressing that I pray will never end. I'm still growing. Although I'm feeling secure in some areas, I still have a long way to go in others.

Nobody put a gun to my head to get me to write this book. I did it for two reasons: to set the record straight about me, so that all the lies could be answered by the truth, and because the timing was right. There was a feeling inside me that was like a flower in tight bud, wanting to unfold into a blossom, under the warmth of the truth. Now, having reflected on the past, I find that I'm still in awe of the present and the future. Sure, I've survived—the fact that I'm still here, still active, shows that—but I have to reach even higher plateaus.

Funny, if we didn't know sadness, we'd never know joy. My life has certainly not been the average one. Sometimes I'd ask God, 'Why me?' As a little girl I expected to become a fashion designer; instead I wound up a movie star. I expected to have one husband and seven babies. Instead I had seven husbands and one living baby, my darling Cheryl. I made my first movie without ever considering that my walk-on would be anything more than a one-time job. If I'd been given a magical glimpse into my future, if I could have foreseen everything that was going to happen to me, all the headlines my life would make, all the people who would pass through my days, I wouldn't have believed a syllable of it!

All those years that my image on the screen was 'sex goddess'—well, that makes me laugh. Sex was never important to me. I'm sorry if that disappoints you, but it's true. Romance, yes. Romance was very important. But I never liked being rushed into bed, and I never allowed it. I'd put it off as long as I could and gave in only when I was in love, or thought I was. It was always the courtship, the cuddling, and the closeness I cared about, never the act of sex itself—with some exceptions of course. I'm not masquerading as a prude, but I've always been portrayed as a sexy woman, and that's wrong. Sensuous, yes. When I'm involved with someone I care for deeply, I can feel sensual. But that's a private matter.

I've always told the truth, but never before have I told *all* the truth about myself. I think it's because I've been so close to God these last two years. I wasn't born like this, the woman I've become. It took a plunge toward the bottom, and the hand of God pulling me up slowly to the surface, for me to emerge as a New Woman.

I'm a positive person now, taking responsibility for myself and my affairs. For years, I was in a holding pattern, and I didn't know what I was doing with my life. I believed that even if I wasn't doing anybody any good, well, I wasn't doing anybody any harm, either. But I was doing harm to myself letting the essential me slip away.

But the essential me is still intact. I still love music—melodic, orchestral music, and the sound of violins and cellos. Give me anything that's romantic—Chopin, Tchaikovsky, Rachmaninoff, Mahler. Minor chords affect me more than major chords.

I like colors to be definite. I'm not a baby blue or a baby pink girl. Black, white, strong red—those are my colors. If it's yellow, let it be bright yellow. If green, make mine an emerald green. I don't care for muted colors, except the beautiful lilacs and lavenders. But that's my romantic side coming out again.

I love sunshine; who doesn't feel terrific when the sun is shining and warming you? But I also love rain. Real, pouring rain, not the drizzling kind. If it's going to rain, then rain! Don't just futz around. A heavy rain, and me indoors, enclosed in my own privacy. Reading or snuggled up on top of the bed, with a throw over me, watching TV. And afterward—everything so clean, the buildings fresh-scrubbed, the grass so sweet-smelling.

If I don't laugh at least three times during the day, I've had a bad day. I've got to have a minimum of at least three good laughs. I wouldn't have survived without my sense of humor, and thank God I have always been able to laugh at myself.

I'm very close to God. I read the *Daily Word* and I have learned to meditate. I'm still getting used to this New Woman—after all, she's only two years old! She's very different from the old me, and I respect her. She's more disciplined, and a lot less gullible and persuadable. For example, I don't sign business papers without reading them first. I trust my business managers, but I still read every word and put in my two cents' worth. I never used to. I used to say, 'Well . . . in my heart I don't feel that's right, but if you think so . . .' It had always been so easy to let others do things for me.

After all, that's what I paid them for. 'Don't you worry, darling, I'll take care of it,' they'd say. And I'd say, 'Oh, thank you,' and go off and sip again, or read a book, or watch TV. But now I say, 'Hey, just hold it right there! I'm not going to sign that!'

These days, if something begins to go wrong, I don't turn my back on it and hope it will go away. I pull it up short. 'Let's face this unpleasant situation now, before it gets any worse.'

I'm not pretending to know all the answers. In some cases, I'm still learning what the questions are! But I am beginning to recognize what kind of woman I am and where I'm going. Looking down the years has been as much of a revelation to me as I hope it's been to you. I haven't had an easy life, but it sure hasn't been a dull one. And I'm pretty proud of the way this gal has held up.

One final word. This book has definitely been a collaborative effort, and I'm grateful to those who have helped me, but in the end it's my book and my life and I take full responsibility for both.